ALL IN

ALL IN

Jamie Heaslip
with Matt Cooper

Gill Books

Gill Books
Hume Avenue
Park West
Dublin 12
www.gillbooks.ie

Gill Books is an imprint of M.H. Gill and Co.

978 07171 8597 9

Print origination by O'K Graphic Design, Dublin
Edited by Rachel Pierce
Proofread by Jane Rogers
Printed by CPI Group (UK) Ltd, Croydon CRO 4YY

This book is typeset in 13.5/17 pt Minion
Title and chapter headings in Frutiger Light

The paper used in this book comes from the wood pulp of managed forests. For every tree felled, at least one tree is planted, thereby renewing natural resources.

A CIP catalogue record for this book is available from the British Library.

5 4 3 2

CONTENTS

THE BEGINNING OF THE END

Aviva Stadium, 18 March 2017,
Six Nations Championship, Final Game,
Ireland v England

England at Lansdowne Road. A chance to stop them winning the Grand Slam. This is my 96th game for Ireland, to add to the five test matches for the British & Irish Lions. The final game of the Six Nations. An opportunity for Ireland to redeem a disappointing campaign, for me to nail a spot on my third Lions tour, this time to New Zealand in June.

We come down through the tunnel for the warm-up session about 45 minutes before the game is due to start. There's nothing unusual during my physical and mental warm-up, as we do line-out drills, a few scrums, passing movements. When it happens, we're doing the piston drill, with guys holding tackle bags, where we would work in groups: one player taking the ball, hitting into the tackle bag at force and laying the ball back for the following players to pick up and move on to hitting the next obstacle, pause then do it again. It is an important drill done at speed and with force, between the 10m and 22m lines. It gets the heart racing, gets the body ready for what's coming and it's part of the usual pre-match routine Joe Schmidt puts us through every time. We do it dozens of times before each game. It's just standard stuff. Until now.

I hit a tackle bag with force and feel something go in my back, and, immediately, my left leg feels as if all the power has been switched off. There's no pain, but my leg is dead. It just won't work. All sorts of thoughts go through my mind. The obvious one: what's wrong? Then: is this going to last and for how long? Do I tell anyone? If I look for help, will I be stopped from playing the match? I say to myself, 'You're grand, like, what are you talking about? You'll run this off, you're fine, just get up. If you were really injured, you'd have massive pain and you don't.' And there's another, quieter voice whispering that I'm funking out because I didn't have a fantastic match last week against Wales and that I'm scared now and that's why I'm imagining an injury. And then I have this devil on my shoulder telling me to shut the fuck up: 'You've got your match bonus, you've got your bonus in your contract, get on the field for five minutes and then come off, right.'

There is no pain and that, as much as anything else, is wrecking my head. If I'm injured so badly that I can't play this game, then surely I should be in physical pain? I'd understand that and I wouldn't be so confused by what's happening.

I don't know what to do, but I do know I have a responsibility to the team. I walk over to the physio and explain, as best I can, what's happening to me. We start a fitness test there on the sideline, then quickly realise that we shouldn't be doing this in public. I have to get into the dressing-room. I normally wait to be last in after the warm-up, a little superstition of mine – unless I'm captain, in which case I lead the team back in for the final moments before we return for the anthems. Now, though, I go in as fast as my leg will let me move.

In the dressing-room, the physio and doctor perform a quick fitness test. There are only a few minutes before we have to return to the pitch for the anthems and then the kick-off and we're all under pressure here. My leg is still dead. I put my weight on the toes of my left leg and try to lever myself upwards to standing on my toes, but my heel can hardly rise off the floor. There's absolutely no way I could run, jump, turn, lift in the line-out, push in the scrum, move at anything near the pace of international rugby. I'd be a liability to the team. And there's nothing the medics can do to fix this.

The team doctor, Ciaran Cosgrave, turns to Joe Schmidt, who came over to check on me, and tells him that I'm not able to play. Joe doesn't blink or argue with him, trusting his judgement immediately. He doesn't commiserate with me now that I'm useless to him. There's no time for that and no benefit to it. He's all business. He tells Peter O'Mahony that he's playing now, at number 6, and CJ Stander that he's switching from 6 to 8. He yells at Dan Leavy not to go into the shower because he's now on the bench. I don't argue because I know he's doing what he has to do, and that he's right. He doesn't give me a backwards glance as the team and subs head out the door of the dressing-room, along with the coaches, medical staff and everyone else.

I sit there in the sudden silence, stunned. I keep trying to do the test on my leg, as if its powers will return magically and somehow I'll be able to run out after everyone and reclaim my jersey and play against England. I shower, hoping the heat of the water will bring the leg back to life. I put my socks and boots on again and repeat the fitness test on my own. No good. This foot won't lift an inch off the ground. I have another shower and try again. And yet there is still no pain. Why is that?

In those moments, I'm more confused than distraught. But I remember that I have to think of others, people who'll be worried about me. My family will be worrying when they see the team run out without me, so I text my wife, Sheena, and my dad, Richard, and tell them I'll see them after the game. That I'm okay. Then I get dressed and I walk down the tunnel on my own, out to the subs bench, to watch the match. It's thrilling to watch the team as they set about tearing the English apart, but I have to admit to feeling a little sorry for myself. I should be out there, that's the only thing I'm capable of thinking.

This is all new to me because I've rarely suffered an injury. There's only a short list of them. My eye-socket was broken when I was a 17-year-old playing All-Ireland Division 3 rugby for Trinity College, which is why my left eye sometimes seeps tears. I had three concussions in nearly twenty years. I did my shoulder AC joint once but played through the pain in each subsequent game. I played with syndesmosis, an ankle injury, and came back to play again the following week, even though I could only run in straight lines. I cracked three vertebrae but was playing international rugby again within a month and never had any subsequent issues arising from that, as has been confirmed by leading medical specialists. I don't suffer muscle strains or tightness. My bones don't break. I joke that I'm Wolverine, and I slag my friends who seem to be injured for every Monday training session. I don't even miss those. It's why, just a month before this England game, I signed a new contract with the IRFU, to take me up to after the 2019 Rugby World Cup, even though I'll be 36 years old by then, because everyone knows that I'll be fit, available and good enough for that.

What I don't know is that my entire career has just ended.

CHAPTER 1

ANCHORED

Joe Schmidt once told me that I wasn't 'anchored to rugby'. He said it to me as I was telling him my career might be coming to an end, and I think he intended it as reassurance. I didn't ask him to elaborate, but what was important to me about it was my feeling, satisfaction even, that it meant Joe got me, understood me, that he had a real sense of who I am as a person. He realised that I didn't fit the stereotype of a rugby person who had no interests or perspectives beyond the game, and I was glad that he knew that about me and that he didn't judge me adversely for it.

I suppose that phrase could be interpreted different ways, but I have my own view of what an anchor does. On the plus side, it provides stability and safety and helps you to stay rooted to your moorings, no matter what buffets you. It keeps you in place. Those are good things, clearly. But not always. An anchor also prevents you from moving when you might need to and can limit where you can go and how far you can travel. If you're anchored, you're stuck fast.

I can imagine what many other players might have taken from such a comment from Joe, given that I've heard almost as many of them talk fearfully of him as talk respectfully or gratefully. They might have seen it as a criticism, and not only that but as a warning that he didn't regard them as being committed enough to their job and that there might be adverse consequences if they didn't knuckle down and change their ways. But I also think Joe knew me well enough to know that I wouldn't be bothered by such an opinion and wouldn't take it as a suggestion to change my approach if I somehow managed to get back to playing. While my ways of doing things in my professional life were always evolving, and I always took his advice on that, my attitude to rugby's place in my overall life had been consistent througout.

I love rugby, and if I hadn't been playing with Leinster or Ireland, I'd have been lining out with my mates on a Saturday afternoon for the pure fun of it. I loved winning – and worked myself to the bone to win – and could get enormously frustrated when I lost, but I also knew when to let that go rather than allowing it to dictate my mood and my life beyond what was, after all, my job. I've sometimes watched, amused or aghast, as some people within the game, and some pundits and fans outside the bubble, blow up its perceived importance out of all proportion. It's only a game. It's not life or death.

A few years ago, during a press conference, I made a comment that was misinterpreted but that I've had to live with ever since. I said that, outside of what I needed for work, 'I don't watch rugby'. The qualification in my statement wasn't noticed by many people. It was represented as meaning that I somehow didn't like rugby or didn't care about it, that I didn't have the right attitude to playing the game just because I wasn't getting up early and watching super rugby from the Southern Hemisphere or even the other internationals. Some people apparently wanted me to declare as a fan. I did and do watch rugby. I watched what I needed to watch and I did it for work, not for enjoyment. I looked back at my training sessions, I previewed teams, I reviewed our games, I watched lots of it. But when I'm on, I'm on, and when I'm away from it, I'm away from it. I needed that separation, to allow me to see the bigger picture.

I always had a natural curiosity about life outside rugby. Yes, I loved playing and was proud of my achievements in the game, but I wasn't defined by rugby or consumed by it. I wasn't solely a rugby player when I was a player, just like I'm not solely a former rugby player now, nobody beyond what I did with an oval ball. It played a big part in my life, but it wasn't my whole life. It informed my identity, but it didn't provide my identity.

In the reaction to my comment, I realised that some people had their narrative of what I was supposed to be as a rugby player, an identikit I was supposed to fit, one that wasn't going to tolerate tongue piercings, dyed hair or a baseball cap worn backwards, which are apparently symbols of 'disrespect' to the sport. Coaches and journalists aren't slow to tell you when they think you're overstepping the mark – their mark – and as I became better known, fans weren't slow to pitch in either, influenced by what they'd read in the papers or, in recent years, on social media.

I see it differently. I've met too many guys who treat professional rugby as the same sport they first played as eight-year-olds. I had my dreams back then, too, of being Simon Geoghegan, the flying Irish winger who was the brightest spark in the Irish teams of my childhood, the ones that often got beaten because they weren't good enough. But dreams don't sustain you. Once I turned professional, I stopped playing rugby just for fun and I worked as hard as I could to be the best I could be for as long as my career was going to last. I was very much aware that it was a business in which I had a job, and I approached it like that. I think my peers in the game – even those who didn't like me – would acknowledge that I took it seriously and gave it my all.

I wanted to learn about all the things that could make me the best player I could be. I became interested in performance, wellness, nutrition, fitness, finance and a whole range of other things in my efforts to build a broader understanding of the professional system and my place in it. I got the best people in their fields, nutritionists, performance mentors, masseurs, whatever was needed above and beyond what Leinster and Ireland offered, to provide the services that would make me the best.

I was aware, at all times, that it would come to an end, and possibly not at a time of my own choosing. I thought I'd be doing well if I got six years at the top international level, so I was going to get the best out of it in terms of performance and I worked accordingly. I decided I was going to get the most out of it financially, too, from the contracts with Leinster and Ireland and from the commercial endorsements. And I was going to use it all as a platform for my future beyond the sport. I wasn't going to allow the conventions of the game and limited expectations prevent me from taking the opportunities that would arise to do other things. Rugby would open doors for me and just because other people wouldn't step through the openings, and frowned upon those who did, that wouldn't stop me.

I realised early on that I was a cog in the rugby machine and that, ultimately, I was disposable. I had to maximise my return from my investment in this sport. I knew that my employer on the other side of the table wanted to get the most out of me for their money. I had to do the same from my side. It was the same if a sponsor was employing me to promote its brand. I came to realise that I had a brand, too, and I treated it as a business in which I had to create value and then capture that value, just as they did with theirs. I admit I probably wasn't as discreet about this approach as others were and being upfront often got me into a bit of trouble. But my attitude was, 'Well, fuck it, I'm going to do the best I can to get the most out of this.' There would be a long life to live after rugby was gone.

Professional rugby is still a young sport, which means it hasn't yet worked out all the imbalances inherent within it. The IRFU is a hybrid, with the voluntary blazers and the über professionals working side by side, dealing with both amateur and professional games. That makes things even more difficult than they would be otherwise. The game has been professional for 25 years, so people are still learning as it evolves. It's not perfect and there are a lot of things that could be better about it. That said, Irish rugby has done many things better than other countries, as success for the main clubs and country during my time playing shows. A lot of that is down to Joe Schmidt, to whom I also owe a lot. I know what I've done for myself, but I also know and thank all the people who have helped me along the way.

There are an awful lot of people looking to control the players at professional and international level, but I wanted to control what I could of my own life while knowing that I had to be part of a team or teams. Joe may have made that anchor comment about me, but he also said that I was the most professional player with whom he had worked. He said that to other people who then said it to me. I'm proud of that. It shows that I delivered on my ambitions in rugby.

I had the confidence to back myself, both on and off the pitch. I believed in my ability to face up to bigger opponents and to look them in the eye. In school I often got into trouble with coaches and teachers who might have mistaken self-belief and confidence for arrogance. I understand it now, in retrospect, but I wanted the best, to be the best. What was wrong with that?

~

I think that ability to see the bigger picture may have had a bit to do with my upbringing and the characters of my parents, Richard and Christine, and also the travelling we did as a family when I was a child.

I'm the youngest of four and by quite a distance. I always joke that I'm the one that got past the keeper. Graham, the eldest, is twelve years older than me, Richard Jnr ten years older than me and Joanne, my only sister, is eight years older. We call myself, my mum and dad 'the family within the family'. I probably was a bit spoiled and indulged, and my siblings would say that I got it a lot easier than they did. Joanne left school at seventeen, as she didn't do transition year, Graham joined the army and Richard went off to Japan for years after he finished college. My Dad held a number of senior positions in the Irish Army, finishing as a brigadier general, which meant he was regularly posted overseas. As a result, it was often just me and my mum in the house, so no doubt I did have it easier.

My mother, Christine, is a formidable woman. She's funny but very organised, too. There was no rugby interest in her family. My granddad, James Whelan, was an amateur boxer. She is a very can-do person and she had to be as the family moved around a lot because of Dad's work, to Limerick for a few years, to Fermoy in County Cork and to Cork, and on various foreign postings, before Dad settled the family near the Curragh army camp and a home in Naas, County Kildare, shortly before I was born (in Israel, when Dad was on peace-keeping duties with the United Nations (UN)) on 15 December 1983.

Mum ran a crèche from the house for years, on and off, depending on where Dad was working. There were always other kids in our house when I was growing up. I broke a couple of their collarbones playing rugby around the yard. Imagine doing that now. She'd probably be sued or shut down for health and safety violations, but back then it was simply a case of, 'Ah sure, look, these things happen.' She also did counselling work for the Samaritans in her spare time and still does.

My father, Richard, is very much in the army mould, very disciplined, very big into proper behaviour. He's from Janesboro in Limerick and he played rugby, first for Shannon RFC, then for clubs at the various places where he worked. He's very structured, quite old school and traditional in his thinking. He doesn't drink alcohol, never did, and is very strong in his religious faith. When I was in school, I had to go to Mass every morning for the whole six weeks of Lent, no choice in the matter. He gives out to me a lot to this day for cursing so much. 'You've a mouth like a soldier sometimes,' he complains, but that's the retired army officer in him.

He attained the rank of lieutenant colonel in the Irish Army and established the elite Army Ranger Wing (ARW), which is a special ops unit within the Defence Forces. Then he went to work with the UN in the 1990s, serving as a colonel across various peace-keeping missions and then as a brigadier general as the Irish observer to NATO. Dad never spoke much about the work of the ARW. I know it is designed for the physically capable and the mentally robust, but from what I've heard it is all about structure and discipline, and I've no doubt he would have established a really strong work ethic among those troops. He didn't talk much about any aspect of his work at home, regarding it as confidential, but talking to people who worked with him, I've heard that he had a very matter-of-fact approach with soldiers and officers alike. That fit with his personality alright, and he also brought a bit of that home with him.

Dad was tough, but always fair. Discipline was a big thing for him. So was a keen work ethic. He used to throw all of these clichés at me, like 'Nothing's worth doing unless you do it well,' or 'When the going gets tough, the tough get going,' or his favourite one, 'Talent is nothing without discipline,' and he just hammered them into me. He'd tell me: 'You don't need to be the toughest, or even the strongest, you just have to have a certain mindset.' Clearly, a lot of it rubbed off on me, even if it may have taken me a long time to realise that. I might have rolled my eyes at times, but I heard him and much of it seeped in. For example, Dad's the reason why I train on the pitch in a jersey and shorts, never in a tracksuit. 'Train as you want to play,' he told me, and that included wearing what I would wear in a game, nothing more or less. I did as he told me. I was the product of nature and nurture. I realise now that there's an awful lot of him in my character.

But then, there are differences too, things that I rejected consciously. For example, I never for a moment considered a military career, to follow in the footsteps of my father and my eldest brother. I always regarded the army as being too disciplined, too much following orders and not being able to question things. I don't like doing stuff just because I'm told to do it. I don't like repeating the status quo just because someone says that's the way it's always been done. I don't like stereotypes, don't like being put in a box. I've always had a slightly rebellious streak and I've been told I have a stubborn side. And I hate to say it, but I probably got that from him, too. But in terms of how to be a man or a father or a family man, I couldn't have had a better example. My dad puts family first, no matter what. He was never going to be missing in action, down in the pub or anything like that. As a non-drinker, he was always available to drive everyone home after a night out, and then would still go out and do some ridiculous hiking event or whatever the next day. He's a very disciplined man, and still is, doing things like organising walking tours of the Second World War battlefields.

Dad has had quite the career himself. There are three pictures in our house of him as a teenager, standing in his uniform at the graveside of President John F. Kennedy in November 1963 in Arlington National Cemetery. He is among the group of 26 Irish cadets who performed the Queen Anne Drill, also known as the Funeral Drill, as part of the interring ceremony. Jackie Kennedy is in one of the photos, that's how close he was to the mourning party. Dad was a member of the 37th Cadet Class, which had greatly impressed Kennedy during his visit to Ireland earlier that year when they performed the Queen Anne Drill at Arbor Hill in memory of the leaders of the Easter 1916 Rising. When Kennedy was assassinated, a request was made, apparently a personal request by Jackie Kennedy, that these Irish soldiers be brought over. The drill is very solemn and performed in silence at a very slow pace, without the barking of orders, and it lasts for about three minutes. Dad's photo shows how close he and the other Irish soldiers were to the very high-profile people at the ceremony, but he says that he was so focused on the job at hand that he didn't really process who all the famous people were. There are loads of remarkable details in the story of how they got there, but probably most notable is how, when they flew over to the USA on the same flight as President Éamon de Valera, they brought their rifles on board as normal luggage and stored them under their seats for the flight.

Dad's career brought him all over the world, and me and my mother with him. I loved moving about as a child. I was born in a city on the western shore of the Sea of Galilee called Tiberias. Dad was serving there on peace-keeping duties with the UN. We left before I was six months old and I had one trip back to see the place when we were living in Cyprus, doing the usual tourist things of seeing the Wailing Wall and the Dead Sea. I never took an Israeli passport and even though I was born there, I don't know if I would be entitled to one, if I ever wanted it.

My first detailed memories are of living in Cyprus, on an army base in Nicosia. We were there on and off for a couple of years when I was of primary school age. I had a great time. I thought it was a fantastic adventure. I got to live on an army base and we played sports all the time. It was brilliant during the summer. My brother was a lifeguard at the pool and as I loved swimming I was there from nine o'clock in the morning, heading off on my own from the house to meet whoever was around, safe because my big brother was working there. It was always sunny and we were always outdoors. On Sundays after Mass we sometimes drove down to Salamis, on the Turkish side of the island, and went snorkelling around the ancient ruins.

I also went to school there. I was picked up at my house by the school bus at about 7am. I went to an international school, which was very different from the Christian Brothers school in Naas that I would later attend. We did French and German lessons, subjects I'd never have done in Ireland.

Whenever my older siblings were there – which wasn't too often – they weren't as keen on being there as I was, but they were doing different things, partying and being teenagers. I was left largely to my own devices, indulging my fascination with ants and snakes and all that sort of stuff. On the occasions I stayed indoors, I played with Lego. I was massively into Lego. I had an almost unhealthy fascination with Lego Technic. I built anything I could get my hands on. I loved the methodical processes of figuring out a problem and finding a solution.

The lack of supervision meant I could get up to little bits of trouble. In the pre-division days, before the 1975 Turkish invasion, the old main road across the island used to run into the army base. It sat just inside the Greek side of the dividing line that marked it off from the Turkish side of the island. There was a wire fence around our camp on our side of the road, then there was the road itself and then on the other side, also fenced off, a minefield, with Turkish outposts beyond it. I kicked so many balls across the road and over that fence to see if they would hit anything that would set off a mine. It never happened. I had a set of binoculars and I could see the Turkish soldiers at their posts, starting about 150m away, looking back at me. One time when I looked over a guy was pointing a gun at me. I imagine he only did it to put the shits up me, but it worked well at the time.

When we were leaving Cyprus, Dad bought a car there to bring home to Ireland because they were so cheap. It meant a long drive back through Europe, so Dad decided to make it an educational tour, taking in lots of war history-related tourism. He brought us to Auschwitz and then over to Normandy. I think I was about eight and my poor sister was seventeen, having just finished her Leaving Cert. She was forced to spend weeks of her first summer after finishing school in the back of the car with me, our parents in the front.

It was a trip to remember, though. As a child I was very interested in those war magazines that used to be published monthly and have some kind of toy or a memento attached as a freebie to entice you to buy them. But I developed an interest in the stories beyond the toys when Dad brought us to Normandy. The battlefields and burials gave me an appreciation of the scale of war. The cemeteries really got to me; the sheer size of them was mind-blowing. We think of Dublin's Glasnevin Cemetery as big, and it is at 124 acres, but it was built up over hundreds of years. In Normandy, the thousands of bodies were placed there in just a few short years, and they are just the ones that could be accounted for. The Normandy beaches fascinated me, too, going onto the battlements and imagining the sand full of people, many of them landing to almost certain death, scrambling over the already dead, many of them young men not much older than me. While as a child I probably got bored easily, an awful lot of it did sink in.

It was the same at Auschwitz. It was only later in life that I understood what I'd seen there; things I saw on that trip seeped into my mind and became powerful memories in adulthood. I can remember the tracks for the trains leading the people like cattle to their fate, but most especially I can still see all the many, many shoes piled up, belonging to people of all ages who were brought there to be murdered. Thanks to my parents, from an early age I had the sense that the world beyond the Ireland I knew was often very different.

I got more of that from Dad's next big posting, in Kosovo, during the Balkan Wars of the 1990s. The dangers meant that we stayed in Zagreb, in Croatia, but we weren't really allowed to stay there too long. Dad's job wasn't great. He was literally counting the rockets flying over his head. And I was like, 'What happens if they collide above you?' He was in a building without running water for much of the time.

I really liked Zagreb. It was very different and it played to my impression of what Eastern Europe would be like. This was just before I went into secondary school, so I was about twelve years old. They were big into outdoor sports there, with swimming and water polo being particularly popular. They had these amazing outdoor pool facilities built on a massive scale. It was great for a kid. Dad was off working, so Mum would bring me to the pool most days and she'd sit there reading while I tried to make friends with all sorts of people. We spent time in Dubrovnik, before anyone had heard of the place and way before it became the tourist trap it is now. We also spent time in Sarajevo, so I was well aware of what the people there went through during the Balkan wars.

The last foreign posting that involved me was to Belgium, when Dad was sent there as the Irish observer at the NATO headquarters, even though Ireland is not part of NATO. It was a quasi-diplomatic role, which meant he couldn't get prosecuted for things like illegal parking. I tried to persuade him to let me drive the car, on the basis that they could do nothing to punish me, even if I was just fifteen years old, but he was having none of it. It was all a bit boring, to be honest. Belgium wasn't exactly exciting and I was a teenager who just didn't want to be there. Dad also ended up spending a lot of time in Macedonia and Kosovo, organising new homes for refugees, in his role as one of four senior Irish officers working with the Organisation for Security and Co-operation in Europe.

I was in Leaving Cert cycle by then, so Mum used to go over to Dad in Belgium without me and I'd head down to stay with my cousins in Ballyvaughan in County Clare. We have a big family down there. My dad's father married a second time, after his first wife had died relatively young, but my grandfather also died before I was born. It meant my dad had several half-siblings and their children were older than my own siblings, so it was their children, who were my age, who I used to hang out with. They have a house down in Ballyvaughan that still doesn't have a television, it's proper old school, and I used to have a great time with them, playing football and hurling, going to camps and generally mucking about together.

I think my parents got the balance right for me when I was growing up. Dad's work involved travel and obviously he wanted his family with him, or rather those of the children who hadn't grown up and moved on to other things. That meant that I was brought to various places and saw different things and it all stood to me. But they were also conscious of giving me the opportunity to grow up in a steady environment in Ireland, to go to school, to make friends, to play sport. I got a sense from it that I was a lucky person, that I enjoyed a certain degree of privilege, but I never got the sense that I had to give out hell to myself for being a child of a certain class. You are born into what you are born into, so get on with it.

I had a great time growing up in Naas. I always had jobs of some type because even from an early age I liked having my own money. I had three jobs in the first summer I was properly employed, in 1998 when I was fourteen years old. At weekends, I washed dishes at the golf club in Naas and collected glasses at a nightclub in Johnstown called The Sound House. During the week I worked at the local cinema, which was where my love for movies started. I also had a car valeting service that I used to run with a buddy, Paddy Bough, during the summer months. It was great fun as well as providing us with cash.

I played all different sports as a child, whatever was going, but I watched a lot of rugby because both of my brothers were playing with the Curragh RFC, and Graham also played with Connacht. In time, rugby became the main sport for me, a case of 'monkey see, monkey do'. I actually started as a centre in underage club rugby, and it wasn't until we got to the age where there were eight-man scrums that I was moved to the pack. There I started as a number 6 blindside wing forward, then I ended up at number 8 from the age of fifteen and that was that. At that time the style of rugby being played meant the traditional number 8 role suited somebody who roamed around and tried to play a bit of football, with my early experience of the backs helping a bit.

I was the first of my siblings to go a private school and to play rugby at school. I went to primary school at Naas CBS and played underage rugby with Naas RFC before I went to Newbridge College for secondary school, partly because of the rugby they played. I had been spotted already as having some talent. It wasn't a scholarship, though. There was no discount on the fees or anything as an incentive to move school. In fact, I'm pretty sure that Graham and Richard Jnr helped my parents with contributions towards paying my fees.

Newbridge was a co-ed school and rugby was the main sport. I'm really glad it was co-ed. I'd kissed all the girls by the end of second year and it meant that we were all cool with each other for the rest of the time. Some of my best friends to this day are girls I went to school with back then. It was academically good, too. I loved science and was hugely interested in biology, maths and physics and did those subjects for my Leaving Cert, which proved helpful when I later went to university.

I didn't do transition year and I was what was called a day boarder, which meant organised study after school, with dinner, and I'd get home about 10pm or so. Sometimes I'd board full-time for a few weeks if Dad was away with work and Mum went to visit him. The one constant was that I played lots of rugby. Newbridge College wasn't one of the Leinster powerhouses in the schools game, but we did well in my time there and I got picked for the good teams from a young age. I played two years on the Junior Cup team and we made it to the final one year.

It was the first time I was introduced to the idea of using visualisation in sport. There was a lot of talk about how the boxer Steve Collins was getting help from a guru called Tony Quinn, and somebody in Newbridge came up with the idea of copying some of it. We used to do some stupid things, like closing our eyes and imagining we had balloons tied to our hands and when we opened our eyes and looked around, we'd see that everyone had their arms in the air. We'd put our hands in cold water and visualise them being warm. We were told to put all our problems and worries into a box in our heads and to visualise blowing up the box. I'm not sure how much it helped in getting to the Junior Cup final, but it didn't save us from taking a big beating from Blackrock College.

I got called up to a few Leinster camps and that made me realise that I had something and I started to get ambitious. When I was fourteen, I was up against guys at the camps who were a year older than me and at that age the physical difference can be huge. I started off fearing that these guys were monsters. Sometimes I could hold my own and sometimes I couldn't, and my ego would take a bit of a bashing. At that age you come up against players who have big reputations, word of mouth goes around that such and such is going to be a big international star in the future, because they have the skills or the speed or the strength that you think you don't have. Few enough of them do, though. Things happen as they get older. They might get injuries, others might catch up, they get distracted. Sometimes they've had it too easy at youth level and can't cope when things go wrong as the games get faster and tougher.

I was just fifteen when I went into fifth year and started playing senior rugby and coming up against guys who were eighteen years old. Again, I found that I was able to hold my own and I started realising that I could give this a go. But I never thought that I could actually make a full career out of it. That path just wasn't clear. There weren't any of the academies there are now, but in a way I may have been fortunate.

As a fifteen-year-old I was gutted not to be selected for the Leinster schoolboy trial, but I made it for the 2000/2001 season and found myself first on the Leinster team and then on the Irish schoolboys side. It helped that I had friends with ambitions, such as Breffni O'Donnell. The two of us were both going, 'Oh! This is good! We're not too bad at this.' Unfortunately, we only got to play a couple of matches that year because games were cancelled due to the foot and mouth crisis.

I came out of school at the age of seventeen weighing about 116kg, which was probably about 10kg more than I should have been carrying, given my age and height. I had been in good shape prior to that. Same as any Irish teenager who played sport, I was just flat out all the time and that kept me trim no matter what I ate – meat and two veg from my mum each day, sambos to beat the band. But then I developed severe acne in fifth and sixth year and was put on Roaccutane to treat it. That proved to be good for my acne but there are some potential downsides to the medication and my reaction to it was that I piled on the weight. I was chunky. I could always move, but this was too much weight – and it wasn't like I was a ripped 116kg. It all led to a pretty embarrassing incident at my debs when the class photo was being taken. I was standing up on a kind of platform with the lads at the back and as we were stepping down off the platform, my pants split, right up the ass, with all the girls looking on and laughing. A lot of photos of that went around.

My mother bolted almost as soon as my Leaving Cert was over. Two weeks later she was gone to Brussels to be with Dad, leaving me with the keys to the house in Naas and instructions to mind it. It was hilarious. I went from having to live by the rules according to reasonably strict parents to having complete freedom. It used to drive my brother Graham mad because he's a neat freak. He'd come over to the house to check on me and the house and I'd have all my buddies staying over and it'd be a bit of a mess.

The deal I had going with all my mates was that anyone could stay over, and bring a friend if they wanted, as long as they didn't go near my parents' bedroom. We had a loose arrangement that everyone came over once a week and helped me clean up. I rarely even showered in the place, going to the gym instead because it was less messy and I'd get a towel there that I wouldn't have to wash at home. To make it all a bit more manageable, I basically lived in the sitting room. I brought down my mattress, had my PlayStation there and that was all I really needed. That was how I thought about it at the time. Looking back, it was piggery, absolute piggery. But they were fun times.

That was the only time I was short of money. I worked and had enough to buy food but spent more on partying. I didn't have to worry about bills, but let's just say I was busy entertaining. Weetabix with water somehow became a staple meal in the house. It was the making of me, though. I had to learn to look after myself. That came in handy when I moved to Dublin in September 2001 to attend Dublin City University (DCU), to do a four-year degree in medical and mechanical engineering.

I went to university because even though I had played for Ireland Schools that year, Leinster didn't pick me for the Academy. That was actually a lucky break in the end. The intake to the Academy each year was low, nothing like the volume there is now. By not getting chosen, it meant that I went and lived the full university experience, got my degree and also continued to develop my rugby in a club setting. I stayed in digs in Glasnevin, close to the DCU campus, and went home to Naas on a Friday evening and then back to Dublin on Sunday. Medical engineering was a full-time course with lots of hours of lectures and practicals, so I was busy even before I added in rugby.

There was no senior rugby team at DCU, so I was allowed to join the Trinity College (TCD) senior team. I had to wait to do that, though, because Dad wouldn't allow me to play for the senior team in first year as he didn't think I was ready. So in 2002, when I entered second year at DCU, I started on the senior team at TCD. At that stage no one was giving me education on diet or nutrition. I just turned up for Wednesday and Friday training with TCD under-20s and played a match on Sunday.

I was still carrying that 116kg in weight and desperate to shift it, but Dad persuaded me to avoid weightlifting until I got older and, as he saw it, better able for it. The easiest way to get around the city, from Glasnevin in north Dublin to TCD in the city centre, was to cycle. As I cycled from place to place, the weight just fell off. I lost over 12kg and then I started rebuilding from that lower base over time.

When I was in college, I was out every Tuesday or Wednesday in Dublin and then out on Saturday night in Naas. I did that more or less every week for four years. My mates lived on Pearse Street, just out the back gate of TCD, which was handy after training. I was doing the college thing to the full, except most people in college don't go out at the weekend because they're working in their part-time jobs. I was going out at the weekend because I was either with the team or out with the crew in Naas. The rugby didn't suffer from the partying, though. We won the All-Ireland League (AIL) for the under-20 age group, the first time I ever remember winning anything.

At the time there was an Ireland under-19s side that catered for players like me who didn't do transition year and therefore came out of school a little bit early. The coach was Willie Anderson, the former Ulster and Ireland second-row forward and captain. I trained a bit better under him, but I was going between the two colleges and having the time of my life and wasn't entirely serious about it all. I played a few games with the senior team, but it was really in third year that everything started to happen for me.

Coaches Tony Smeeth and Hugh Maguire were in charge of the TCD senior team and they gave me free rein to carry the ball and wander the pitch, but they also taught me a great deal about the needs of the game, how to be part of a team. Tony had a lot of vision, but Hugh was old school when it came to discipline. I definitely pushed his buttons at times, but it was a good relationship. He tested me and if I stepped out of line, he let me know about it. I'd get a quick clip across the back of the head. That wasn't too uncommon because at the time I was young and I questioned everything. I wouldn't do anything just because I was told to do it. Rugby wasn't the army and I didn't have to be an obedient soldier.

In 2003, my third year in college, I started, belatedly, with the Leinster Academy, largely on the back of my performances with TCD. There was a side-effect to training with the Academy in that it meant I couldn't take up a work placement, as part of my degree, with one of the medical device companies because they were nearly all in Galway and Cork. Leinster requested that I stay in Dublin, which was difficult for my coursework, but DCU was very accommodating. I was permitted to write a 20,000-word thesis instead, which I had to complete within a month. Once that was done, I was more or less free to train and play rugby from February 2004 to the September that marked the start of fourth year.

My availability meant that I could be called in as training fodder for the Leinster team, offering opposition as it went through its drills, or even for the Ireland A team when they were training. So I trained and played a lot of rugby, and a lot of PlayStation, for much of the year, which to me was living the dream. But at the same time, I also started to develop a sense of investing in myself. It convinced me that if a contract offer came up for the next season, I would take it. It was the start of a formula: plan for the worst and hope for the best. I'm an eternal optimist but I believe in that expression: the harder I work, the luckier I get.

During that season we had a great run of form for TCD in Division 2 of the AIL. On the final day of the 2003/2004 campaign, playing at home to Sunday's Well, a great club from Cork, word came through that our promotion rivals Old Belvedere were getting beaten away to University of Limerick Bohemians. We were leading 10-0 at half-time, and three more tries would secure a bonus-point win and with it the Division 2 title and promotion for TCD. Within fifteen minutes of the restart, I scored three tries. I can only really remember one of them and getting a bit of a slagging because as I strolled in under the posts I wagged my finger in the air in celebration.

That was an incredible moment, but it was what came in the summer of 2004 that made me as a player. I was selected for the Irish squad to compete in the under-21 Rugby World Cup in Scotland. It was played between May and June. We got to the final of the tournament, beating Australia along the way. In the final we got to play against the Baby Blacks, New Zealand.

This was the one game that brought me wider recognition. Even though I was having success with TCD and was working with the Leinster Academy, I still saw myself as something of an outsider, the guy from Naas, from Newbridge College, not exactly a powerhouse in Leinster schools rugby, who had struggled to get picked for teams. As far as I was concerned, if it was between me and somebody from one of the elite schools, like Blackrock College, then I'd get passed over. No more. I had a bit of a fuck-you attitude at the time and it helped, even if people liked to tell me that it didn't.

There was a certain disbelief that we had reached the under-21 final. We weren't getting any media coverage up to that point, but then a crowd from the IRFU turned up in Edinburgh for the final, alongside the suddenly interested media. We'd been massive outsiders when we'd beaten Australia in the semi-final, even though we'd already beaten

Argentina and France, but the Baby Blacks was a step up again. Most of them were on Super Rugby contracts; most of us were still in college. It was boys against boys, but they were conditioned like men; it was professionals against amateurs.

One of their team, Ben Atiga, had already been capped by the All Blacks by that stage, and Jerome Kaino and Luke McAlister would be by the end of the year. Stephen Donald, who had kicked the winning penalty in the World Cup in 2011, was there, as well as Ben Franks, Piri Weepu and John Afoa. They'd beaten the Six Nations Grand Slam champions England 42-13 on their way to the final, and it's fair to say that no one gave us a chance of winning.

The game was played in the Hughenden Stadium in Glasgow and we got absolutely spanked. They'd obviously done their homework on us. I'll never forget the first kick-off: they just put it straight on me and I caught it and … *bang*. I got a good old-fashioned rucking. There was no citing commissioner then. We won the ball back and cleared the line, which was fine, but they made their presence known early doors and it was the toughest game I'd played in my career so far. They tore us apart.

We'd done well to get to the final playing a fairly basic game. We'd boxed clever because we weren't that expansive in what we did with the ball for fear of turning it over. We used line-out mauls, carries from the pack and then we'd hit it up the middle with one of our centres. We tried to suck our opponents in and then go wide. It worked in other games, but it was no bother to them.

We got beaten 47-19. We gave it a go and probably didn't deserve to get tanked by that much. We conceded 14 points in the final ten minutes, when we had a man sent off, harshly, just minutes after the referee failed to send off one of their men for a punch. It didn't make a difference to the outcome, but it made a tough day tougher. They were on a different level from us, with three- or four-minute spells where they ran us all over the park, changing angles, moving us all over the place, passing where we didn't expect it. McAlister and Atiga in the centre ran the show after the pack, who mullered us, gave them the ball. They were also way ahead of us physically. Either in defence or attack, they were just streets ahead of us in all ways. They had much better technique and skills and were way fitter. They were simply better than us. They could take tackles with ease, were strong enough that they only needed a few men in the ruck and had plenty of people ready to rampage forward all over us. And they were faster. We did well to hold them to six tries once they had softened us up. Nine of them had Super 12 experience. We were amateurs. Game, but amateurs.

I managed to score a try and assist Shane O'Connor to get another, and I can honestly say I worked as hard as I possibly could have. Afterwards, we weren't down in the dumps. We all went out and partied because no one had expected us to win, ourselves included. Everyone was surprised we were even there. That was the mentality of the time.

That the vast majority of that under-21 team didn't even make it to interprovincial level, let alone international level, says a lot about where our system was then versus where it is now. The New Zealanders had systems for producing talent and bringing it through that I think we only have now in Ireland, fifteen years later. They had guys ready to play professional rugby soon after leaving school, which is the way it's getting in this country. We had good players who didn't get a chance at the time, especially at Munster: Shane O'Connor was a great second-row, Brendan O'Connor, a back-row, Denis

Fogarty and Dave O'Brien at number 7. Gareth Steenson was on that team, too, and he couldn't get in at Ulster. He ended up having to go abroad and then had a great career at Exeter. Dave Gannon, the captain, spent time at Connacht before moving to New Zealand on his release. Tomás O'Leary did make it at Munster and with Ireland and would have had a British & Irish Lions tour in 2009 if he hadn't shattered his ankle. Tommy Bowe made it on to that 2009 team, but he missed the under-21 final through injury. Maybe three players who would eventually become full internationals is as good a return as you might expect, but many of the rest of them should have been part of the interprovincial set-up that decade.

It did the business for me, however. Mark McCall, now so successful with Saracens, was our boss for the Six Nations in the spring of 2004, but that summer he had left for a job at Ulster and put Mark McDermott in charge of us for the World Cup. McCall wanted me to join him on a full-time contract in Ulster. I had one year left at DCU and asked if it was possible to transfer to a university up north to complete it, but that didn't work out. My dad was firm about me finishing my degree, arguing that if I was a good enough rugby player, there'd be a contract there for me in a year's time. I couldn't avoid Dad at the time. He had retired from the army but had decided to do post-grad studies in international affairs, at DCU of all places. Few students ended up having lunch with their dad in college but at least, given he was on a pension, I could make him pay. I wanted to take the contract on offer from McCall, but reluctantly I took Dad's advice. As it happened, I was really glad that I did.

At that point, what I really had was a sense of self-belief ... and some frustration. I felt that the offers were confirmation that the work I'd been doing over the past year was paying off. Even better, from a personal point of view, was the nomination for the World Young Player of the Year Award 2004. I was put on the shortlist with Jerome Kaino and Luke McAlister. That November I remember sitting in TCD having a beer after a match, watching the two of them playing for the All Blacks in the autumn series. I had met them in London that month, at the awards ceremony. I didn't win – I didn't expect to – but it made me wonder: why were they already at the top level of the game when I still hadn't played for Leinster? That was the frustration. It made me even more determined to develop my game and become a top-class professional like them. If I was their equal on this shortlist, why couldn't I be on shortlists in the adult game with them? It was time to go all in.

CHAPTER 2

ALWAYS POSITIVE

M y professional career could have been ended as soon as it had started, before I'd even won my first cap for Ireland.

In early August 2006, at the end of my first full season with the Leinster team, where I started 26 games, I was notified that there was an issue with a potentially failed drugs test. A letter from the Irish Sports Council (now Sport Ireland) started what was probably the scariest, if thankfully brief, period of my life. It began: 'Dear Mr Heaslip, this is to inform you of a negative finding following the testing of your A-sample ...'

The letter with this news had been waiting for me at home in Kildare for some time before I got it. I'd been off on a four-week jaunt in the USA and Costa Rica at the end of the 2005/2006 season. A friend of mine had gone to live in New York and myself and a friend went to visit, to stay with him and his missus. We stayed for about ten days but, ironically given what was about to happen, one of his housemates was a complete dope-head who smoked a load of weed and I was so paranoid about being around even the smell of it that I ended up sleeping outside on the flat roof for the three weeks, just so I could be in the fresh air and not risk inhaling the smoke. I went from there to Costa Rica for three weeks. Getting back to Ireland was a problem: I lost my passport and while the British embassy was of great help in getting a replacement Irish document for me, American embassy officials got very antsy about my request for a fresh visa to travel back to Ireland via Florida. For some reason, and for the only time ever, my being born in Israel became an issue for some over-zealous bureaucrat, leading to a testing three-hour session of intense questioning. It was a preparation for the anxieties to follow.

Dad collected me at Dublin Airport to bring me home to Naas to spend a bit of time with him and my mother before I went back to my flat. He had all my post for me and I went through it as he was driving and we were chatting. I noticed one that seemed a bit odd, with an official mark on it from the Irish Sports Council. I opened it and to my horror it said that my A sample had failed a drugs test taken after my last game before the holiday, at the Churchill Cup in San Francisco when I was playing for Ireland A. Upon confirmation of receipt of this notification my second, or B, sample would be opened and examined, and a decision would be made as to whether further measures were to be taken against me.

I was in shock as I read it. I hadn't done anything wrong. I looked over at my dad, the former army officer, the stickler for discipline, and wondered what I should say to him. My head was spinning. What would he think? What would he do? I didn't think too long about it. I couldn't hide this from him. Instinctively, I knew that I needed his help.

'Dad, I think this thing is saying that I failed the fucking drugs test,' I said.

I think he continued driving, but my dad, being my dad, all serious and brutally direct, immediately asked, 'Have you taken anything?'

'Not that I know of,' I said. 'Like, I mean, we were given protein shakes and stuff by Leinster, but I haven't taken anything beyond that. I haven't gone off and looked for something else, from anywhere else, you know what I mean?'

I knew I wasn't a cheat. I knew I was clean. I knew I was careful. It wasn't like I'd built myself up to be a huge player or anything like that – I wasn't then, and never have been, someone who has the size to lift weights like other players can. But now I started second-guessing myself. Had I taken something dodgy without realising what it was? What the hell had I eaten or drunk in recent months? The letter didn't tell me what I was supposed to have in my system, just that I had potentially failed a drugs test. WTF? So much stuff was going through my head: what do I have to do to confirm my innocence? Who do I have to convince? What if word gets out before I can do that? Would anybody believe me? I'd be shamed and my family and friends would be ashamed of me. Would I ever be able to play again? If I was handed down a ban, would I ever get another contract at Leinster or, come to that, anywhere else? Would I ever play for Ireland? There is a cliché about 'the longest trip ever', but that 45-minute trip back to Naas felt like the longest 45 minutes of my life. My head was spinning.

Two things gave me confidence. One was that I knew that I was innocent, which meant there had been a mistake and this could be proven and rectified. The other was that my dad had my back, immediately. Once you're straight with him, once you tell him and he believes you, then that's it, he's with you. There are five people I could call if I ever killed someone and had to bury the body, and Dad is one of them. Whatever needs to be done, within reason obviously, he would do it for me.

'Not a word to your mother, right. We're going to get to the bottom of this first, not a word to your mother yet,' he said.

Grand. When we got home, I went and made my first phone call, to Professor Arthur Tanner, at the time the doctor with Leinster. Arthur was a hero, a great man. He fought off pancreatic cancer once, but sadly it returned and got him a couple of years ago. But at the time he was a man who all of us players, even young professionals like me who had only come to know him in recent years, knew we could trust. I called him and he was incredibly calm, telling me that the negative finding could be caused by any number of different things that I didn't know about.

He asked me the obvious question: 'Have you taken anything?'

'No,' I said.

'Look, you can tell me, I'm the doctor, what goes between us is private,' the usual spiel.

I was like, 'No, I haven't taken anything, right, not that I know of. I swear.'

'Okay, grand,' he goes. 'That will be the case then. We'll work from there.'

Basically, the way the system works is that the testers, once they open a sample, look for what are called 'markers' that alert them to the possible use of illegal performance-enhancing drugs. One of those markers is the individual's testosterone to epitestosterone ratio. And that, it turned out, was where my problem lay.

While testosterone is the hormone responsible for the development of male sexual characteristics, it is also thought to regulate a number of functions alongside sperm production that are relevant to athletic performance, including bone mass, fat distribution, muscle size and strength and red blood cell production, all of which are clearly of benefit to an athlete. It is why some dopers try to introduce additional or artificial testosterone to their bodies – and why the doping authorities seek to catch them through testing.

Epitestosterone is an endogenous steroid, one that occurs naturally and forms in a similar way to testosterone. In most healthy males the two are found in more or less equal measure, a one to one (1:1) ratio, although, according to some university studies, some young men, especially athletes, have been shown to have much higher amounts of naturally occurring testosterone. It has been established that introducing additional testosterone to the body does not affect the levels of epitestosterone in the body, which means the normal, naturally occurring ratios can change. This is why tests to determine the ratio of testosterone to epitestosterone in urine are used to find athletes who might be doping. If the ratio is outside a particular band of approved measures, it's a big warning sign that an athlete may be doping to introduce additional testosterone, although it is not in itself proof that an athlete is doing so.

Thankfully, in my case an explanation was quickly established. The ratio levels that constituted a positive sample had been changed on 1 January that year, down from either 5:1 or 6:1 to 4:1. Dr Tanner's hope was that the figures from this latest reading would prove to be consistent with my measures in all of the previous readings, before the base was changed on the test – and they were.

However, even that wasn't the end of it. The doctor told me that there would have to be detailed examination of my B sample, which would tell what was natural in my testosterone reading and what might not be natural. In other words, the examination of the B sample would be conducted on the basis of searching for artificially introduced testosterone – of which, I knew, there would be none. He warned that if that was the case, I might have something else to worry about because a problem with my hormone levels could indicate a cancerous tumour.

'Like, that's great,' I said, 'if I'm clear, it could be because I have cancer?'

I went to Conor O'Shea's brother, Donal, the obesity professor, and he took my sample, did all my bloods and did a full check to make sure I didn't have cancer. Thankfully I didn't, but what was agreed was that I did have higher testosterone levels than is normal for most people. There was nothing in the B sample that was in any way artificial or added, it was simply that my naturally occurring testosterone levels were above the stipulated 4:1 ratio. As Dr Tanner had anticipated, a review of my previous tests discovered consistently high levels of natural testosterone. It is a physiological anomaly. I'm lucky. It may have been what kept me free of injury for almost all of my career and why I rarely get hangovers.

I got a formal letter from the Irish Sports Council to confirm that they had not detected any prohibited substances in my samples. The whole process went on for weeks, but it was rectified pretty quickly, to my great relief. I didn't mention the episode to anyone until years later. For years it was literally just myself, my dad and Arthur Tanner who knew about it. I don't even know when my dad told my mum, but I don't think he did until much later after the event. I know why we kept quiet, because there would have been people whispering about there being no smoke without fire.

If I had been careful up until 2006, I was absolutely paranoid after that experience to make sure that nothing could go wrong with any subsequent testing. I became ultra-careful. I wouldn't take boo-diddly for a cold, not even a Lemsip; I'd let it run its course naturally rather than take something. I'd never take anything unless it came from one of the team doctors and I wouldn't take antibiotics unless it was absolutely necessary. I was very careful about supplements, too.

I could not begin to estimate how many times I was tested during my career, before and after that incident. It happened after matches, where I might be delayed for hours as I waited to hydrate enough to be able to provide a urine sample, at the Leinster training ground or at my home. If I went away for a holiday, in Ireland or abroad, I provided notification of where the testers could find me, although I don't think that ever happened. Blood or urine, I provided it whenever asked, no questions, no objections. While I believe the processes that are in place work well – and I don't think rugby has a problem with people cheating the system – I like the idea of adding another layer, that of biometric passports, to keep an easily accessible record of all data. Everything should be put together by club and country and by the testers. I reckon that in my case, they went and looked back at old samples they'd kept at the Irish Sports Council and saw not just that my sample was natural but that it was consistent with all of the previous findings. A biometric passport would have helped to make that process faster.

There was one other occasion that gave me the shivers. A drug test involves you peeing into a cup with somebody standing there with you as you do it. You bring it over to the assortment of polystyrene boxes on the table, all numbered and sealed. You pick a box at random, open it and inside it there are two bottles, for the A and the B sample, with tamper-proof seals and numbers to identify them. You open them and divide the sample into the two bottles and then, with the tester still watching, close both bottles, making sure the number on the top matches the number on the container holding the urine. It's easy to take it for granted that everything is in order, but one day, thankfully because of some sixth sense, I checked the bottles and caps before I poured the sample in and found that the numbers were all different. I freaked out. If I had filled and handed them over without checking, I could have been in massive trouble afterwards, not because of anything in the sample but because of the perception that someone had interfered with the containers. The testers were very apologetic and embarrassed and they opened a different box, which had units that matched up, but ever since that day I triple-checked everything.

~

The issue with the drugs test scared me badly because I knew what I wanted: to be the best professional rugby player I could be, one who was going to win at the highest level. That eureka moment after the World Rugby Awards in November 2004, when I realised that I was well behind where I probably would have been had I grown up in New Zealand, had lit a fire in me. But I felt that I couldn't talk about it because I'd be seen as bragging or getting above my station. I wasn't going to start saying, 'I'm one of the best players for my age in the world, so play me', but I did want to be able to say, 'I have something here and I want to use it to get me places. I want to try and achieve things.' Being ambitious isn't being brash.

I still had to complete my degree at DCU, but during that 2004/2005 season I got more and more time training with the full Leinster team under Declan Kidney. But I was made to wait before I got onto the pitch for a real game. My first appearance was at Donnybrook as a late substitution in a game we lost to the Ospreys, 16-12. It was in March 2005, at a time when the Six Nations was on, and many of our front-line players were away with Ireland. I came on for Victor Costello with just 12 minutes left. A week later I got on to replace him in an away win down in Galway against Connacht after coming on with just 20 minutes left. I spent most of that season playing AIL Division 1 rugby with TCD and it got me noticed because I was picked on the Irish Times/AIB team of the season for that level. I was building towards the next season, when I would finish college and become a full-time, paid, professional rugby player.

I can't remember much of those first two brief appearances for Leinster. That shouldn't be considered unusual by anyone. What do you remember of every day you went to work? I can't tell you what the score was in each game I played, who played alongside me, who was in the opposition, what happened during particular plays, what I did or others did. I remember how I felt at different times, stand-out moments, things I saw played back on many occasions. But what I recall about the big games in which I played is likely to be different from what you remember as an observer, or indeed how another player saw it.

Almost no sooner had Kidney introduced me to the senior squad than he was gone. It caused consternation at the time, the idea that Deccie would ditch Leinster before the end of his first season – on the back of another disappointing Heineken Cup quarter-final exit, a pretty humiliating 29-13 home defeat to Leicester – to go home to Munster. I didn't take too much notice of that aspect of it because it wasn't really relevant to my position, but looking back on it now I can fully understand why he took that decision. Working with Leinster, he was living away from home and his family six days a week. People move jobs all the time and do so because they take all the other factors in their lives into account. Why should rugby be different?

What was of concern was how this would affect me. A little bit of me wondered if this was bad news for me, that the man who had given me my first professional contract, had played me off the bench in the Celtic League while I was still a college student and playing AIL with TCD and who, I assumed, had planned to use me next season once I was a full-time professional was no longer there to put me in. I wondered if I should be worried that a new coach wouldn't be interested in playing this unknown kid, particularly as I didn't have the physical bulk and power of the retiring Victor Costello and had a different way of playing.

The optimistic side of me always wins out, though, and I saw this as an opportunity to benefit from a new coach coming in with a clean slate. Crazy as it may sound, I already saw myself almost as the incumbent Leinster number 8 as I looked around and saw who else was available. Of course, Eric Miller was an international number 8 and had gone on a Lions tour, but I saw him as a 6 in the back-row I expected to be part of.

The identity of the new coach, when he was announced, surprised nearly everybody: an Australian called Michael Cheika. Few people had heard of him. He hadn't played international rugby and he had been coaching for only a few years.

It was only afterwards that I discovered that I caught something of a lucky break. I may have Mick Dawson to thank for my breakthrough. The Leinster chief executive subsequently told me that Cheika had it in mind to bring in a southern hemisphere number 8 as one of his early, most important signings. Mick never told me who Cheiks had in mind, but he urged him to hold fire, telling his new coach that even though I was coming through the Academy, I was ready for the first team. It was a big call for an executive to make; Cheiks might have thought that Mick just didn't want to spend money on a new signing.

I was excited as I went into 2005/2006 pre-season training. I had enjoyed my summer, going to San Diego with college friends for a few weeks, getting the tongue stud put in – to the horror of my parents, who were grateful only that I hadn't got a tattoo as well – and surfing and playing golf, before going to Las Vegas. When I came back, I saw only opportunity. Cheika made an immediate impact with the training regime he set for us. The difference between what he did in that pre-season training and what was in vogue when I finished my career was enormous, although what Cheiks did with us was regarded as near to cutting-edge at the time.

He brought in volume running, aerobic long-form training that was used in Aussie Rules football. We'd do an hour of running, loads of sets of 400m runs, then 300m, 200m, 100m, 50m, down to 25m and 10m, as fast as we could, until we were wrecked. I'll never forget the Killiney Hill sessions he then added in. Just up past the public car park there is a grassy knoll area on a hill and the path is just behind it. We'd start there, run down through the trees to the very bottom, turn and run back up to the knoll, making a kind of S-bend. After getting to the top, you waited until your heartbeat dropped and then you went again. The first week we had to do eight reps, next week ten, the following week we did twelve, all volume. We got really fit, but I suspect that as far as Cheiks was concerned it had the added benefit of weeding out those he felt weren't tough enough. Hardness was a big thing with him, mentally as well as physically. He reckoned that people have to go through this kind of suffering to bring them together. He didn't really care if you struggled through it, as long as you got through it. It wasn't how you did it, it was that you managed to do it and didn't give up. I loved it. It suited me. It allowed me to make an impression.

Not enough of an impression to get picked for the first league game, though. I had done well in pre-season, so I was a bit shocked when I wasn't picked for the first game in the Celtic League, away to Ospreys. I had started in a couple of the warm-up games, but Eric Miller was picked for that match at 8. I wasn't happy. I decided I would go and talk to Cheiks in his office about it. I didn't have an argument with him because I knew, even then, that once a coach had named his team, he wasn't going to change his mind. But I wanted him to know that I felt ready to start, that I had done the work and deserved to be in the team. I imagine he may have thought I was being cocky, but he listened to me and he didn't hold it against me. Perhaps it was what he was looking for. I came off the bench during that game and started the next one, against the Gwent Dragons. After that, I was picked for every big game that season, playing 26 times for Leinster and becoming an established player.

I was lucky that I got to play alongside two very talented international back-row forwards that season. Eric played mainly at 6, although he continued to struggle with injury. He had a fantastic way of working out what was going on during a game, could see things going on that others couldn't. I think it probably frustrated him at times that others weren't on his wavelength. Keith Gleeson was at 7, causing havoc at every ruck, defensively quite astute and well able to act as a very good link player between the backs and forwards. He wasn't that fast, which he'd admit himself, but he kept himself in great shape and was a really good professional, someone to emulate. He made the best of his attributes and I learnt from that, both in making myself the best I could be but also in improving my link play.

My job was fairly simple under Cheika. I could roam more or less where I wanted and not worry about the finer details of rucks and the like. He just wanted the 8 to roam, get on the ball and play. My self-analysis at the time was that I had good feet and a nice turn of pace, could read the game very well and was able to interlink with the backs, looking for space and attacking it. I felt that I had to be a different player from Victor Costello, who I succeeded at Leinster, because I didn't have his power. He was such an amazing athlete and power forward – who I loved to watch – that all he had to do was run over people. I was never going to be as strong as him.

Cheiks had the Aussie mentality of 'If you're good enough, you're old enough', so even though I was still only 21, he kept putting me in. It probably helped that he was a former number 8 himself and had strong views about what was needed in the role. He had brought in Mike Brewer, the former All Black, as his forwards coach and Mike was a tough nut, very demanding. Mike had lived in Dublin for a few years and was critical of what he thought was the softness of the Leinster mentality. It meant that he didn't always get on with Cheika's other appointment, the former Australian out-half David Knox. He was quite the character and he encouraged the type of flamboyant attacking play that delighted our backs. But I also found Knoxie to be enormously encouraging, helpful and insightful.

You'd have to ask other people what they made of my self-confidence or ambition at the time. I'm aware of the stories that my ebullience didn't go down well with some people inside the team or outside it. Some things came as a bit of a surprise to me. I remember before Christmas 2005 we gave Bourgoin a bit of a thumping in a Heineken Cup game at the RDS. I scored one of the eight tries and did one of my celebration things, jabbing the middle finger of my left hand in the air as I carried the ball over the line tucked under my right arm. Later that week Brian O'Driscoll (Drico) came up to me and admonished me, saying, 'You know, we don't do that type of thing here.' I was more than a bit surprised. Brian was our captain, Ireland's captain and had led the Lions on tour that summer before that injury in the first minute of the first test took him out. I didn't answer back, but I remembered him doing these little signs after he scored tries for Ireland and the fuss there was about all of that, which he had ignored. He had dyed his hair blond only the year before, so he knew all about being the subject of comment and tittle-tattle.

It's funny how the age gap plays out in rugby. Drico is only five years older than me, but at the start it was like he and his friends in that Leinster team, people like Shane Horgan (Shaggy) and Denis Hickie, were of a different generation. I remember once walking into the dressing-room and Drico was doing a celebration for Shaggy's thirtieth and I thought, 'Wow, he's old.' After I retired, Shaggy wrote a piece about me for one of the newspapers in which he said he didn't really know me that well. I would have enormous respect for him, not just as a player but for what he did to improve the culture at Leinster and also for the advice he gave me regarding contracts when Fintan Drury acted as agent for both of us and on how to be a leader as my career progressed. But he was right. We didn't become friends as such.

There was something I came to realise early in my career: your teammates don't have to be your friends. It's a workplace. Yes, you have a common purpose and you have to bond with each other to achieve your goals, but that doesn't mean they are your friends outside work, or even that you want to spend much time with them at training or camps or social functions. I think that's the way for anyone in any job and sports shouldn't be any different.

~

The highlight of that season for me – my breakthrough season, when I became an almost automatic selection as starter – and the best day of my career to date was our victory away to Toulouse in the Heineken Cup quarter-final. Nobody gave us a chance. In those days, Toulouse were European's stand-out side, not just the reigning Heineken Cup champions but at that stage the only team to have won the competition three times. The team was stacked with great players: Yannick Nyanga in the pack, with backs like Fritz, Jauzion, Poitrenaud and Élissalde. They even had Trevor Brennan, the former Leinster and Ireland back-row or second-row, who had gone down there and reinvented himself and become a regular in a team of stars. They were renowned for playing brilliant, attacking football from all parts of the pitch, off the basis of a formidable streetwise pack.

It wasn't just that Toulouse were regarded as practically unbeatable at home in Le Stadium, it was that Leinster were regarded as too soft to win on the big occasions. Our backs were regarded as brilliant on their day – when you consider we had Shane Horgan, Gordon D'Arcy, Brian O'Driscoll and Denis Hickie as our three-quarter line that day, with

Argentina's Felipe Contepomi conducting the orchestra from out-half, that was a fair assessment – but the feeling was that our forwards would not be able to compete, either physically or mentally. Results in previous seasons – European games that Leinster should have won and contrived to lose – had written that narrative.

I ignored much of that. I hadn't had the bad experiences of some of the older players, so maybe I was naïve about what I believed we could achieve. I hadn't been part of the team that had failed against Leicester a year previously. Neither had Cheika and his management. Our form in recent months had been patchy – not helped by key players being away with Ireland – but we emphasised getting the performance right on the day and if we did that, then the result would follow. But there had to be a plan to deliver that performance. That plan was to do what few teams do when they go to the ground of a team regarded as unbeatable: it was to take the game to them.

Cheiks had us believing in ourselves. He had hammered into us that we had to keep attacking, no matter what, to keep them on the back foot, because if they developed a head of steam they would roll all over us. Defending was not our game. Taking control of it, with Felipe Contepomi pulling the strings, was the game play and we executed it. We played as they had been expected to, as if we were the French side. We had big powerful forwards, but we ran with the ball, passed it well, hit the attacks from different angles, ran from keep.

We won 41-35 before a capacity 37,000 crowd at Le Stadium, but that scoreline was misleading. We hammered them, but they got two converted tries as consolation deep into injury time. We got a standing ovation from the home crowd as we left the pitch, which is rare. Their own players were slated, star out-half Freddie Michalak, in particular, was booed as he was substituted. We had got at him, which was the key to winning. Hickie's try from inside our own 22 is remembered to this day as one of the best ever scored by Leinster.

We had prepared for this match properly, but we treated it only as a stepping-stone. Much was made of how many Leinster fans travelled over to see it, about 6,000 of them, which hadn't been our experience of support to date, so it was a breakthrough day for them as much as for us. We didn't do a lap of honour at the end. Instead, we waved from the centre of the pitch to the travelling fans. We didn't want it to be seen as the celebration of an achievement but merely the acknowledgment of a means to an end. We wanted to go on and win the entire competition.

That Toulouse game was one of the toughest I'd ever played, a preparation for the internationals that would be part of my career later on. It was faster than probably anything I'd ever played up to then and it was physical, too, lumps taken out of each other. And I loved it. Winning helps, of course, but I did feel this was what I was made for.

There is no doubt but that the win gave the team a great lift. We blew them off the park. We scored great tries. The set-plays that Cheika had introduced gave us success. We were better than we had been. But people got carried away. We would discover we weren't as good as we thought.

The semi-final was played at Lansdowne Road – effectively a home game – against a Munster team that had been somewhat fortunate to beat Perpignan in Dublin in their quarter-final the day after our French success. We were the favourites, probably on the basis that if we could stand up to the Munster pack as we had to Toulouse, then our backs were clearly superior to theirs. There was also a feeling that, like us, they tended to choke in the big games, even if in their case it had been in finals rather than semi-finals.

There were all sorts of reasons why we ended up taking a 30-6 thumping that day, but some still stick out for me. I remember that week of the game there were players in our squad who sold their allocation of tickets to Munster fans. I was furious, but I didn't say anything at the time because I was one of the younger players. It always drove me mad, the number of people in Naas, in Dublin, lots of places in Leinster, who were Munster fans, who were somehow embarrassed to support their own province. I took it personally when I heard people from Leinster making a big deal about Munster, some of them even being friends of mine who had bought into the whole Munster thing a few years earlier. On the bus journey to the ground on match day, I was taken aback to see that the streets around Ballsbridge were full of red-clad fans drinking pints and waving flags. It was made worse by the fact that I saw lads I knew from Kildare wearing Munster jerseys.

And then I remember coming out onto the pitch at Lansdowne Road to this sea of red jerseys and flags. It must have been about three-quarters of the crowd and I was like, 'What the hell is going on here?' The sea of red in the ground proved to be something of a distraction from the job at hand, even if you're supposed to put things like that out of your head and concentrate on the game. I remember talking to Mick Dawson about it a few years later and he told me that was the moment when the administrators realised they needed to do something about this. It's hard to imagine now, given the success and support Leinster enjoys, but back then there was a disconnect between the fans and the team. They couldn't relate to us, weren't proud of us, didn't see themselves in us. Ironically, the majority of the team were actually from outside Dublin, not that anyone seemed to notice.

Cheika knew there was more to the result than who had more supporters in the crowd. To go from the high of the performance of winning in Toulouse to getting so bullied by Munster and by the occasion meant that there were more fundamental issues to be solved.

In retrospect, the result came about because Munster were ahead of us at the time. They played a very forward-dominated game in that period and it gave them the edge. You had Ronan O'Gara (Rog) and Peter Stringer (Strings) controlling things from half-back, putting the pack into the right positions. You had Paul O'Connell (Paulie) calling the line-outs and being so dominant there. From the scrums you had Anthony Foley (Axel) picking and going all the time, driving them forward. They were ahead of everyone else because they were so in sync with each other, as well as being big, powerful men. Leinster at the time were trying to play a different, more varied game, but we weren't yet all in sync because not everyone was singing off the same hymn sheet as to what we wanted and how to get there. We also may not have had the same strong values or culture as the Munster squad did, and that goes a long way. They had a very different mindset in terms of how they trained, how they prepared and how they played, whereas we were probably way more scattered in ours.

I think I did reasonably well personally in that game. It was a battle for me, going up against such a good back-row that featured Axel, Denis Leamy (Leams) and David Wallace (Wally), but I felt that I did as well as could have been expected of me. It certainly didn't count as a personal setback in my ambition to become a member of the national team.

CHAPTER 3

STEPPING UP AND STEPPING BACK

f I was fortunate that my arrival at Leinster coincided with Victor Costello's retirement, my first call-up to the Irish squad, in autumn 2006, coincided with Eddie O'Sullivan's decision to start phasing out Anthony Foley, even though he was aged just 32, creating a space for a replacement specialist at 8. What I had learnt from watching him was that he could see where the space was and would wait for the game to come to him. He had a very smart footballing brain. He wouldn't chase the ball mindlessly around the park, because sometimes people think that's what they've got to do, to keep getting onto the ball, going around the corner and carrying into traffic. But there's such width in the field to be used and you can get the ball to those positions by kicking wide. Anthony often stayed in wide channels because he could see that defences were not always well organised, certainly not as well as they are now, and would condense towards the middle, leaving space on the outside. Why would you run where people are when there is this space outside them? So he kept the width and next thing, two, three passes and he's in. Anthony could see the bigger picture as he played, he never suffered from tunnel vision.

I wouldn't say that I was Eddie O'Sullivan's biggest fan, even if he was the first coach to pick me for Ireland. He couldn't even get my name right at the first couple of international camps that I attended. Twice I had to correct him because he kept calling me by my brother's name, Graham, who he had coached in Connacht. I really didn't appreciate that and it's not something that ever happened with any other coach.

Eddie also got things into his head and couldn't shake them out. For years he wouldn't pick David Wallace, who in my book is probably the best back-row forward for Ireland I've ever seen, definitely one of the best I've ever played with at any level. He's class, athletically gifted, an unbelievable specimen of a human. He had strength in contact, his general speed, his fitness levels, his all-round strength and power and acceleration were superb. He was as fast as most backs, but he could have the engine of most forwards and then he was as strong as anyone, but he was a great pair of hands as well, a great link player, very strong over the ball, and defensively quite astute. I think he was like the Australian number 7 David Pocock before there were any David Pococks. He is also one of the nicest people you could ever meet. It took years for Eddie to select him, even though Wally was doing it all the time for Munster. Players pick up on that, don't like when things are obvious to everyone else but the coach, when the man in charge won't allow the evidence to interfere with his preconceptions.

Eddie certainly seemed to form quite a few about me, too. Years later, in his new career as a pundit, Eddie said that I was immature when I first joined the squad but also a real professional who listened to every bit of advice, personal or tactical, that was given to me. What's immature about that?

After I retired from playing, Donncha O'Callaghan told a story about me from when I first came into the Irish squad in

2006. In his column for *The Times* he described me as the tide
that lifted all boats in the squad, someone who showed the
Ireland players that, despite their belief in themselves, they
were not actually the hardest-working athletes they thought
they were. According to Donncha, a fitness test was set for the
squad. He spotted that I, the new fellow, was well able to keep
up, so he decided to up the pace to put me in my place. When
he didn't, he called a repeat set. So we did another. Donncha,
getting a bit annoyed now, called a third set. Wally refused
to take part, but we did another. As Donncha told the story,
he gave up at that point when he realised that I was ready
to go again. He wrote that he walked away thinking, 'This
guy's fitter than me . . . he's next level,' but also feeling excited
that I would drive standards in training and push everybody
higher. And yet Eddie thought I was immature and that this
was an issue?

Eddie later also told a story publicly of how, when he first
brought me into the international team, he told me that if I
scored, 'all I want to see you do is shake the hand of the person
who passed you the ball'. Did he tell Brian that? I doubt it.

But Eddie did give me my international debut in November
2006, against the Pacific Islands, in the last game to be played
at the old Lansdowne Road before it was demolished to
make way for the construction of the current ground. He
also brought in Stephen Ferris (Fez) and Luke Fitzgerald
(Lukie) for their first caps, although he played Fez at 7 when
most people would have said 6 or 8 was his natural position.
However it was calculated, I was nominated as the 1,000th
player to be capped for Ireland. It added another layer of
excitement to the day. Somewhat typically, however, Eddie
went out of his way to create an issue for me. The colour of
my boots offended him. I wore white boots. Big deal. I liked

them. No sooner had Eddie picked me than he told me – at the captain's run, the day before my first full Irish game – that I'd never play an international wearing white boots. There are ways and means of delivering messages to players, and that's not a message you deliver to a player on the eve of the biggest day of his career so far. He didn't explain why, which was also typical of his attitude at the time. I'm guessing he was some kind of traditionalist, because this was in the days before people wore boots of every colour under the sun, but back then it was just, 'wear black'. I was annoyed and distracted. I had to compromise by wearing a pair of black boots with big white trim because I was genuinely afraid that I would be dropped and that he'd make me look foolish for refusing to change my boots. I took them from a bag of free stuff Adidas had delivered into the kit room. I did it, but I also promised myself that I would never again be told what colour boots to wear. It would be white all the way from there.

We won the game 61-17. It's strange what moments can stand out from games. What I remember of that game more than a decade later was Shaggy getting into a fight with Alesana Tuilagi, Manu's brother, the giant Leicester wing who had come on as a sub. I just happened to be on hand and it fell to me to step in between them and I was terrified that I was going to take a thump from one of them and get myself knocked out.

When I started out as an international player, I wanted to have performances that included stand-out moments that would get me noticed. I think that's in the nature of most players. Even if you are there for the team and to help the team win, you still have to look after yourself and do what you can to make sure that you're picked again. But what I learnt quickly is that you should never chase a game to try to make those big moments for yourself. You have to feel a game out and fit in where you're needed. When you get your chance to do something special and eye-catching you take it, but you can't go out of your way to try to make those moments happen or to be involved in every single thing that's going on.

I did a solid job in that Pacific Islands game, tidying up messy ball and driving close in when required. I wanted to show that I could carry out all the basics as required. I dropped one ball at the very end and was furious with myself for it in case it left a lasting impression. I had played in big European games earlier that year, but the pace of the international game – even though I'd been warned – still took a bit of getting used to. As you might expect, the tackling by the Islanders was pretty tough, as was trying not to bounce off them when I tackled them. That said, as the result showed, they were nothing outstanding. It was an introduction and there would be many tougher games ahead.

I now had thoughts about being part of the 2007 Rugby World Cup the following autumn. There was a Six Nations to come first in the spring, but even if I didn't get into the team or squad for that, there would be 30 players going to the World Cup. While Leinster was my obvious priority for that season – with some people telling me that the second season would be somewhat tougher than the first – I was ambitious enough to want to be part of a World Cup team.

I thought I had a good chance, especially when I was picked for the extended squad for the 2007 Six Nations. Those were the days when you had seven rather than eight substitutes on the bench, but the coach always brought a twenty-third player with the squad for warm-up in case anyone pulled out at the last minute. I had filled that role for two games: the France game at home, which was the very first international played at

Croke Park, and the Italy match away. Maybe I was just being overconfident at the time or it was youthful exuberance, but I thought I was in a very good position coming into the World Cup to get a place on the plane and maybe start in one of the so-called easier, lesser matches. After that, who knew what might happen?

A couple of things made that an outside bet, however. Ireland had come close to winning not just the Six Nations Championship but a Grand Slam. It was only a last-minute try that gave France victory at Croke Park on the first day and after that Ireland went really well, including the famous 43-13 win over England.

Then I didn't get a chance with Leinster at the business end of the Heineken Cup because we got hammered by Wasps 35-13 in the quarter-final. That came as a big shock to us because even though we were short Drico in the centre, we thought we had plenty to allow us to take them on. But they shut us out with a massively aggressive defensive approach. Eoin Reddan (Reddser), the Limerick scrum-half who would later come back to join us in Leinster, had a day to dream of, scoring two tries, including one intercept when he read a move off the back of one of our scrums. We were quite naïve that day, throwing big passes out the back, allowing their defensive system, orchestrated by Shaun Edwards, to push up on us and eat the space we wanted to create. It was put down as another learning lesson, but we weren't moving forward as quickly as we wanted to and it was a pretty bad experience coming so soon after what was regarded as a very good Six Nations for Ireland.

I still had chances available to me to make an impression, though. I was picked to go to Spała for part of the overall Irish squad's warm-up during the summer, a sign to me that

I remained very much in the mix for selection. The place has become infamous in Irish rugby folklore and, in truth, it was grim. Spała is in Poland, an Olympic training centre, but it was an industrial outpost and that's what the campus itself was like. In fairness, it had exactly what we needed for training: good weightlifting facilities, proper tracks to run on, a pitch to train on. It wasn't glamorous or anything like that and the food wasn't particularly amazing, but it was exactly what it said on the tin.

We were bored to bits there. There was definitely no wi-fi and we were depending on our DVDs for a bit of entertainment, using the hard-drives on our laptops. Somebody brought a PlayStation to connect to the TV, but there was no TV. We were in this facility in the middle of nowhere, as if the Berlin Wall hadn't come down and we were still stuck in communist Eastern Europe. We got up in the morning, trained, did weights, maybe a pitch session and then took our turn in the cryochamber at some stage during the morning. Then we did the same again in the afternoon. We did it for a week and it was such a grind, we were knackered the whole time.

I liked the cryochamber, the deep-freeze unit that was supposed to aid recovery and that was all the rage at the time – and that later, without much evidence, was blamed for sapping the energy of the team so close to the actual World Cup matches. It might have been that, or it might have been the overall extent of the training, but the post-mortems after the tournament didn't really prove anything about the so-called Spała effect. In any case, I quickly came to think that pre-season training trips were something of a waste of time because the facilities were just as good back home. This particular not-so jolly was justified on the basis of the cyryochamber being the latest and greatest thing, and I know

Wales bought into it and used it for a long time. There is good science behind it, but I think for the Welsh it was more about Warren Gatland getting the group together for a tough experience and bonding over it than it was for the alleged physical improvements it brought. It was a fad of the time.

One of the real problems for the squad was that Eddie seemed to have picked his team and wasn't deviating from it, no matter the form of those on the list or those working to get onto it. I had gone to Argentina in the summer for our pre-World Cup tour and had won my second Irish cap there, against the Pumas. I played well in the first test, which we lost 22-20, but was dropped from the second when Fez was put in at 8 before leaving the pitch injured. The end score was 16-0. It's said that there are times when it can be a benefit to have missed a defeat and I wondered if this would hold true for me. Whenever you are fighting for a place on a team or squad, there is a tendency to engage in a bit of wishful thinking.

I suspect I got the run out against Argentina merely because Eddie didn't bring the first-choice xv on the plane and not because he was genuinely interested in helping me make the team or even the squad. For all his talk of going there with his mind only 60% made up about the World Cup selection, it became a running joke in the squad that the xv who didn't travel were 'the untouchables' and the rest of us were extras in *Lord of the Flies*. Those who could survive and make the biggest impression would make the cut for the World Cup squad, but even then would only play on the team if Eddie was really stuck. There may have been a certain logic to Eddie resting his best players during the summer, but it didn't do much for the morale of the rest of us. And it was to get worse during the tournament itself when Eddie tried to give his key players time to play their way into form, while most of those outside the starting xv were left to scratch their backsides for over a month.

I also knew I was a candidate in the area of the squad where Eddie had the most options available to him. He was bringing Simon Easterby as his first-choice number 6, David Wallace, now finally in favour, at 7 and Denis Leamy at 8, if they stayed fit. The choices for the remaining two or, at best, three places were between me, Neil Best, Fez, Shane Jennings, Keith Gleeson and Alan Quinlan. In the end, he went for three: Best, Fez and Quinny. All three were best suited to playing number 6, though, which didn't make sense to me.

I'll always remember getting cut from the squad. I was rooming with Gavin Duffy, the Connacht centre or full-back, when we played Scotland away in one of the warm-up games, the day before Eddie was naming the World Cup players. I got to play against Scotland, which was good, but we lost 31-21, which didn't exactly help the chances of any of us who were outsiders for selection. We came back that night to stay in Killiney Castle and wait to find out our fates.

Eddie could be an awkward person during the camps when it came to normal conversation and interaction. It was a standing joke that he pretended to be talking on the phone if he saw you coming towards him in the corridor, and then he'd get caught out by the phone ringing. Gav and myself were at each other all the time, 'Have you got the call yet? Has he sent you a text?' The nerves were at us. But I thought I was in with a chance when he didn't come near me, until there was a knock at my door. I opened it and Eddie was standing there, and he just delivered the news that I was out.

I didn't try to argue my case. I just asked him why, accepting my fate but also wanting to know where I'd gone wrong. He said, 'You're too small.' Well, that wasn't useful feedback. I had no problem with him picking Denis Leamy ahead of me for the team in 2007 on the basis of his experience, strength and playing ability, but as far as I was concerned, I was big enough, fast enough and strong enough to be part of the squad.

In fairness to Eddie, he was one of the first coaches to bring in a really good systematic approach to the game with Ireland. He got some very good results. His flaw was that he favoured particular individuals and didn't think of the collective. He paid the price for that by sticking with them too long and not bringing through other talent quickly enough. Maybe we weren't ready, but he cut me, Tommy Bowe, Luke Fitzgerald and Rob Kearney from that squad. We all started the Lions series less than two years later and I don't think we were that far off being ready in 2007, at least being part of the squad.

Michael Cheika was one of the first people to call me when the word got out that I'd been dropped. 'Look, mate, take a couple of days off, blow off a bit of steam, do whatever you got to do, come back and you'll get a real good run of games for us,' he said. I went back to Naas, got out of my mind drunk, middle of the day, on a random Tuesday, with loads of lads showing up to drown my sorrows with me. After that, I went hard at it with Leinster and pretty much tried to do everything Cheika told me to do. A lot of players were away for the World Cup and he kept saying to me, 'Opportunity, opportunity, opportunity'. So that's how I looked at it.

Some of the lads going to the World Cup were very good as well, getting in touch to tell me that they were sorry I hadn't been picked, people like Mal O'Kelly and Gordon D'Arcy. They said the same kind of thing as Cheika, 'Keep doing what you're doing, it will come good for you.'

That didn't make it easier as the tournament got under way in September ... and Ireland performed so poorly. I remember going to a pub in Ranelagh called Russell's (now the Taphouse) to watch the Georgia game, which we only just about won, 14-10. And I was a bit torn watching it, thinking I should have been there, wanting Ireland to win, but also wanting others to realise that it would have been better had I been there. At different stages of your career you want to make different teams, different squads, and when you don't it affects you in different ways. You can go into yourself and blame the world or go, 'Okay, hold on, how can I get better to make that next step? How do I take the learnings here?' I always took the positive approach. I didn't consider that I probably should have been grateful that I had been spared involvement with that disaster, although I probably would have done my nut holding tackle bags in training with no prospect of getting a game.

I didn't particularly believe in Eddie's philosophy as to the type of game he wanted to play – which I felt was very limited in its approach – so I went to other coaches, particularly at Leinster, who helped me to get better as a player, people like Colin McEntee at the Academy. But it wasn't the end of me with Eddie. After the World Cup debacle, he had to be seen to make changes because he came in for some heavy criticism on the back of Ireland's performance. That meant I was back in for the 2008 Six Nations. But I didn't feel grateful for the recall or any love for Eddie. He didn't tell me that he suddenly had a different opinion as to my abilities … or size. He was a man under pressure. I was one of his joker cards, along with the likes of Tommy and Rob, the players he could have brought to the World Cup and now had to bring back into the fold.

He didn't start me against Italy in the first game of the Six Nations, which was at home, preferring to keep his World Cup back-row of Easterby, Wally and Leams in place, but I was on the bench. It turned out to be a very poor performance and we just about won it 16-11, hanging on with a nervy finish against what was a very poor team. It was a performance full of handling errors and poor execution, which betrayed the clear signs of a team lacking belief and confidence. I got on with 11 minutes to go. Simon Easterby had been sin-binned 10 minutes earlier and when his time was up, I was sent on instead. I would play every remaining minute in the tournament.

I was in a somewhat strange position. I wasn't carrying the baggage of some of the senior players and their World Cup disappointment. I had a future to play for and the past performances on the pitch for the other players meant little to me. But I was also playing for a coach who I felt didn't rate me and I wasn't feeling any desire to play for him, no matter how much I wanted to play for Ireland. Still, I could see myself playing for my country for many years if I did things correctly because it certainly didn't look like Eddie was going to serve his full six-year contract.

I got my first Six Nations start in the next game away at the Stade de France. This, as some people warned me, might be a mixed blessing: many fledgling Irish careers had gone off the rails because of a pasting in Paris. It was a bizarre game. We lost 26-21, but just after half-time it looked as if we could lose by over 40 points. Then, with about 30 minutes to go, we started a comeback, as if someone had flicked a switch, and in the last few moments battered away at their line to get the score that would have levelled the game at least. But someone kicked the ball away and that was it. The frustrating thing was not winning after making our comeback. We got punished for turning over possession in the first-half cheaply, as the French in that era always did.

Even though we lost the game, I loved playing in it. Now I was playing at the level I wanted. It was such a step-up in pace from what I was used to that I spent the first 15 or 20 minutes sucking as much air into my lungs as I could. I remember looking up at the clock and thinking, 'Wow, that little time gone.' After that, I found my groove. The ball stayed in play a lot and any game where that's the case you'll find it hard to catch your breath. It was good, I really enjoyed it, but I also felt that I could have played for another 10 or 20 minutes at the end of the game: it was a bit of a weird one. It was a good performance and people said it might be a turning-point, even though we lost. It turned out to be a false dawn.

We did hammer Scotland at home in the next game, but they were poor. Even if they had beaten us in the World Cup warm-up the previous autumn, this game was the seventh in a row in the Six Nations in which we'd beaten them. I had a good day, doing the grunt work but also ball-carrying, and we won 34-13.

Our next game was at home to Wales, coached by Warren Gatland, of course. There had been an added frisson in this fixture in recent seasons caused by the fact that Eddie had been Warren's assistant at Ireland and had got the nickname 'Dagger' for his alleged involvement in Gats' sudden and highly controversial sacking from the job in late 2001, despite a serious upturn in Ireland's performances under his direction. It didn't escape the headline writers that this was the chance for the one-time victim to turn the knife. It might have been expected that the performance of the previous 120 minutes – the second-half of the French turned by a willingness to attack with the ball, and a good run-out against Scotland – would have persuaded Eddie to go all out for the Welsh. Far from it.

After the game we were accused of being devoid of ambition and ideas, desperate merely not to lose, suffering from a fear that the coach had transmitted to us. We were accused of looking like one-trick ponies who were told not to engage with the Welsh in a high-tempo game. Wales weren't great, to be honest, but they were cuter, only kicking to touch twice in the whole game and denying us much of our line-out platform. They kicked well, knowing we had no real counterattacking strategy, that our whole attacking game was based on planned setpiece strategies. They could and should have won by more than the 16-12 scoreline, our four penalties keeping us in touch.

We went into the England game at Twickenham the next week with all sorts of rumours swirling about that Eddie was going to be fired even if we won, that in fact he had been told by the IRFU after the Welsh game that he was finished, notwithstanding the extraordinary six-year contract he had been awarded before the World Cup. We were without Drico, who was injured, so Rog was made captain. We started brilliantly and went 10-0 up within eight minutes with some great attacking rugby. And then we conceded 33 points without scoring again. We allowed Danny Cipriani to look like a world-beater. The day had an end-of-an-era feel to it and within days Eddie was gone.

Different people in the squad took Eddie's departure in different ways. Some were genuinely very sad about it because they'd had success under him and had established good personal relationships and they felt it at a human level. They tended to be the most senior players, the ones he had always picked. Some liked him but agreed, reluctantly, that change was necessary and therefore quietly welcomed the decision. Some of us might have been a bit short of feelings of sympathy for him. He'd been ruthless in despatching us when necessary, and now it was his turn to feel the sharp end of the axe.

He was moved out quickly. There was no post-tournament review. There wasn't any need for one. He had been Ireland's most successful coach to date, but subsequent events under better coaches suggest that he didn't do as well as he could have with the talent available to him. He established structures, but he also became inhibited by them. He became too reliant on certain players and wasn't prepared to accommodate others. Although I know this is a criticism that others have levelled against Joe Schmidt in recent years, he at least had the achievements to back his decisions.

Eddie won three Triple Crowns (the once-cherished achievement of beating England, Scotland and Wales in the same season, something that had been rare previously), but he didn't win a championship, let alone a Grand Slam, even if he came so close in 2007, losing the championship only on points difference. But the 2008 outcome was Ireland's worst championship since 1999 and lowest Six Nations finish. Our world ranking had reached third under him in 2003 and 2006, but now it fell to eighth. We didn't reach the quarter-finals of the 2007 World Cup despite him talking, somewhat unwisely because of the expectations it raised, of actually winning the thing. You can point out that only France had a better win:loss ratio during his six and a half years in charge, but in that time England won a Grand Slam and a World Cup in 2003 and reached another World Cup final in 2007, the same year we'd beaten them by 30 points in a Six Nations game. More damning, perhaps, was that Wales won Grand Slams in 2006 and 2008 when its club teams were nowhere near as good as ours.

What disappointed me about Eddie as a coach was that there wasn't a whole lot of communication with him. I wanted that as a young player coming in. I was lucky that Paulie was there running the line-outs, making it very clear what I had to do. I wouldn't have done a whole lot of line-out jumping prior to that and Paulie definitely brought that part of my game on. He also brought me on with a level of expertise needed in the field in terms of attack and defence. In fairness, Niall O'Donovan, the forwards coach, was a big help around that time, too, but a lot of it came from the other players, not just Paulie but great men like John Hayes, O'Callaghan and Wally, who helped massively in terms of telling me what I needed to know.

Nonetheless, when Eddie was ditched, I was a little bit apprehensive about what the new man coming in might think about me. You can never be complacent about holding your place. I've experienced a change of coaches on a few occasions during my career and it's the same every time. You worry, even if you probably shouldn't, and I say that as one of the more optimistic of players. I'd just broken into the Irish squad and I was in a good spot, but now I feared that I might be back to square one again. But I was happy enough when I heard that it was Declan Kidney who would be getting the job. Deccie had been the one to give me my first professional contract with Leinster, during that one year he had spent in the job as head coach before hightailing it back to Munster. And he had given me my first senior starts that season. Although that didn't necessarily mean that he would see me as an international player.

I didn't have any truck with all this stuff about him potentially having problems gaining respect or buy-in from the Leinster players because of the way he'd walked away from us after just one season. Maybe I was a bit too wet behind the ears at the time, but I believed it wouldn't be an issue. Looking back now, I can see that what might have been more relevant to players and caused some apprehension was that he was coming from the winning Munster environment, with two Heineken Cups on the shelf. You couldn't blame non-Munster players for fearing that he might favour the lads he knew, because he wanted to play his way, which they already knew. But Deccie had worked with a lot of the non-Munster lads at various levels in the Irish set-up, going back as far as his uncomfortable time as Eddie's assistant in 2002/2003, and he had given a good number of them their starts. He had a reputation for backing people and letting them grow into the team.

Before Declan took over from Eddie we went on tour to New Zealand in June. It was hardly an ideal follow-up to a disastrous Six Nations, to put it mildly. Michael Bradley, the former international scrum-half from the amateur era and for a long time the Connacht coach, was put in charge. We beat a Barbarians side at an exhibition game in Gloucester and then set off for New Zealand, my first time down there, and Australia.

Despite playing four and a bit games in the Six Nations, I was unsure if I'd get picked, especially as it was noted that I was suffering badly from jet lag. But I was picked and found myself in a team that was a mix of guys who were realising they might be coming to the end of their international careers, and some who were starting to get themselves established. Quite a few had been to New Zealand a couple of times and didn't want this to be yet another bad day on the park.

We pushed them hard, but there wasn't a commonly shared belief that we could beat them. There wasn't the same unity in the squad that came later. We matched them until half-time, when the score was 8-8, and then after half-time, boom, they just got at us, had their purple patch and made up a gap that we weren't going to be able to bridge. We were beaten 21-11 and I was taken off after 60 minutes, to be replaced by Shane Jennings.

It wasn't a great game. I was up against my old friend Jerome Kaino at number 8, but it was my introduction to Richie McCaw at 7. I wanted to give a fair account of myself and it was exciting to be there, but what I remember most of the game was that the weather conditions were absolutely atrocious. I have never been as cold. The game took place in Wellington; it's a cricket ground, huge and bowl-shaped, so the wind gets whipped around it. Brian was interviewed after the game and he looked blue. After the game a good few of us didn't even change out of our gear to shower, we just walked in our boots, jerseys, shorts, everything on, straight into the showers, just to get the hot water onto us, we were so bloody cold.

It was my second experience of the All Blacks, but my first at senior international level. They were to become the benchmark for much of my career. What I was to learn that day, for the first time, is that they always get to what you think is the top and then kind of switch it up again, to go that bit further. They find whatever the thing is that will give them that edge, which might be small, marginal, but enough. We went from there to Melbourne and an 18-12 defeat to Australia. There was no disgrace in that, but we weren't looking for moral victories. And most of us were looking for performances to impress the new coach, who was there as an observer even if he wasn't yet in charge.

We had three games in the November series to find our way with Deccie. I scored a try in our facile 55-0 win over Canada and then our next game was against the All Blacks at Croke Park in November 2008.

There's always a sort of Irish optimism going into games with the All Blacks, even if the evidence doesn't support it. Just because we were playing them at Croke Park, where some people seemed to believe nationalistic magic would transform us, there was a feeling that we could finally win against them, even though Deccie had only started work with us and we'd been so dismal in the Six Nations. We hung in against them for the first 35 minutes and then Tommy Bowe conceded a penalty try just before half-time. After that, the floodgates opened. That was my first real introduction to Brad Thorn. I thought we were good, but we weren't even at the races. We lost 23-3.

It wasn't all bad news, though. We had some good moments in the game against an already unbelievably good team that we could sense was building towards the 2011 World Cup to make up for the shock defeat in the quarter-final in Cardiff against France a year earlier. They had such depth to their squad and a whole bunch of great players to bring off the bench when needed. The pace at which they played the game was incredible and yet when you thought you were coming to terms with that, they would change gear again. They were ruthless in exploiting our mistakes, but at the same time incredibly scabby, not making any mistakes themselves, not giving us any chances to score. We didn't get a lot of penalties off them or easy access points, as we call them. We learnt a lot from that game, that we had to get the penalty count against us down, that we had to be better in building territory and keeping possession. But we held our own for a while and that gave me a little bit of belief that we had things to build on.

We needed that belief the next week because we had to beat Argentina at home to hang on to our eighth-place world ranking before the draw for the World Cup. That was the key thing, but for some there was a desire to extract a measure of revenge for the 2007 World Cup defeat. It was an ugly, nasty game, but Tommy got a try and Rog kicked four penalties and we won 17-3.

That wasn't the end of 2008 for the Irish team, especially when it came to creating a platform for 2009, the best year of my sporting life. There was a renewed energy after Deccie took over. I felt that I didn't have any ownership of the way we had played before, under Eddie. Now a new system was evolving, but nothing was set in stone and everything was up for discussion. He wasn't saying, 'It's my way or fuck off.' It was, 'This is my way, but we are trying this system out and if you feel something could be done a little bit differently, then fine, we'll discuss it.' Declan and his staff did not dictate to us. Even if he wasn't going to be the greatest tactician in the world, he provided a fresh set of eyes and was a much better people person than Eddie.

That showed in a session he held at Enfield before Christmas, in which he asked the squad to break into small groups and discuss the issues they felt were most important to the development of the squad. The agenda was entirely up to us. The various group leaders would then report back into a general group discussion.

During those discussions, an issue came up that has acquired almost semi-mythical status in Irish rugby. I don't remember a whole lot about what happened in that now famous Enfield meeting, even though everyone else, even people who weren't there, seem to have a detailed recollection of it, but as I recall it Rob Kearney in his group with Rog raised questions about the perception that some Munster players might care more about playing for their province than they did for Ireland.

At that stage I had been in and around Irish squads for nearly two years and I hadn't a problem with the Munster lads. Far from it. In my early days I wasn't trying to set standards, I was just trying to learn and do my best. At the time it was probably seen as being a very Munster-dominated Ireland pack, but as far as I was concerned none of that mattered to me or to them. I always felt accepted and was made to feel a valuable part of what we were doing by more experienced players, whatever colour their club jersey. We were playing together for Ireland and winning was all that mattered. If it was the media that raised the issue, implying that the Munster players cared more about their club than their country, it might equally have been true that there were also players in Leinster who cared more about playing with their club. Neither was right. But if it happened, it was on an unconscious level. Anyone who thought it would never have said it.

Rob, in fairness, called it as he saw it – that it was a perception some had, even if others disagreed or denied it. It was a brave move because he was only in his early twenties and not long in the squad. He called out a room that included the last Lions captain, lots of Lions players, guys who had won Triple Crowns, who had lots of experience. But it had to be said, because the team weren't going to get along while there was any perception of a divide. But as far as I was concerned, this wasn't confined to a Leinster and Munster thing, it extended to different cliques that had formed in the squad. That's dangerous because it can breed negativity; three or four lads get together and it can be like 'them versus us'. Rob's intervention lanced a boil: it didn't start a row where people fell out, but it created a situation where people were determined to prove that it wasn't true. That stood to us when we regrouped for the Six Nations at the start of 2009.

CHAPTER 4

THE DREAM SEASON

The year 2009 was a stand-out success in my career. At the time, it was a mainly joyous ride. In retrospect, it set a level that could never again be fully emulated, even if the desire remained, and intensified. On the back of that year my professional pride could have been deemed sated, if I'd been that type of character. Others enjoyed the same success as I did, being part of a Grand Slam, Leinster's Heineken Cup win and being picked for a British & Irish Lions tour, but it was still a personal pleasure to be savoured, especially when I made the shortlist for World Player of the Year.

Ireland brought me the first success. It was Alan Gaffney, Ireland's backs coach, who said to me: 'You can't win a Grand Slam or Six Nations on day one, but you can lose it.' That is so true. Two years earlier, Ireland's ambitions had been curtailed, even if the season wasn't derailed, when Vincent Clerc scored a last-minute try to win the game for France at Croke Park. As twenty-third man that day, I can remember how deflated everyone was, not just by losing the first rugby international ever at Croke Park but because it also lowered the ambitions for what could be achieved in the rest of the campaign. We won our remaining games, but that try denied us the Grand Slam. And the championship was lost on points difference when France scored a last-minute try in their final-game win over Scotland.

If you win the first game of the Six Nations, expectations increase but the pressure is positive; lose the first game and you know that if you lose the next one, you face a potentially disastrous season, so the pressure to win that second game, to get back in the mix for the championship, becomes enormous. The first game sets the tone. It can go wrong afterwards, of course, as I would discover in future seasons, but winning the first gives you momentum, one of the most important things in any sport.

We started the 2009 campaign in Croke Park against France, the defending champions. We weren't anywhere near being favourites – as the French almost always beat us then – and it turned out to be every bit as tough a game as we had expected, especially in the first-half. We were 7-6 down when, in the 33rd minute, I scored the try that gave us belief, possibly the best try I ever scored, but very much a team effort that I was in a place to finish.

The try was constructed on the training ground and implemented in real time, largely as planned, but with off-the-cuff invention near the end. Jerry Flannery threw into a shortened line-out on our 10m line on the right-hand side of the pitch, finding Paulie at the tail, who immediately released it to Tomás O'Leary, who spun it, without taking a step, to Rog. He passed beyond two forwards, who were loitering in the middle of the pitch, to Wally, who was in the centre, as we had planned, and he turned and delivered to Tommy, who came over from the right wing at full speed. He passed to Rob, who had come up from full-back, and he made good yards, fending off a few tackles. When he was caught, but before he was brought to ground, he offloaded to Tommy, who had stayed on his shoulder as a support runner after delivering the initial pass. Tommy took it and bombed on for a good 20m or so before he was brought down, but Drico and others were there to provide quick ruck ball for Tomás. By this stage the French had lost about 50m and their players were in all sorts of unexpected defensive positions. Tomás flung out a long pass to Paulie, who was in towards the middle of the pitch, and he pirouetted out of a tackle as he popped a pass to Rog, who quickly shovelled it on to me, coming at pace right down the centre of the pitch where I'd been running, waiting for this opportunity.

I was about 30m out when I got the ball but breaking through the French line was fairly easy because it was a prop and second-row forward that I had in front of me to go through. It was a hole into which I could run, but that was only the first thing I had to do. I saw Poitrenaud, the full-back, ahead of me. I thought that I wouldn't be able to outrun him, so I started making a beeline to my left. Suddenly I realised that he had overrun his line to tackle me as he came across. I stepped away, off my left foot, to the right, a pretty big side-step when I looked back at it, and immediately he was in trouble, side on to me and unable to make the tackle. I could see the posts and suddenly realized that the try was on for me. Médard came over from the other wing in an effort to jump on me. I just trusted myself to hold on to the ball while using my momentum to carry me over the last few metres. Somebody told me afterwards that I went over the line like a barrel of beer being thrown into a cellar. I'll always remember that description. I touched the ball down properly as I was brought down to ground, but I placed it again, just to be sure there would be no debate. I felt euphoric as I got up and had the pleasure of seeing all my teammates going absolutely ballistic, not just because we had scored but because it was such a good team try that I'd been able to finish off. This was a turning-point on the scoreboard and, as important, in our self-belief that we could play top-class rugby and get scores as good as this. This was now a game we thought we could win.

It was still an incredibly tough second-half. Drico scored a great solo try. Paulie did exactly the same again at the tail of a line-out, just outside their 22 this time, but it was a much simpler try. When Rog passed to Brian, he side-stepped their centres and went in near the posts. That left us 20-10 up, but then they brought it back to 20-18. Many previous Irish teams had let such leads slip and what had happened two years earlier must have come to mind for those watching. I never thought of it. It was all about focusing on the task at hand. With a little more than 10 minutes to go, we got in again. Gordon D'Arcy had come on as a sub in the centre for Paddy Wallace, who had taken a bad cut over the eye. We'd been battering their try-line for a while, but it was a combination of Darce's footwork and his sheer strength that got him over for a converted try. We ended up winning 30-21 and we were on our way.

But to what? Already people outside the camp were talking Grand Slam, on the basis of one result. It helped that we had Italy up next, away from home, and then England at Croke Park. Even if we had been very poor in beating Italy at home the previous year, we knew we should be good enough this time, even on their home turf.

The first-half was possibly best remembered for an assault on Rob that should have brought about a red card but didn't. He was flying down the wing when Masi came in and clotheslined him, when he could have hit him with a proper tackle and hurt him legitimately. I legged it over from the other side of the pitch to remonstrate but came in shouting at the wrong guy. Masi only got a yellow card, which was ridiculous, especially as Rog got one later for tackling a guy without the ball, which, while fair enough, was far less serious. We led 14-9 at half-time in what was a fairly brutal physical game, but we pulled away in the second-half, winning 38-9, with two of the converted tries coming in the last five minutes and giving a boost to our points difference.

The English game was one of the toughest imaginable, a world apart from what Ireland had done to England at Croke Park two years earlier. If England had been blitzed by the occasion then, they were mentally and physically much better prepared this time around. It was 3-3 at half-time because Rog missed a couple of penalties, including one we would have expected him to get, straight in front of the posts, about 38m out, which hit the post. Drico was a real captain for us that day, getting the try that gave us an 11-6 lead. There were many times when Drico blew me away with what a player and leader he was and that was one of them. He was immense that day, he just took the game by the scruff of the neck, drove us along, inspired us to go to another level. It was one of the greatest performances I've ever seen. Yet we struggled to hold on to the lead. But then we had a bit of good fortune when Danny Care got himself yellow-carded only three minutes after coming on as sub scrum-half. Rog nailed the penalty to bring us to 14-6. Job done, it seemed, and I was replaced by Leams. Then they got a converted try and there were seven seconds left as Rog restarted. But we hung on and now all the real speculation began, that we could do something no Irish team had done since 1948: win a Grand Slam.

I had one embarrassment ahead of me that night, though, at the post-match reception at the Shelbourne Hotel. My punishment was that, in front of about 400 people in the ballroom, I had to get up and sing a Snow Patrol song *a capella*. The reason for that was my failure to accept an invitation from the group to come and perform for the squad earlier that week.

It was a genuine mistake on my part, but I paid a high price for it. Drico's mate Damien O'Donoghue worked in MCD at the time. Everyone in the squad was given informal jobs and he knew that I was in charge of organising the entertainment for the players when we were in camp and he said, 'Would you like Snow Patrol to come in to you guys on Thursday night?' I was distracted when Damo rang me as I was on the side of the pitch at St Mary's College during our week off after the Italian match, watching their school team play Newbridge College. I thought he meant they wanted to come in and say hello, not that they would play a private gig for us. I thought it was too much, that we were going to see them the following Sunday night and would be going backstage, so there was no need to be meeting them now.

I'll admit now, although I didn't at the time, that I wasn't that big into their music, so I wasn't particularly pushed. I said, 'No, thanks.' Damo rang Drico and as captain he absolutely hung me afterwards, asking me in a team meeting to explain my decision. I said I didn't realise how big Snow Patrol were. The whole squad went mental with me and wouldn't buy it when I suggested that I'd thought they wouldn't really be into it. I didn't live it down for the rest of the season. Even John Hayes used to slag me about it and I doubt he had any idea who Snow Patrol were. O'Callaghan made me write a letter to the band, to apologise, saying the team didn't want Snow

Patrol thinking we were so up ourselves that we'd prefer to go to the cinema. I didn't lose my place on the entertainment committee, but from then on I had to get every decision ratified by two other members. And I had to sing at the reception. I did 'Chasing Cars' but didn't know the words or the tune and I had to play the song off my phone in one hand with the microphone in the other so I could work out what words to sing. You can only imagine the reaction given they all had been on the beer.

I learnt my lesson that night and subsequently got Mumford & Sons in to do a few songs for us on another occasion, not long before they broke big. That ended up with me having a rugby tackling competition with Marcus Mumford at about 3am, definitely one of the most bizarre moments of my career. We were pretty well fuelled by drink and I imagine he'd give a different answer as to who won, but I can tell you that he held his own for a while; he is a big unit.

We had a week off again before the Scotland game, but when we got back into camp the Monday before going to Murrayfield, we discovered that Deccie had a shock in store for us. He had decided to drop four players and, to my horror, I found out that I was one of them.

Deccie was always going on about honesty, so I decided to go to his office and let him know how I felt. He said he wanted to reward the other guys for training hard and playing at a high level with their provinces. Well, that's what I was doing, too. I told him I wasn't happy with his decision because I was on form. It was nothing against Leams, who replaced me. He was a quality player. But that wasn't the point. I hadn't done anything to warrant being dropped. I had my say and Deccie, being who he is, just sat there and nodded and said that he understood but that he had difficult decisions to make.

Once I'd had my say, I told Deccie that I'd be Mr Positive and he wouldn't have to worry about my attitude around the squad that week. There'd be no moping. I understood that we were trying to build a squad mentality – where we all pulled for each other, no matter what – so I had to buy into that. And I would. I probably did bitch privately to Rob, who was my roommate, and one or two others, but I tried to be as positive as possible for the week, even if I was hurting. On the day of the game, Deccie pulled me aside and thanked me for my behaviour over the course of the week, on and off the training pitch. I really appreciated not just that he said it but that he had noticed. Many coaches wouldn't have and if they had, they still wouldn't have bothered to say anything.

As it happened, I got onto the pitch at Murrayfield pretty early during the game because Leams got a bad injury to his shoulder in the first-half. In the second-half, I was able to have my big game-changing moment. Paulie called a line-out on me at the back, not far outside the Scottish 22, and I tapped the ball down two-handed to Strings, who had been picked to start at scrum-half ahead of Tomás. Their number 7, Barclay, shot off the back of the line-out towards Rog, in anticipation of the pass, and Strings spotted the gap he had left. The second I hit the ground I saw Strings, who was known for nearly always passing instead of taking it on himself, take off with the ball on a break. I just ran straight towards the Scottish line as Strings went on this crazy, swerving run, which, he told me afterwards, was an effort to buy time as he waited for support to arrive, hopefully before too many Scottish defenders did. I was screaming at him to pass, but I thought he couldn't hear me. Then, at just the perfect second, he turned and popped the ball to me as I ran up at full pace and went, almost unopposed, to the line. I suppose I took a risk, waving my finger in the air, ball in my left hand and not held against my body for protection, as I roared, with relief as much as anything else, as I crossed the line. It meant that there was a referral to the TMO to see if I had grounded the ball properly. Thankfully, I had. I don't think I would have ever lived it down if I hadn't. We won in the end, 22-15.

Now it was down to us to win in Cardiff. When I was dropped for the Murrayfield match, my fear was that we would win there but that I wouldn't get back into the team for the Wales game. Even though I believed in the whole squad thing, and had proved it with my behaviour prior to the Scottish game, not being involved in the Grand Slam game would have left me feeling short-changed by the whole thing. The others who were dropped had to worry about whether or not they would be recalled – Paddy Wallace wasn't, whereas Jerry Flannery and Tomás O'Leary were – but I probably had less to worry about because of Leamy's injury. If it was doubtful that he would be able to take his place as a sub for the game against Wales, then it was most unlikely they would pitch him in to start.

The outcome of any Six Nations match, no matter what is at stake for the teams or their form going into it, is never guaranteed. Teams looking to do the Grand Slam or win the championship can freeze, no-hopers can lift themselves unexpectedly. There was a history of Irish teams denying others their Grand Slams, most notably England in the foot and mouth-delayed fixture in 2001. Ireland had gone into a Grand Slam decider previously against England at Lansdowne Road in 2003 and ended up losing 42-6. Wales had something to play for in this game, other than the normal professional pride of winning on their home ground. It was something of a long shot, but Wales could win the championship if they beat us by 13 points. Gats started winding it up in the week before the game, going on about how much the Welsh players disliked us. We took no notice, which was easy enough given that it was pretty pathetic sledging. We were focused on delivering our own best performance.

I found out on Tuesday that I was definitely in the team to start, so I just went about it in the normal way, shutting out all the noise in the media about the importance of the game. We didn't need to be told what was at stake. We knew we needed to win. I don't recall being particularly tense as we travelled over on Thursday – but I don't get that way anyway – or of anyone else being more nervous than usual. The day of the game, though, on the drive through the crowds thronging the stadium, the noise outside and then inside, there was no escaping that. Come kick-off time, it was almost impossible to hear what we were saying to each other on the pitch. I found it all thrilling.

It was a nervous game on the day. Leams ended up on the pitch not long after the start, despite carrying that shoulder injury, playing for far longer than he or anyone else had ever expected. About 10 minutes in, Fez got kicked on his right index figure and the bone came shooting out the back of his hand. He shouted, 'Paulie, my hand's wrecked', and then he said he was playing on anyway. It was disgusting to look at, one of the few sights on a pitch during a game that actually came close to turning my stomach. There he was, walking about with this bone sticking out going, 'Come on, let's get on with it.' The doctor insisted that he had to come off and Leams replaced him. He thought he was on as a 10-minute blood sub, and slowly it dawned on him that he was there for the rest of the game, despite his banged-up shoulder. It was that sort of day.

We were 6-0 down at half-time and anxious that if they were to get another score, we'd be chasing the game. There were lots of players in quite a bit of pain, Rob in particular because of a back spasm. Drico showed real leadership in the dressing-room during half-time, telling everyone, 'I believe in us'. Paulie went around saying, 'We're unbreakable, we're unbreakable.' It would have been easy to buckle under the weight of expectation and the adverse scoreline, but as well as belief we needed a strategy. Paulie wanted us to pick and go and do it again and again. He believed that we could hammer away at them, take them on up front, in the same way Munster had succeeded in recent seasons. And when we went back out onto the pitch, that's how Drico got his try from a ruck two yards out, just like he did in the game against England, showing incredible strength and courage. When Rog converted, we were in front. Then we had one of those glorious inspired moments when Rog hit a crossfield kick for Tommy that sat up perfectly when it bounced and he grabbed it over his head. He took a punch to the sternum from Gavin Henson as the Welsh full-back tried to tackle him, which meant that Tommy really was gasping for air as he sprinted for the posts. But he got there, and our balloon was fully inflated now that we were eight points, more than a converted try, ahead.

It didn't take long for the air to start leaking again. We were dominating possession and territory, but not only were we not getting the scores we needed, we were giving away penalties in our anxiety. I admit that I was among the guilty parties on that score. They kicked two to bring the game back to 14-12 in our favour. Then they got a drop goal to go a point ahead and it could easily have been a try instead. There was only four minutes left, but there was no panic. We also got an extraordinary bit of luck. The Welsh hadn't been kicking from play to touch all game, but then Stephen Jones botched the rules on kicking to touch from inside his 22 when the ball was passed to him from outside it. He kicked it straight to touch, an unbelievable error on his part. That meant we had the line-out inside their 22 and the opportunity to score.

We launched a couple of drives, got the play in towards the post and, taking a pass from Strings, who had come on for Tomás, Rog kicked a drop goal for the three points we needed. And that should have been that – we were 17-15 ahead with only one more play to come in the time available – but there was more drama to come.

Wales were going through the phases, but we were aligned defensively and they were making slow progress. They were still just inside their own half when, right in the middle of the pitch, Paddy Wallace, not long in as a sub, went to steal the ball at a ruck but was penalised. It was, in retrospect, the correct call, but on the pitch it was hard to process. While we would still be champions if Wales missed the penalty, what we wanted was the Grand Slam. I can't really remember if I registered that Jones was taking the kick instead of Henson, who we all knew had a big boot on him and a far longer range. Jones, possibly tired, didn't hit it properly. I was standing near him as he kicked it and I could see immediately that it had gone very high into the air, which meant it might not travel as far as it needed to go. I looked down the pitch, following the flight of the ball, and I could see Geordan Murphy getting excited, preparing to catch the ball under the posts because he realised that the ball was about to drop short. He was right, he caught it and ran with for a few seconds to waste time before kicking it dead into the crowd. Time up. We had won. Cue bedlam.

I can hardly remember how I felt in the immediate moments after winning. What I do remember is looking into the crowd as I walked with my teammates on the lap of honour and seeing grown men cry and being taken by how important this was to other people, as well as to ourselves. I saw my dad and my friends, making it all the more special. It was the cliché, a dream come true. A little part of me thought that this was happening only four years into my career and I should enjoy it because it would be the only time, that devil on my shoulder having his say, driving me on.

It was madness back in the dressing-room, noise, back-slapping, adrenaline overcoming exhaustion, but one man was somewhat detached from it. Paddy Wallace looked shell-shocked, still unable to process what had, and almost had, happened to him. You couldn't talk to Paddy. He didn't know what to do with himself. I felt sorry for him because he should have been enjoying this, not worrying about what hadn't happened. But the thing was that I had given away two penalties that Wales had kicked successfully, six points. I said to him, 'Mate, had I not given away those penalties, we'd have won easily. Your penalty wouldn't have mattered.' It was true. I would have been more responsible for us losing if we had, but in all likelihood that's not how people would have remembered it.

We had a great few days afterwards, celebrating, although not altogether. If you look at the Ireland team of 2009, there was a big age gap between some of the more senior players, like Rog, Brian, Paulie and Donncha, and the younger ones like myself, Lukie, Tommy, Fez and Rob. Most of the older guys were married, some had kids and some, like John Hayes, slipped away home while we celebrated. I particularly remember going to the Druid's Chair pub in Killiney and the sheer joy of the celebrations. All sorts of people got the credit, the players, obviously, but also the backroom staff. While Declan Kidney, in that subtle way of his, had done a remarkable job of transforming the confidence of the squad, he had also brought in others who assisted him brilliantly. Gert Smal had come in from South Africa and he was a terrific forwards coach, particularly on the detail of how to run line-outs. Paulie loved him for it. Smal took it to a new level and he was so committed, we hadn't wanted to let him down.

I remember Deccie saying to us: 'This means a lot for a lot of people.' It was a distraction for the country. Winning the Grand Slam brought positivity to people at a time when things in the country weren't exactly great, with the recession already in full flow … and about to get worse.

∼

I went back to Leinster in late March with the winning mentality and a desire to achieve more. Leinster had won the Celtic League the previous season, but in those days the prize was awarded simply on the basis of league position, not after the play-off system with final that is in place now. While it was great to win silverware at the end of the 2007/2008 season, it was somewhat overshadowed by Munster winning the Heineken Cup again. They got all the kudos. Our achievement meant something to us, but others largely ignored it.

One of the things that drove us forwards in 2009 was the desire to disprove a column written by Neil Francis, the former rugby international, who had sneeringly called us 'Ladyboys' when we went out of the Heineken Cup the year before. I thought it was a cheap jibe because the game was different from what it had been in his day. For someone who liked to think of himself as clued in, Franno didn't seem to realise or understand what had happened at Leinster. Cheika had literally cleared house. You look at the picture of the squad he had inherited in 2005 and the squad he had in 2009 and it's very obvious what had happened. He got rid of people who were not buying into the way he wanted to play and who didn't have the mindset that he demanded. He transformed the personnel. If players couldn't be paid off, he just told them not to come to training because he didn't want them and their attitude around the place. Maybe Franno's criticism, albeit unfairly stated, might have had some relevance a few years earlier, but not then.

Some of the players hated Cheiks because he very much had his favourites, the lads who, if they delivered for him, he liked. It was a tough environment if you didn't perform or if he just didn't take a liking to you. Some players won him over, like Rob, who delivered once he got his chance. I think Cheiks loved an underdog story, he loved supporting the guy he felt might have had it tough. He's from Randwick in Australia, the son of immigrants from Lebanon, and he had it tough coming through in the sport himself and trying to be accepted. I'm told that the way he played the game was hard as well, at a time when there were very rarely any citing commissioners or anything like that. He could be quite emotional, too, and I think he felt at times that, emotionally, we didn't get to the place that was required to win games.

I discovered myself how I was becoming one of Cheiks' favourites when I didn't get the blame I deserved for an incident in Biarritz on a pre-season tour. I was room-sharing with Eoin O'Malley (Chubbo), a young player just out of the Academy who was trying to establish himself and we went out one night and got absolutely bananas drunk. When we headed back to the hotel I couldn't find my room key and for some reason I thought that Eoin was asleep inside the room, had locked me out and wasn't opening the door on purpose. I got a bit mad and started putting my shoulder to the door. Suddenly, it split widthways at the handle, more or less in half, and the top half collapsed inwards. I stood there in shock and then Leo Cullen was standing beside me going, 'What have you done?' The next minute, Chubbo walks up asking the same and I'm going, 'Are you not meant to be inside?' Leo was disgusted, knowing that, as captain, he'd end up having to deal with this. He told us to go inside and sleep and we'd deal with it in the morning.

We didn't get that long. What may have been minutes or hours later, when the two of us were dozing off, the door flew open and Cheiks stormed in and started roaring at Chubbo, swearing at him that he was a 'little shit' and that he would sort him out for doing this. I was pleading with him that I was the one who did it and he should be addressing me, but he ignored me completely. I knew that was totally unfair. He roared at Chubbo – who most definitely was not one of his favourites – that he was going to pay for this tomorrow morning and then he finally left the room. We were looking at each other, fairly speechless, when suddenly Cian Healy (Church) stuck his head up from the foot of one of the beds and said, 'Do you think he saw me?' Chubbo and myself were now looking at each other, wondering where the hell Church had come from. It turned out he had needed a place to crash because he couldn't find his room key either, and he had taken advantage of our broken door to get in and make himself at home on the floor. When Cheiks came thundering into the room, Church just pulled the sheets down to cover himself and dragged himself in under one of the beds as much as a guy of his size can. Church had only just about managed to work his way into Cheiks' favour and was terrified that he would end up getting the blame for this too. It seems that Cheiks had somehow missed him, and Chubbo took the blame for the whole thing.

The next morning I went downstairs and met with the hotel manager to ask how much it would cost to repair the door. I arranged payment, and then went to Cheiks and admitted full responsibility and apologised. He told me that he was disappointed with me, but after that it was business as usual.

There were quite a few changes at Leinster that season. We were a mentally harder, better team in 2009. The foundation of the team was the Leinster lads who had a won the Grand Slam, but there were other top-class Irish lads who hadn't been part of that and who were looking to win something themselves. John Fogarty came in from Connacht as a hooker and Simon Keogh came home from Harlequins to add cover for the three-quarter line. We had great foreign players, too, such as Rocky Elsom in the pack and Chris Whitaker at scrum-half, both Australian, and the man who turned out to be the greatest Leinster foreign signing of all, Isa Nacewa. He was from New Zealand, although he had one cap for Fiji in 2003, which meant he couldn't play for Ireland subsequently under the residency rule. CJ van der Linde came in as a prop after winning the World Cup with South Africa, although it would turn out that his influence would be limited by a foot injury.

We also had significant coaching changes that season. Cheiks had brought in a lot of people to help with the evolution of the squad, people like David Knox and Mike Brewer. They were gone by the time the 2008/2009 season came about, but they were invaluable to me while they were there. Knoxy looked after the backs, but he encouraged me to get involved in playing with them. He wanted me to carry off the back of the scrum and get into short number line-outs. Brewer was really good, too, because he provided insight from New Zealand, who were way ahead of us then, on how to play the game. He had a very hard edge to him but was also very interested in trying to get me more involved in all aspects of the game. Being coached by both Cheiks and Brewer, two former back-rows, was hugely beneficial in encouraging my development. But we didn't have their input any more. Mike Brewer had gone to a job with Scotland, so the recently retired All Black Johnno Gibbs came in as forwards coach. Kurt McQuilkin, an old Leinster favourite in the centre, was in charge of midfield. Alan Gaffney, Leinster backs coach under Matt Williams nearly a decade earlier and then Munster coach before he went to a job with the Australian national team for two years, returned to double up as Leinster and Ireland backs coach.

Leo had replaced Drico as club captain, probably because Cheiks wanted somebody who would be around all season and not dragged off regularly to Ireland sessions. Leo wasn't in favour for the national squad at that time, although he would be later, so he was a good choice. It also helped that Leo had genuine presence, both as a player and as a person, and had the experience of winning a Heineken Cup with Leicester during the two seasons he had played with them. When Leo and Shane Jennings (Jenno) came back from Leicester, they were used to playing in a far more confrontational, tougher league that was probably at a higher level than the Magners League was at the time. This was long before the Pro14 overtook the English league. At the time, we probably needed their different take on things. It's great to have the majority of your squad from the province that you're playing for, but it's always extremely helpful, as in any organisation, to get that outside perspective as well. Leo and Jenno came back in with different eyes on things from when they had left originally. Their success with Leicester demanded respect, too. They had done it in England and now wanted to do it with us, especially in Europe.

Leo was driven. The story that went about was that he had a photo from the 2006 semi-final, of the Munster players celebrating, pinned up at the end of his bed. Apparently, it was to provide motivation or something, even though he hadn't played that day because he was on his two-year stint with Leicester. I used to slag him about having a photo of a load of blokes at the end of his bed. 'What's that about?' I'd ask him. He just ignored me.

My problem with Leinster was that while we could hit the heights, we had no consistency. We were hot and cold, good at home and terrible away, and it didn't make sense to me. Part of that may have been down to the process of players preparing differently for European games than for league matches, of caring more about their performances for the international side than club, using Leinster as a stepping-stone or a stone in their shoe. All it needed was for a few to behave that way and it could derail the collective.

Perhaps we had allowed negativity to shroud us at times. Once negativity enters an organisation, it spreads like a cancer. That's dangerous for the mindset of the group, the culture, the values and also in terms of lads wanting to play for each other. What you cannot have is players saying that some other guy, one they don't like, is not good enough, or that others they like should be in when they shouldn't, or that the coach is playing favourites. Any successful team I've been involved in has been defined by the same key attribute:

everyone is pointed in the same direction. You don't have to like each other, but you definitely have to agree on what you're trying to achieve. You must have the confidence in the people around you that they can do it and you can do it. Once you lose confidence in someone, that's a threat to the whole group because you're going to try and cover their job and then you're going to mess up your own job in the process. Thankfully, we largely eradicated those problems towards the most important stage, the end of the season, the success of the Irish team providing something of a template.

In our group stage for the Heineken Cup we had drawn Castres, Wasps and Edinburgh. We won four of the six group matches, starting and finishing with a win against Edinburgh, but, most important, hammering Wasps 41-11 in October at the RDS, scoring six tries. Then we had another big win, 33-3 at home in December against Castres, to set ourselves up nicely. Then things then went off the rails a bit. We lost the return fixture in France 18-15, and then in January Wasps got their revenge with a 19-12 win. The important thing, however, was that we dug in to get the bonus point for losing by seven points or less in both fixtures. We knew that if we beat Edinburgh at home in the last game, we'd be okay, unless Wasps did something extra special down in Castres, in which case we'd need a bonus-point win. We kept hearing from the crowd that Wasps were losing in France, so we just concentrated on our own game on a very wet day. We couldn't get any tries, though, and all our scores in a 12-3 win came from penalties. Meanwhile, Wasps were within a score of Castres with just five minutes to go when the French got another try to seal victory. Yet again we were in the quarter-finals, but we were drawn away from home, against Harlequins in England.

This game was to be a defining one for both clubs. It would be for ever remembered by many as the so-called Bloodgate game, one that damaged the reputation and career of the Harlequins coach, one of the great number 8s of the game, Dean Richards.

Our attacking plan was largely to give the ball to Rocky and let him batter holes. My job was to follow him around the pitch and stay close. In defence, he was detailed to tackle as much as possible and I would poach at the resultant ruck, or vice versa. The game turned out to be nearly all about defence because our first-half was error-ridden, full of poor decision-making, appalling kicking, many dropped balls and too many turnovers. Harlequins were just as bad and let us take a 6-0 lead. In the second-half we produced what was our best defence performance in my time at Leinster until then. They kept coming at us, often on our own try-line, and we held them out, tackling ball carriers with ferocity, putting bodies on the line. Remarkably, the same xv who started were allowed to finish the game. Instead of being worried about being able to sustain our performance, Cheika didn't want to disrupt the cohesion and unity by taking anyone off.

Although we hung in, their full-back did get in for a try, but fortunately they missed the conversion and Mike Brown, who wasn't their normal kicker, missed a penalty. And that is where all manner of controversy broke loose. Dean Richards had replaced his kicker, Nick Evans, early in the second-half with what seemed to us to be a knee injury. But with about 10 minutes to go Richards sent him back in, saying that he had only been replaced temporarily, even though that had been 28 minutes earlier. In order to put Evans back on they had to take off Tom Williams, who appeared to be covered in blood. As he walked off, in a gesture that further aroused the suspicions of our guys on the bench, he threw a wink at a teammate.

Our bench thought he was faking it and demanded, as the laws allow, to see the source of his blood injury. Harlequins refused. We discovered in the following days that Williams had been handed a capsule of fake blood, purchased in a joke shop, and bitten it to create the illusion of blood. It was blatant cheating and they almost got away with it.

I didn't see any of this happening or the commotion on the sideline. All I saw was Nick Evans back on the pitch and I realised he was probably there to attempt a drop goal or to kick a penalty if they got one. In the closing minute they got into position for Evans to attempt a drop goal, but we forced them backwards, and by the time he took the shot he was 40m out and missed. What would have happened had he scored, I don't know, considering what was discovered afterwards. To be honest, we weren't too bothered, because we had won, 6-5. That meant we would now have a repeat of the 2006 semi-final against Munster on 2 May.

Lansdowne Road wasn't available because of rebuilding work, but thankfully Croke Park was because the IRFU and the GAA, having foreseen the possibility of an all Irish semi-final, had secured special permission at the GAA Congress to make the ground available. Those of us on the Irish squad were used to playing there, but it was a special venue for some of the other Leinster players who hadn't and who had GAA backgrounds. We were regarded as the underdogs this time and looking back at it from this distance, it is a bit hard to understand why Leinster were written off by so many beforehand, when you look at the players we had, particularly our foreign additions. That said, Munster had more players selected for the British & Irish Lions that summer and in the quarter-final had absolutely hammered a good Ospreys side 43-9. But, in fact, that had prepared us better and sometimes, for all the preparation and skills involved, one team can want it more. I know Munster said they wanted it, and to this day feel they had prepared properly, but we hadn't tasted what they had and we needed it. I remember Wally saying afterwards, 'Every time we carried the ball we were hit by three fellas.' It was probably just one of those days when it all came together for us, beyond even what we had planned to do.

It also happened to be more of a fair fight when it came to the crowd, which was 50/50 this time round. Friends told me afterwards that they had never seen Croke Park more colourful, that it surpassed All-Ireland final day with all the blue and red jerseys and flags. Coming out to the field provided a rare wow! factor. It remains one of the coolest moments I can remember from my career. The sight of the blue and the red chequered around the entire stadium, the ear-splitting level of noise, I felt that as a club team we had finally reached the top level. I was always proud to be a Leinster player, but everyone was with us now.

Everything clicked for us on the pitch. Our first try came off a planned move, a dummy switch that put Rocky into clean space in the middle of the field. Our confidence lifted. We called moves as we were running, we were constantly calling what we were seeing, it was real heads-up, confident rugby. And then Felipe Contepomi got injured. For all of the talent we had in the team, in the three-quarters in particular and Isa at full-back, we depended on our number 10 to pull the strings and that's what Contepomi did, which is why we and the fans loved him so much. His injury meant that he had to go off and Johnny Sexton replaced him.

Johnny may have been something of an unknown quantity to the more occasional Leinster supporter as his game time that season had been limited by the presence of Felipe.

Johnny believed in himself and didn't suffer nerves. I had no fears about him replacing Felipe. None. I had played so much with Johnny, particularly in 2007 during the period when so many players were away at the World Cup, that I had no doubt about his ability or his temperament. He was one of us, an Academy lad, and he was driven, and because of that I automatically backed him to do every bit as well as Felipe had been doing for us. It was only afterwards that I realised just how well Johnny did, given that he had to take a penalty straight away coming onto the pitch. It must have been a huge moment for him, but he kicked it as if it was the most natural thing in the world. A lot was made afterwards of that photograph of him screaming at Rog in the corner, when Rog was on his knees after Darce's try, that the sledging was disrespectful and unnecessary. He tried to say afterwards that he hadn't been out of order, but we were all shouting stuff at each other, we were all so geed up that it went a bit mental.

The really telling moment in the game for me was turning to the stands after Drico's intercept try and seeing the Munster fans streaming out and lots of Leinster fans singing 'Cheerio'. Having been there in 2006, it was great for the boot to be on the other foot. We won 25-9 in the end and, in retrospect, it was the end of an era for them and the beginning of one for us. We were now the top dogs, having had to live with Munster getting all the kudos in recent years. Or at least we would be if we finished the job off by winning the final, which was going to be against Leicester at Murrayfield.

Leicester were going to be a hell of a team to beat. Like Munster, they had won the Heineken Cup twice and had just become English champions again. They weren't a pretty team, just abrasive, persistent and ruthless. We were underdogs yet again. I was lucky that I had plenty to occupy me during the week before the game. We had been chosen to do a press and sponsor day for the British & Irish Lions on the Monday, much to Cheika's fury. He agreed to it when a private jet was arranged to fly us to London and back, and only after I had done that morning's training. I also sat exams at UCD on Wednesday for the master's course I was doing part-time. I was focused on the match, of course, but my down time was also full.

I enjoyed a great moment as the teams came out onto the pitch for the game. It was a really proud thing to know that there would be as many Leinster fans going as Munster would have brought with them and that they were going to the same lengths, begging, borrowing and stealing to get the money together for tickets and travel. If they could get them. I only found out afterwards that many of my friends from Naas couldn't get tickets, but in fairness to them they kept this quiet from me so as not to distract me from the task at hand. As it happened, at the time European Rugby Cup was based in Dublin and there was a guy my age who used to work there, Eugene Delaney, who was also from Naas. Eugene, being Eugene, got it sorted for them. He gave all of my mates jobs on the pitch as flag-bearers for the pre-match formalities, which meant they could stay on in the ground to see the game. When I saw them all there on the pitch beforehand, as they started to call to me as I walked out, well, it was a great uplifting moment for me.

We were the better team on the day, but it was all so tight. It was our toughest game of the season, but the Harlequins experience stood to us. Alesana Tuilagi was one of their big-name players on the wing, but I remember Rocky absolutely smashing him with a tackle early on in the game and I thought, 'Tone set'. No one was flinching. It was a helter-skelter game, going back and forth, hammer and tongs. Many of the lads shipped big knocks but carried on despite the pain. Nobody was willing to be removed. There were lots of players who had big games, but Johnny, the sub against Munster, drove us on from out-half as if he had been playing there for years. They were big into the sledging, Leicester. I got a bit of it when I knocked-on and Craig Newby slapped me in mock congratulations as I was on the ground. I ignored it.

We went in behind by seven points at half-time but equalised about 10 minutes into the second-half. The try came after a Drico grubber kick forced Leicester to put the ball into touch in their own 22. Rocky won the line-out and we went through the phases, driving it on, everyone pitching in to make sure the ball remained secure. The ball was slow, but when my chance came, I took it. I drove forward, Shane Jennings latched onto me for extra power, putting the rocket boosters on, and I went through Ben Kay and Newby and got the try. There's a picture of me lying there on the ground, ball in my hands, almost under my neck, and a big smile on my face. For some reason I can't explain to this day, at that moment I thought of Scott Quinnell scoring for the Lions against Australia in 2001. He had scored, he was lying on the ground smiling, and I did that. I don't know why, I just thought of him at that instant and did the same, but I knew immediately that it was a big moment in the game because while we still weren't in front, we weren't chasing the game any more. And it was Murrayfield, too, where I had scored against Scotland just a couple of months earlier. I had joked beforehand, 'Ah yeah, I always score tries in Murrayfield,' taking the piss, so maybe that's why I was smiling to myself.

It gave us the momentum, even if it was more than 20 minutes later before Johnny nailed the penalty that gave us the eventual three-point win. We had just nine minutes left to hang in there. I never panicked. I remember another moment in the game, just after that penalty, when someone put a kick down to their end and I just took off after it. It was one of those perfect moments when I was into a game and I was in this kind of constant flow, not even thinking, on autopilot. I think it was Tom Croft who caught the ball and I got right on top of him, tackled him into touch and the crowd went absolutely mental in response. I just felt then, knew, that it was going to be our day and everything was going to go our way because we had put the work in, suffered the bad nights after games, the horrible games, such as when Munster beat us out the gate in the semi-final three years earlier and Rog jumped over barriers into the crowd to celebrate, all that sort of stuff.

It didn't all go smoothly, though. I dropped the ball with five minutes to go and Johnny was doing his usual shouting and I was just going, 'Relax, next ball,' citing the mantra that we had, that we couldn't change a mistake but we could make sure we didn't make it again. Afterwards, Bernard Jackman said that I looked calm and that transmitted itself to the rest of the players. That said, we still had to work our socks off.

I'll never forget the moment when I realised we'd won it. They had the ball around halfway for what felt like ages and the terror was that we might give away a penalty, which, had they kicked one, would have meant extra time. There was a ruck and I piled in, trying to kill the ball or at least to slow it down enough, gambling that we were still outside the kicking range. Anyway, the ruck piled up and then there was a loud whistle and I remember thinking, in a brief flash of new panic, 'I hope to fuck I haven't given anything away'. I hadn't. No penalty. It was over. Church was standing over me and grabbed me going, 'Wahh', which was scary enough, followed by 'We've won!' I think I just fell over then. It was a combination of being bolloxed and an overspill of emotion at what we'd achieved.

Winning shut up all the critics. That was a big part of the satisfaction. But we were our own most relevant critics. We weren't soft, we did care and we'd shown that.

CHAPTER 5

LIVING AS A LION

The British & Irish Lions can be hard to explain to those who aren't rugby supporters but it matters to the fans … and certainly means a hell of a lot to the players. My own affection, indeed love, for the concept of a team made up of the best players from four countries – Ireland, England, Scotland and Wales – that travels to play against the best players in the Southern Hemisphere started as a teenager, in 1997. I had been sent for a month to the Gaeltacht at Ring, in County Waterford, and we had no access to television there. That meant I couldn't see that year's tour games against South Africa. These were the days before social media, so it meant we couldn't even find out the results of the test games, which took place on successive Saturday afternoons. But we were allowed family visits each Sunday – out to get fed – and my friend's dad recorded the games onto VHS and we went to his house nearby in Dunmore East to watch them as if they were live. They were three thrilling games and Irish lads like Keith Wood, Paul Wallace and Jeremy Davidson were stars in the series, which the Lions won. Afterwards, there was a tour DVD brought out, *Living with Lions*, the first real fly-on-the-wall, behind-the-scenes documentary of a rugby tour, and it was brilliant. I was hooked.

It meant there was almost a childish anticipation for me when it came to the possibility of being selected to go and huge excitement when I was picked. In the old amateur days, I'm told, players used to receive letters to their home, informing them of their selection and what they had to do and of the minimal expenses they would receive. I heard a lot of players simply couldn't afford to go because the earlier trips went on for months, but that for those who could go the experience was often one of the best of their lives, for the friendships they made as much as the games they played.

That had all changed in the professional era and now selections were announced at a press conference broadcast on TV. I already knew I was in the extended squad, from which they'd make their pick, because you get a letter confirming that weeks in advance. I was hopeful I'd get in – having read all the stuff in the newspapers where everyone makes their predictions as to who will get selected – despite being dropped for that game against Scotland. Friends and family asked me where I'd be when the squad was announced so they could be with me when the news came through. I remember sitting in the David Lloyd gym in Clonskeagh, where Leinster were based at the time. It was early in the week of the Munster semi-final game. The tension was huge, sitting with Rob and a group of the players, not knowing if I'd make it or not. The announcement has great pageantry and hype to it, which adds to the sense of occasion. I had taken nothing for granted, so the feeling when my name was called out was amazing. I had really made it.

It certainly helped to ease the tension I was feeling about the Munster game. I was about to enjoy one of the most extraordinary experiences of my professional career in one of the most relaxed atmospheres I've ever experienced, although first I had to finish out the season with Leinster safely. Tomás O'Leary broke his ankle weeks later and missed the trip and Alan Quinlan was suspended for an alleged eye-gouging incident in our Croke Park match. Jerry Flannery got injured at the first Lions training session in London and had to go home. It's obviously hard luck when that type of thing happens, but you have to continue training and playing to the maximum even if you might want to avoid taking risks. I've seen guys tense before a selection is announced, more worried about not hurting themselves in training than training well, but I always worked on the basis that the minute you start trying to look after yourself in training, that's the minute you get hurt. So I just kind of ploughed on and didn't really think about it.

We met up in London before heading off, and I admit that I took a chance of going out on the lash in Dublin the night before we were flying. We had won the Heineken Cup the previous Saturday after all. I got home about 5.30am on the day of the flight to get my bags and Lukie collected me in a taxi to go the airport about half an hour later. It took him about ten minutes banging on the door to wake me up. I'll never forget meeting Ian McGeechan (Geech), our head coach, for the first time because I didn't have the freshest of breath or look the freshest in general and the first thing he said to me was, 'I'd be worried if you weren't like that.' And I was just like, alright, I'm in a good place here so.

We were so lucky to have Geech as head coach and Paulie as captain. Geech is from a different era, when the players went away on tour for a long time. His manner is excellent, he is so decent, he made it all about the players, didn't make demands of us to do commercial stuff that ate into our time. Geech had a vision of how he wanted things, from his own previous experiences as a Lions player and winning coach. Alongside that, you need a captain who understands the vibe of the players and what they need as a group and what's the right thing and the right time. Paulie had that in spades. Everyone respected him for it. He has really good emotional intelligence, gauging people and the squad and getting them to buy into the common goal, as well as being such a good player and professional and being able to lead by example on and off the pitch. There was a bit pressure given that the previous two tours in Australia and New Zealand had been lost, the second in 2005 in humiliating fashion, and talk that if we lost this tour the Lions concept would be heading for the knacker's yard, but Geech and Paulie made sure that pressure never became overbearing.

Going on tour with strangers is a bit odd, but I just made it my business to get to know people straightaway. Other than the Irish lads, I knew some of them anyway because I'd played so much rugby against them and I had made connections. It was great to watch how others went about things, what they did in training, how they prepared off the pitch and I got into conversations in which I learnt so much. I asked questions of everyone – other players, coaches, physios, strength and conditioning people – trying to glean whatever knowledge I could. I learnt more by training with people or against people on tour than I did playing against them on the pitch prior to the tour. And while it may go against the whole ethos by which I worked throughout the rest of my career, I found that we bonded over having a few drinks. We had to because the time we had together was short. It wasn't a holiday, but it wasn't a normal professional set-up either. We went out the night after every game and took it easy the following day. We played some really tough games and got so much out of them.

Once I got there, the ambition was to make the test team. It's harsh to say, but in my head there's a difference between a Lion and a test Lion. The distinction isn't always made and the players who get to tour deserve to be there – which is why Gats made a big mistake bringing in some players in 2017 to make up the numbers in a midweek game before sending them away again, devaluing what it meant to be a Lion – but you want to be the guy who plays the tests.

It meant so much to me to get on to the test team, to be the best of the best. I didn't go out in 2009 with the expectation that I would be in the starting team, reckoning that Gats, as a member of the coaching staff, would urge Geech to go with Andy Powell, the Welsh number 8. He was a lot bigger and stronger than me and a very different style of player, into full-on conflict, but fortunately for me Geech wanted something different from the crash, bang, wallop style that the Boks were likely to use.

I have a picture at home from right before that first test in Durban, one of the few I have from my career, taken by Inpho sports photographer Dan Sheridan without my even knowing because I was so absorbed in my pre-match routine. I'm sitting in the dressing-room with my head bowed and my hands clenched, looking like I've just taken communion. This was about to be a major 80 minutes in my life and I had to have my game-head on.

Unfortunately, South Africa blew us away in the opening quarter, the World Cup-holders deciding they weren't going to be embarrassed in front of their own fans. They went at 100 miles per hour and beat us up in the pack, particularly destroying us in the scrums. We probably didn't have tough enough warm-up games to prepare us for this.

They were 13 points up by the end of the first 20 minutes, a converted try and two penalties. Even when Jamie Roberts and

Drico combined brilliantly in the centre to send Tom Croft in for a converted try, we gave away another two penalties, had a try by Tommy Bowe disallowed for some midfield infringement and went in 19-7 down at half-time.

They got another try early in the second half and after the conversion were 26-7 up by the end of 50 minutes. We looked dead and buried. But we weren't. With five minutes left we had the score back to 26-21, after Croft scored a second try and scrum-half Mike Phillips got in for one as well. We had outscored them on tries, could have got more and yet we'd lost.

We could have crumbled after that, but we didn't, which was further tribute to the way Geech and Paulie led us and moulded the group. There wasn't a lot of review going on during the Lions tour, the concentration moved so quickly to the next game. It's only a decade ago, but there wasn't the same level of analysis back then. I felt I had done well in difficult circumstances in the first test, even if Tom's tries meant he got most of the back-row plaudits from the press, but I was still anxious about getting selected for the second test. When I heard that I'd made the team, I was thrilled. There were seven Irish in the starting xv – Rob, Tommy, Drico, Lukie, Paulie, Wally and me – and Rog came off the bench later.

That second test is probably the most brutal and toughest game of rugby I've ever played. I'm not alone in thinking it was a bit insane; others who played in it have also said that it was their hardest ever. There were bodies strewn everywhere, both during the match and after it. It was like a war zone. The rules are a little bit different now and the game in general was probably a lot more aggressive than would be allowed today. Afterwards, people told me that it was one of the greatest matches of all time. I didn't see it like that at the time. Who thinks 'this is a great game' in the middle of one? I was concentrated on doing the right thing, phase after phase, not thinking of how exciting it must be for the people who were watching. Anyway, we lost. The brilliance of the game, as others saw it, didn't really matter.

How we lost was a matter of considerable controversy. We had a good first-half, running up a 16-8 lead. We imposed ourselves, both in the backs and forwards. Rob ran everything back at them, no matter from how deep. Simon Shaw was a giant in the second row, having replaced Alun Wyn Jones from the previous week alongside Paulie. Adam Jones anchored the scrum in the way Phil Vickery hadn't been able to do the previous week.

We should have been playing against only 14 men from nearly the very start of the game. Schalk Burger threw Lukie out of the maul using, as one writer put, his eye socket as a hand hold. He got ten minutes in the bin and an eight-week suspension after his citing, although he wasn't found guilty of deliberate gouging. I only became aware of the incident later because I didn't see it when it happened. It wasn't put on the big screen, as far as I can remember, and in any case unless I'm captain, I don't look at those replays because I'm getting on with being ready for the next play. There are others to look after the injured. It's not that I'm emotionless about it, but I compartmentalise and focus on my job. That we didn't see it may explain why we didn't follow in the footsteps of the Willie John McBride team of 1974, which dealt with such incidents of violence by calling '99' and every one of them then ploughed in to punch an opponent, on the basis that the ref couldn't send all of them off for doing so. Thankfully, that doesn't happen these days.

Like they had the week before, this time we started brilliantly. Fatigue and injuries got us when we were 19-8 up, though. Our props Gethin Jenkins and Adam Jones had to leave the pitch and our advantage at the scrums was lost. We couldn't keep the momentum going. They scored two converted tries and a penalty and went ahead with seven minutes to go, before Stephen Jones levelled for us with another penalty.

Obviously, I'll never forget the last few moments of the second test. We were level at 25-25. Leave it at that and we get a chance the following week to draw the series. Rog was on the pitch by this stage, but instead of playing it safe he decided to gamble, to get us down the pitch and into a position to look for a score. So he launched a garryowen, high into the air, and chased it. It was the weirdest thing ever to happen because it was not like Rog was known for going after his own up-and-unders. Normally, with Ireland, he'd put it up and Geordan Murphy or Gerv Dempsey or someone would chase it. I remember thinking, 'What is Rog doing?' He hit Fourie du Preez in the air as he jumped for the ball and it was called as a penalty. I looked at Rog and he was acting surprised that he had been penalised and at the time I thought, 'Well, what did you expect?' It was inside their own half, but in the centre of the pitch, and at altitude it was close to a sure thing. Morné Steyn steadied himself and from 51m the ball hurtled through the thin Pretoria air and between the posts to avenge the series defeat in 1997. It was what might have happened to us in Cardiff on Grand Slam day.

It was only afterwards that I realised that Rog wasn't on the reservation when he took that kick. Rog has since said that he was sparked, he didn't know what he was doing. If that game was being played today, he would have been taken off the pitch for a head injury assessment and likely been kept off with concussion. He'd taken a clear bang to the head only a few minutes earlier and he didn't know what was going on. But as recently as a decade ago, people in the game did not realise the significance of head injuries and played on when they should have been brought straight off for their own safety and for treatment. At the time, though, we didn't realise what had happened to him. I think some of the guys who were further on in their career were a little bit more pissed off than I was with that kick, but I don't know if they realised that Rog was sparked. Was I pissed off about losing? A bit, of course, knowing that we weren't going to win this series, but I didn't let it linger. It's like anything; if you've prepared well and you've given it your all and you get beaten, there's not a whole lot you can do about it. On a personal level, I had prepared as best I could, played well and we got beaten by a single kick.

It was like a triage centre in our dressing-room. Everyone was deflated, not just because we had lost but because we had been literally battered. Injuries are common in rugby, but I'd never seen anything like this. Five of our team ended up in hospital for treatment and, not surprisingly, couldn't play the following week.

Rog, unfairly, took something of another battering from the British press, who were also ignorant of what had happened to him. Thankfully for him and the rest of us, social media wasn't really a thing then, because I'm sure many of us would have been slaughtered online for losing the game, as is the way now. Instead, we discovered that among the fans who were there in South Africa, and even among some of the hosts, there was an enormous sympathy and respect for us, a feeling that we had done everything we could possibly have done.

I badly wanted to play in the third test. We were going to be down players with all the injuries and there were other back-row options, but thankfully Geech stuck with me. We got a cracking 28-9 win in that game, even if it was a dead rubber.

The team for the third test had lots of changes, with the likes of Drico, Jamie Roberts, Gethin Jenkins and Adam Jones out injured. But Tommy Bowe started at 13 and John Hayes and David Wallace were among those who came on as subs. We were relaxed, possibly because of the drinking sessions we'd had earlier in the week, but we were also focused. It was a game I really enjoyed playing. I only remember some moments from different big games, but I look back with satisfaction on setting up Shane Williams for a particularly nice try to break open the game. I remember setting up one for Mike Phillips as well, thinking I was going to get blown up for being around the wrong side of the ruck when I got the ball for him.

Our final test victory may not have changed the overall outcome, but it still mattered. The biggest margin of victory in 118 years was hard-earned. It was the end of a very long season and we could have thrown in the towel, but we wanted to win, for each other in the squad and for the Lions. We rose to the challenge. We did it by being more amateur in our approach than the 2005 lot, who had become bogged down in their level of Clive Woodward-enforced preparation. We bonded. They were good men I shared those weeks with. It was one of those times when losing wasn't the worst thing.

People tell us that we saved the Lions, even in defeat. I have no time for the people who say that it no longer means anything, not in the World Cup era. I would have loved to win the World Cup, but if you look at the crowds wherever the Lions go, the effort of the teams we play against, the enormous historical legacy because you're the best of the islands going against the best of wherever we tour, it retains something special. It's the challenge of trying to bring the best elements of four different teams together in near zero time, to play against a well-established international side. All the different skills, abilities, ways of playing, even egos, people coming out of their trusted environments into a new one, it's just a mega-mix of new and exciting things.

And 2009 was not over for Ireland yet. The November international series would give us the opportunity to test ourselves against some of the best of the southern hemisphere teams, including South Africa, now Tri-Nations champions as well as World Cup holders and victors over the Lions, again. The challenge we set ourselves was to finish the year undefeated, but to get to the South Africa game we had to play Australia and Fiji first.

The series kicked off on 15 November at Croke Park against a good Australian side that had won at Twickenham against England the previous weekend. Our resilience stood to us because Australia were probably better than us, most definitely in the scrums, and we handed them seven points in the first few minutes, which meant we were always chasing the game. We clawed our way level again, but when Rocky Elsom got a try that they converted on the 61st minute to give them a seven-point lead, we were really up against it. We thought Tommy Bowe had scored a try right at the end, but he didn't get the ball down properly, held up by the defenders. From our attacking scrum Drico did more or less what he had done in the Six Nations, burrowing his way over the line, and when Rog converted it we had our draw and retained our undefeated record to date. We gave Fiji a thumping the following week, 41-6, and our ambition now hung on beating the World Champions in what was being billed as the 'battle of the hemispheres'.

Home advantage clearly means a lot because we were facing a team that had won the series over the best of Britain and Ireland. But what also matters is cohesiveness and that is something we had in the Ireland team that the Lions probably hadn't been able to achieve in their short time together. South Africa were missing Pierre Spies and Bakkies Botha, both of whom were a massive loss, but Deccie made the brave call of starting Johnny at number 10 instead of Rog. He had a brilliant day with his place kicking, getting five out of seven penalties, but he couldn't be blamed for the two he missed, given where they were, and some of those he knocked over were terrific efforts. He also had to contend with getting his bearings in freezing fog. It was so dense that it wasn't possible at times to see from one touch-line to the other, let alone the stands on the far side. It was weird, knowing massive crowds were in the stands, being able to hear them when they roared, but not being able to see them.

It wasn't our best playing performance. The scrum was in big trouble again, we handled badly too often, allowed teammates to be isolated in possession and surrendered too many turnovers. But we had unity and self-belief and a willingness, borne out of all that we had achieved throughout the year, to keep them out, even when the Boks were hammering at our 22 in additional time. Drico again led by example, smashing Zane Kirchner and, when he failed to release the ball, securing a penalty. When that was kicked to touch, we won 15-10.

Victory meant the longest unbeaten sequence in Irish international rugby: 10 victories and the Australian draw, not beaten since the All Blacks had been in Dublin a year previously. My personal satisfaction with the year increased when it was announced that I was on the shortlist for the World Player of the Year. I never expected to win it, given that Drico was the other Irish nominee and he'd had a sensational year, but everyone was somewhat surprised when Richie McCaw got it again, because 2009 was not one of his better years.

Still, there was a great satisfaction in knowing that just five years after I had made the shortlist for the Young Player of the Year award, I had now graduated to the top table. The vows I'd made while drinking cans in TCD in November 2004 had been achieved, but my thirst for rugby success, and to make the best of myself, wasn't sated yet.

CHAPTER 6

LIVING AS A PRO

O ver the years, I've met people who asked me what I do and when I said, 'professional rugby player', they replied, 'Right, but what do you do outside that?' If I dug a bit deeper, I discovered that they thought I did a couple of hours' training in the morning and had the rest of the day free to lark about. That it was a part-time job, in other words.

Far from it. I lived my job. It was a full day's work between meetings, individual and team training, video analysis, memorising instructions for forthcoming matches, rest and eating according to the needs of my role. You might think that everybody has to eat, that I shouldn't be making a big deal of that, but professional rugby players have to eat vast quantities of specific things, almost whether we want to or not.

One of the best pieces of advice I ever received during my career came from Mick Kearney, a successful businessman who was manager of the Irish team under Joe Schmidt for a number of years. He sat me down and told me, 'One of the best things you can do is to invest in yourself. You know you have a limited window of time to do what you want, but you also know it will finish, and not necessarily at a time of your choosing, because being a professional rugby player is not a normal career.' He challenged me to make it last as long as possible, injury permitting, and to do it as well as I could because, he warned me, my life would change once I was no longer playing and I might find it hard to cope without the sporting challenge and the income from the game.

There were different times during my career when my desire to be the best professional possible intensified. I wanted to be a good pro from the day I signed my first contract, but there were moments, in 2008 and 2011 particularly, when I consciously wanted to take a further step forward, and again after Joe Schmidt became Irish coach in 2013. Being a good professional didn't mean just doing my best during games, it was about the things I did before and after each game, the preparation and recovery, about investment in my physical and mental well-being to allow me to do my best.

When I started in professional rugby under Cheika, there was little data or science to measure or support what we were doing on the pitch.

Leinster was the first rugby team in the Northern Hemisphere to use GPS tracking of the distance covered by each player in training and in games. Cheika had seen it used in the Aussie Rules game and we started wearing the equipment in training. Cheika favoured volume running at the time, and everyone trimmed down massively as a result, even though that went somewhat against the mantra of the time that players needed to be big, particularly the forwards. I had enough height, standing at 6 foot 3 inches in my socks, but I kept hearing from people around the game, some in the media, some at the fringes of involvement, that I wasn't heavy enough to be a modern-day number 8 and this would restrict my progress in the game. In fairness to Cheika, he never put me under that pressure, encouraging me to concentrate on being a good footballer and not to worry about my size.

Cheika didn't just run the legs off us, he brought in really good strength and conditioning (s&c) people and nutritionists and tried to improve the structure and nature of training according to the data he was getting. He veered towards recreating the game experience in training where possible. Jason Cowman – who later went on to work with the Ireland squad – was in charge of s&c and he was ahead of the field when it came to understanding and implementing the new information in sports science. Equally important, he understood people's reaction to what he was telling them, because sometimes players want to do basic training and not what they think is just in fashion, and the necessity to work within a team structure. Jason and Cheiks were very open to ideas as to how we should be training, as long as there were data to support the proposed measures. Anything was considered – even meditation. They were pushing the boundaries and constantly trying to evolve our training to suit our bodies and improve our performance.

By the time Cheika left us we were no longer doing volume running. Instead, each training session was now very game-based, replicating what we had to do during an actual game. Training was monitored: our metres per minute, the occasions we hit high speed and the volume of high-speed metres accumulated, all were examined to see what we'd be able to do in a game.

I didn't train differently from the other players, but I may have prepared differently for group training. I was proactive about dealing with my physical strengths and weaknesses through prehabilitation (prehab) and rehabilitation (rehab). I did specific pre-training, a lot of core work and stretching, exercises to protect my neck, and I practised efficient running to protect my knees. I was an early adopter of different recovery strategies, believing that there was more work to be done after training to get the real benefits of the session and to protect the body against injury. At Leinster, we used to say that you have to recover as hard as you train. I liked my sleep and had time allotted for naps during the day.

When we'd start a group training session, we'd fire up the body with exercises to the glutes, hamstrings and core, things that had to be properly warmed up before engaging in full training. But I'd also fit in a lot of movement-type drills, which laid down good movement patterns for me and also good running technique. I worked with physios and other specialists to get programmes that were individually tailored for my body type. I was lucky that at Leinster we had some excellent rehab and prehab physios, who helped get my body in the right condition to play rugby. My weekly schedule included at least two hour-long rubs by masseurs, and they were just flush-outs, repairs to the wear and tear from games and training. If the slots were taken, I went elsewhere to get them because I regarded them as essential.

In pre-season I tried to maximise everything because I knew that once the season began it would be all about maintenance – at least, it was for me because I didn't have a lot of injuries. I saw pre-season as the only window for making substantial gains. If I presented in good shape for pre-season, then I didn't have to worry about cutting weight and I could concentrate on building muscle mass and reducing my body fat percentage, which I liked to keep in the 11–13% zone. Any lower and I felt that I might not have sufficient padding to absorb the blows of tackles. I looked to have muscle mass at 90kg plus. I never went more than a week without training, even in the off-season. My belief was that I should always keep myself fit, keep the body ready to go, dial it down during my brief off-season holiday, but then ramp it up in pre-season, keeping it fairly level afterwards.

I didn't have many pre-existing injuries – apart from ankle and shoulder issues I had picked up along the way – but I still went to a physio regularly. Leinster did screening every year to identify various weaknesses, such as a stiff neck, for example, and to counteract the problems identified by that I was given prehab work to do in the gym. I did core work or hip stability work as assigned, or as I had identified as necessary. The main goal was to prevent injuries by strengthening and flexing. I worked to make myself more efficient in movement.

Outside Leinster, I went to physical therapists as opposed to physios; there's a difference between the two that's not recognised as much in Ireland as elsewhere. A physio is good for helping you with an injury, when something is wrong and you need to repair it. A physical therapist can treat injuries, but their focus is on getting your body into the right condition to avoid injury. I went to Mike Carswell once a week, a South African who is a former rugby player himself and who lots of players swear by for getting them into the right condition. He worked my body from head to toe, absolutely stripping me apart. I also went to a stretching specialist, Aidan Kilgannon, who performed myofascial release. That's an unfamiliar term to many people, but basically there is muscle and over it, like a protective sheath, is fascia. The science about fascia is still not particularly well understood, but through use the fascia can get crunched up, which affects mobility and the ability to withstand impact. Aidan used stretching techniques to smooth the fascia, a bit like giving it a good iron to make it smooth and supple again.

My background in medical engineering meant I saw the body as a construction. I did a musculo-skeletal review every morning that I went into training with Leinster. I took the iPad and filled out a questionnaire on how I had slept and how I felt physically. Then I carried out some motion tests, usually five, and logged the results. These data generated an algorithm that pointed up any vulnerability to particular types of injury and the likelihood of it occurring.

I invested in technology to use at home to improve my physical condition. I became interested in EMS (electrical muscle stimulation), which can be used for strength, growth and recovery. I wore recovery skins – compression leggings worn after a workout – and things called fireflies, which I put behind my knee and that delivered painless electrical impulses to gently activate the muscles of the lower leg to increase blood circulation. The idea was to reduce muscle soreness within 24 hours of high-intensity exercise, aiding recovery from any sprains or strains and reducing swelling following an injury. I do like my gadgets. NormaTec, for example, is a great piece of tech. They are basically massive compression socks that flush out all the lactic acid from the legs post-training and push blood up towards the heart. A couple of times a week I'd stick on the NormaTecs when I was watching television. People laughed me at first when I started using them, but when I retired a number of players offered to buy them from me. Even if something might not work, there's always the placebo effect, where you think that it's working.

I had an altitude tent for a while, too. There's good science behind it. The theory is that the tent mimics sleeping at high altitude, with reduced oxygen. In adapting to that environment, my body produced more red blood cells. At training the next morning I was at sea level, but the effect of the night in the tent meant I had much more oxygen available, I wouldn't tire as quickly and I wouldn't produce as much lactic acid. Too much lactic acid can affect the efficiency of your muscles and give a bad burning sensation. The altitude tent helped my aerobic capacity, so I could recover faster and run for longer. I did it for a couple of pre-seasons, but I found that it affected the quality of my sleep, which is, of course, the most important time for recovery from exercise. The tent effectively put me into quite a stressful environment and disrupted my sleeping pattern. It took a while to get used to it and I had to do it for a minimum of four weeks to get the benefits. I tried doing it during the season once and I couldn't. I simply wasn't getting the right sleep that I needed for recovery. Sheena didn't like it either, to put it mildly. The tent I had was a one-man job because it just got way too hot in there. Second pre-season I did it again, and I was more or less sent to a different room for most nights of the week.

I discovered the hyperbaric chamber when Gordon D'Arcy used it after a really bad arm break in 2008. He found one in Capel Street that was used mainly for people who got the bends from deep-sea diving. But it has other uses. There is good science around the benefits of the chamber in recovery from bone injuries. I went there first in 2015 for a vertebrae injury. I did it for a couple of weeks on the basis that it would promote a massive output of stem cells, which is beneficial to their growth and recovery. It worked like this: I walked into this tin-like cylinder, it was closed and I was told, 'We're going down.' The pressure inside the chamber was slowly increased, simulating the body going deeper under-water. I didn't really notice the pressure, but then I'd look at the plastic water bottle I'd brought in with me and it'd be half scrunched up because of the pressure levels. My body was getting that too. I did it for 90 minutes, three times a week. I wore an oxygen mask and received medical-grade oxygen as part of the treatment, but I felt nothing really. I lay there and watched movies.

All of this extra work and effort was part of my drive to excel. I was strong, but I wasn't a muscleman. I was fast, but I wasn't an Olympic sprinter. I was tall, but not as tall as other forwards. Whatever natural talent I had, I built on it by out-working my competition and the opposition. I became known for my physical resilience. I usually played up to 30 games a season for club and country, and I started and finished the majority of those games. It was all down to constant, unrelenting hard work.

Despite the prehab and rehab work, there would have been many times when I was a bit sore going into games. I'd say most professional players are the same. There may have been times when players underplayed their injuries, because admitting a problem and missing a game risked not getting your place again. As a result, everyone pushed through and played at that high level, even if their body wasn't at the optimum level. I was proactive in managing issues, both current and those that had subsided. I never had any chronic injury issues. I had an ankle issue at one stage that we didn't handle correctly, so my ankle gave me hassle in subsequent years. I managed it by icing it for 30–60 minutes while watching television or video analysis. I injured the AC joint on one shoulder, but I was lucky in that it separated completely, which made it easier to have it fixed straight away. My main problem with that injury, which I got in a game against Ulster, was that I was due to fly out to Dubai on a week's holiday the next day and it had to be cancelled so I could get treatment.

I believe I've been concussed three times during my career. The first time was against Scotland at Murrayfield in February

2011. I banged my head off the ground sometime in the first-half and couldn't remember any more of that half, even though I apparently set up Reddser for a try by taking a quick tap penalty. I only remember the second-half, but I played on to the end.

The second was when I was knocked out cold in the 2011 pre-World Cup warm-up game against England. I clashed heads with Donncha O'Callaghan and the big melon head on him, and then I got up to play on. Church looked at me in a line-out and realised that I hadn't a clue what was going on and he got the medics onto the pitch to take me off. I don't how much later I woke up, but I was in the medical room under the stand with my dad beside me and David Wallace on the next bed. He had suffered the knee injury that ended his career and his wife Aileen was there crying and his children were looking on and I looked at them and back to my dad and went, 'What the hell is going on?'

The other time was in early January 2016, in a game with the Ospreys when Ben Te'o and I went to tackle a player at the same time and we clashed heads. I was substituted immediately, but I was back playing quickly each time.

The way players are removed from the pitch quickly now is much better than it used to be. It is done by independent medics, not by coaches who might want an important player to try to run it off. The game is a contact sport, so incidents will happen, but you don't want them to happen as a result of recklessness, and if there is an injury, players need treatment fast. But you go in knowing that collisions are inevitable and you can't be wrapped up in cotton wool.

～

There was another crucial aspect to my preparation and recovery, and that was nutrition. I always treated my body as if it was a machine: what I put into it as fuel, be it food or training, brought about certain results; if I put in the wrong things, then I suffered. Being a rugby professional is unlike most jobs because I had to be conscious every second of the day of what food I was eating and how it affected me. I burnt an enormous of calories, between 7,000 and 8,000 on match day, up to 5,000 at training and between 3,500 and 4,000 on a down day because of my build. I had to eat a lot of food to cover all of that, although I found it difficult to count it accurately. When I was looking to put on weight, I might have started the day with a five-egg omelette followed by granola, and that was just the first of five or six meals.

As a professional sportsperson, how you eat, what you eat and when you eat becomes incredibly important. I probably shouldn't have tried to change my body shape and size after 2009, given how well I was playing, but I was always trying to get better, always looking for marginal gains. I was conscious that even though I was tall and my teams had achieved success, there were still people in the game who compared me unfavourably to other number 8s simply because they were bulkier.

I just felt bad. I was too big, I couldn't get around the park in the way I needed to, couldn't be the kind of dynamic football player that I wanted to be.

My opinion was that I needed to find something different that worked for me. When I came back from that World Cup I said, 'That just did not work for me at all,' and I decided to change. My opinion was that my diet was limiting the way I wanted to play and ultimately it was my opinion that counted. The idea of being a big ball-carrying number 8 just didn't work for me. I'm not a giant heavyweight like Billy Vunipola or Nathan Hughes, who'll carry into traffic all day for you, running over people with their enormous bulk. I think I'm more of a footballing, link type of a player, so I decided to go deeper into the whole area of nutrition to identify what would work for me.

A nutritionist's job is quite difficult because they have to map out the food for a group of people and might not have the time or resources to go deep into an individual's particular needs. I was too trusting at first, going with the general recommendations as opposed to tackling it from a personal angle. Eating the same as all of your teammates is not necessarily a good approach.

I didn't always agree with the food we were provided during camp at the Six Nations or at the World Cup. Some people can eat everything and their body will react fine, but camp is quite dangerous because there's all this buffet-style food on offer. The line of desserts drove me a little bit insane. 'Why are desserts there for guys every day?' I'd complain. 'They wouldn't be getting dessert at home.' The nutritionist would point out, 'Well, they have to get the calories in.' But I'd argue that calories were not all equal and some ways of getting them were better than others. I would have had a very different understanding from other players and nutritionists when it came to the benefits and shortcomings of carbohydrates and complex carbohydrates and how we were meant to load or phase-load these during the week of a game.

I could see from the All Blacks and from being at the World Cup in 2011 the importance of nutrition and recovery. I remembered what Mick Kearney had said to me about investing in myself, and eventually I did a bit of research into trends in other sports, finding out my phenotype, doing DNA sequencing and blood work and talking to people who were experts on those matters. I found myself in agreement with a lot of the work Daniel Davy did at Leinster, but he was working on a part-time basis, so I looked outside Leinster too, privately, and paid for it myself. I worked with Eoin Lacey, a private nutritionist, and his advice suited me and I got my body into the working order I wanted.

There may have been days early in my career when I went into a game under-fuelled or over-fuelled and it affected my performance. Maybe I was trying to lose fat and was eating loads of meat with carbs and I'd just run out of steam during a game because my energy stores were gone. Or I'd have eaten loads of carbs and ballooned up and then felt like a lead weight on the pitch. My physical shape changed as I became more interested in nutrition. I probably got lighter as my career progressed. It had to, though, as Leinster and Ireland were both playing at a much faster pace and I needed to get around the pitch faster, for longer. So I got leaner and I felt much better. Prior to retiring, my fighting weight would have been about 112kg the day of a game, and then I'd operate at 108/109kg during the week, maybe even lighter at the very start of the week.

I wasn't a picky eater, but I was a clean eater. I avoided dairy products and reduced my gluten intake during the season. Over the years I learnt what worked and what didn't. Sometimes the diet became stale and not particularly enjoyable, but I'm quite a routine-based person, so I could handle it. It was tough for me to add muscle. I had to learn over the years the timings of when to eat food, as well as the type and volume. It was probably about halfway through my career when I became satisfied that I was properly on top of it.

Towards the end of my career, I had reduced my carbs intake so much that I ate them only in and around the time I was training at the start of the week, unless it was a heavy leg weights day or a leg weights and pitch session, in which case I ate carbs at lunch and dinner. If it was a down day, without training, I laid off the carbs because I wouldn't burn them off. If I'd just done a pitch session, for example, with an upper body weights session to follow, I'd only have the carbs once, at lunchtime.

I was mindful of how I loaded my carbohydrate intake during the week, limiting the intake and then increasing it massively in that 24-hour period before the game, to develop my internal energy stores and to help me hydrate. I think one gram of carbs holds four grams of water, so you can massively hydrate yourself as well. One of the keys to optimum performance is hydration.

I liked to feel light on the day of a game. So I had a good breakfast and then the pre-match meal. If the pre-match meal was the second meal of the day, I just had a smoothie and some pancakes, and that was enough because my energy stores would be full from the day before. On match day I would drink a lot of coffee, for the caffeine, making a big pot of it after my nap. I might drink up to 800mg of caffeine during the day of a game. I used to get really tired before games earlier in my career, which I think might have been my body's way of dealing with nerves, so the coffee sorted this. I love my coffee, but I came off it for three or four days before every match to make sure it didn't interfere with my sleep. I took it black, the odd flat white or cortado, and I drank bullet-proof coffee, with Kerrygold butter and coconut oil added in, although I know the benefits of doing this are disputed. I also did intermittent fasting on occasion.

It required discipline and some experimentation to get the loads right, but if I was doing all the physical training to get in shape, there was no point in wasting all that time and effort by putting the wrong fuel, or the wrong amounts of it, in the tank. It was just another part of the job, as was getting my head in the right place.

CHAPTER 7

LIVING OUT THE SCRIPT

There wasn't a eureka moment when I decided that I needed to address my mental fitness for rugby. There were important moments, though, such as when the sports psychologist Enda McNulty first came to speak to us in Leinster in 2008, to encourage us to consider the importance of mental preparation. He had become friendly with Cheika, who hoped that Enda could improve the psychology of the team. He arranged for Enda to come and talk to us at a team meeting.

I know Enda formed the wrong impression of me during our first meeting because he told me so later. My body language and dress suggested to him that I'd be the most difficult person in the room with whom to form a relationship, that I'd be his biggest challenge among the players. I was sitting at the back of the room, with my feet up on the chair in front of me and a baseball cap on backwards. But I took in what he was saying, even if he didn't realise that immediately. When I first heard Enda, I hadn't a clue what he was on about – the power of the subconscious, his belief in scripting, how the visualisation of actions activates the same behaviours and pathways as when you actually physically do it – but I wanted to know more. When he finished, I went up to him and we talked more and he reeled me in. Over the next few months, a relationship developed where we would meet regularly in coffee shops all over Dublin and talk.

We laughed about it afterwards, as our work together deepened, but his initial perception of me was quite negative. In time, I came to worry about that because I was learning that too many people were forming the wrong impression of me and many who didn't know me didn't seem to like me. I'd been aware for a couple of years that some people in rugby didn't like how I looked or behaved, that it was seen as somehow inappropriate to the game's 'standards', something that Eddie's issue with my white boots had crystallised for me. There was a time when I had my tongue pierced, wore white boots, had a cap on backwards, wasn't interested in fitting the mould of the jock rugby type, the one that Ross O'Carroll-Kelly parodies. I was determined to display my own identity, no matter how 'inappropriate', but it did bring me into conflict with people who were old school and wanted things done in a certain way, according to rugby traditions. And there I'd be saying 'No' and 'Why?'

Enda's arrival coincided with my own personal realisation that I needed something extra in my game and in what I did to help me achieve that, and that the information or impetus had to come from an outside perspective, beyond the rugby bubble. What Enda did was to put a mirror in front of me. He forced me to ask questions of myself. I realised that while I'm pretty relaxed and straightforward most of the time, I find it hard to hide my emotions and it can show in my body language, which can piss some people off. This was happening both within my teams and with the media, which in turn could shape other people's perceptions. This put me in danger of being pigeonholed as a certain 'type', and a contrary 'type' at that, which wasn't going to be helpful to me and wasn't an accurate reflection of who I was and wanted to be.

The really great thing about Enda, the reason why I could listen to him and discuss it with him, was that he understood what he was saying from insider experience. I could relate to what he had achieved as a player with the Armagh senior football team, winning the All-Ireland Championship in 2002 for the very first time as part of a team full of strong sporting personalities. I respected the fact that Enda had been there and done it. I never liked taking advice from an S&C coach or a nutritionist who was overweight or unfit. There were exceptions to the rule, because there were some guys who knew their stuff even if they weren't living it, but it just never sat with me to take coaching from someone who hadn't done it at the level I was at or wanted to reach.

The other great thing about Enda was that he didn't tell me what to do; instead he got me to probe why I was doing things and how I was doing them, to allow me take control of my processes, instead of following what somebody else set down for me. He had lots of ideas that he had taken from many different high-performance environments and we discussed them at length. I talked to him about the books I'd read about other sports and the techniques used by successful athletes. One of the best books I ever read was Michael Phelps' book, written after the 2008 Olympics, *No Limits: The Will to Succeed*, in which he described the whole process of how he worked to get his world-beating times that year. He and his coaches had worked out a schedule of preparation in order to achieve that, and his process gripped me. For the same reason, I was fascinated by the story of LeBron James, how he was at the top of his game but still hungry to do better, to do more. Guys like LeBron James and Michael Jordan had insane levels of resources, the best money could buy because sport is such a big business in the USA, and they made a huge investment in S&C. What I found interesting was that they also invested in and strove to be the best at the mental side of preparation. Enda was particularly interested in how Rafael Nadal did this too, training himself to stay at the top, both physically and mentally. This was the sort of conversation we enjoyed, looking at different approaches, recommending books to each other, and then I'd take away what suited me best.

When I started playing professionally, I focused on a game from the day before, but Enda got me thinking in detail about the whole week before a game. We worked on how to plan ahead for each game and also for the entire season, like creating a quarterly business plan. We mapped out the season: pre-Six Nations, the competition itself, post-Six Nations, November internationals. We even drew up a plan for pre-season training.

I found that mapping things out removed stress. I would see some guys getting terribly stressed out in the week of a big game, thinking about having to do the sponsorship stuff or whatever, things that were an additional burden when they didn't need one. Enda encouraged me to block off time to decompress and to do business, so that the various demands in my life wouldn't conflict with my game focus. With his encouragement, I began to plan the month ahead, which is something I do to this day, even outside rugby.

Once I had mapped out the month, I'd then map out the immediate week ahead in even greater detail. In rugby, you know your season schedule, when the European games happen, when the internationals are, even the big Pro12 or Pro14 games. I'd book everything in, including my meetings with Enda, factoring them into the optimal time to fit around my training and recovery. Enda got me thinking on that macro level, the actionable steps to take each week. This approach suited me and I became very disciplined. I knew when I was training, when I was going home to have a nap, how long I would sleep for, when I was going to have a massage, or a stretch, or heat therapy. I didn't have think about it or get it organised at short notice, and therefore there was no stress. That might sound like it robbed the spontaneity from my life, but it was the opposite. It allowed me to do whatever I wanted in my own time, in a way that I wouldn't be worried about it afterwards. For me, process gave me discipline and discipline gave me freedom from stress. I didn't have to think about what to do next; all I had to do was go and do it.

Some of my teammates found it funny that I mapped out my sleep for the week, but I found it really beneficial. In the week before a game I'd mark in naps or relaxation time on my schedule. I'd block off 90 minutes and if I didn't sleep in that time, I'd watch TV and hopefully doze off. I realised very early on that sleep is essential for allowing the body to recover from the exertions of playing and training and that it was therefore useful preparation, so I prioritised it. I never felt guilty about taking a nap on the team coach on the way to a game or in the dressing-room, even if some players slagged me for it and it got commented upon in the media. It was an important part of my pre-match schedule, so I just got on with it.

Enda helped me set up my routine and I relied on that rather than going to him when I had a bad game for some sort of counselling. The point of what we did was to establish a system that I could follow, without needing a safety net. We met frequently in the early days, but as I got to grips with how I wanted to do things, the meetings went from weekly to monthly to quarterly. Naturally, I hit roadblocks at different times in my career, but I was in a much better position to handle them and I was never slow to look for outside advice when I felt it would help.

There were days when being a professional wasn't good, when I played a poor game or the team suffered a bad result. It seems like we're programmed to remember the bad moments more clearly than the good. It takes mental effort to move away from that and fully take in the good moments when they happen and use them to your advantage on the bad days. Sometimes at Leinster, we were so focused on what we needed to do and what we wanted to achieve, we got out of the habit of properly celebrating what we had achieved, of enjoying the good times as much as we should have. I learned that all I could do was prepare properly, but beyond that I had to admit and understand that there would be things I couldn't control, such as the performance of my teammates, the opposition and the referee. I never resorted to blaming the referee. He's human, he makes mistakes, get over it. I had bad days myself too, after all.

This was something I learned over time. At the start, there were nights when I only slept for a few hours after a game because even though I was physically exhausted, I was still thinking about the game, processing everything that had happened. It was probably partly due to all the caffeine I drank beforehand, and it would get so that not even a fistful of whiskey could put me to sleep. I soon realised this was a pointless negative cycle of focusing on the bad. I had to consciously work to limit any negativity. I don't buy into the

belief that you learn more from failure than fro.
You learn equally from both. I think people spend t
thinking about their failures, trying to work out the sour
an attempt to ensure it doesn't happen again. I get that, b
I think it's as important to go back over the games you won,
to work out what went right and wrong there. That way, you
figure out the things that worked so you can do them again. I
didn't get stressed before games and I ignored the criticism or
negative comments online. I adopted what I called a 'Happy
Gilmore face' and blocked out the bad and let in the good. I
reminded myself that many of the critics, whether online or
in the media, had never played a game of rugby in their lives.

Stemming from my work with Enda, one of the key
elements of my game preparation was visualisation. Prior to
a game, I put a lot of work into getting into a zone, as if I was
meditating. I wanted to be focused, concentrated, closed to
distractions. Part of this preparation was writing in a journal,
in order to focus my mind clearly. I journalled twice before a
game – once the day before, once on the day. The day before
the game I did 10 minutes of meditation in the morning, to
get myself nice and calm. I'd use an app like Headspace to help
me get there. I then got out one of my Moleskine notebooks
and wrote out how I wanted the match day to go. I visualised
the day of the game, from what I would do in preparation
beforehand to the game itself. I'd write as descriptively as I
could, trying to be tactile as well as emotional, for example
imagining how the grass would feel under my bare feet. From
the start of my career, I was very focused on the goals to be
achieved during a game, such as a certain amount of tackles,
carries, passes, tries or offloads. Aiming for a set of goals
forced me to be active and engaged during the game rather
than being a passenger. Writing it out beforehand helped me

to focus on it. I also wrote out action points on the general team stuff I had to do; attacking, defending, my all-round contribution. The idea was that once I had visualised them like this, I'd go out and do just that. David Wallace loved how I described this process as 'shake and bake'.

When I was journalling, I'd have music from my playlist on my headphones, and then I'd play that same music on matchday to remind me of what I'd written. Listening to that music before the game helped me to visualise doing those actions. Sometimes I would stand up, close my eyes and almost move through the motions, visualising how I would complete them if I chose to.

I know some people think this all sounds a bit hippy-dippy, but I found that visualisation ingrained into my brain the habits and behaviours I wanted to perform, making them feel automatic when I had to do them. It may not have been the exact scenario on the pitch, but it was always close enough. Visualisation creates a path of least resistance between brain and body, making and maintaining that vital connection. If I visualised doing something, such as making a tackle or winning a line-out, there was a better chance I would do it on the pitch when required. If you're exhausted and you're in the midst of a battle on the field, you fall back on your habits. That means you depend on the processes that have become ingrained in your brain and body, week in, week out. The thing with habits is that when you first do something, it is new and awkward, but when you keep doing it, eventually it sticks and becomes natural, something you do without thinking. That's what I was aiming for with the visualisation techniques, and I felt they worked for me.

I used those techniques to prepare for what I would experience in my surroundings during the game. I visualised waves of blue in the stands because it helped me to anticipate the amazing support we were going to get from Leinster fans, or waves of green if it was an Ireland match. It prepared me mentally for what I would see in a full Aviva Stadium, nearly everyone there supporting us, hardcore fans going for it. I was so prepared for it that I focused exclusively on the game and many days hardly heard the crowd because I was in my zone. That also meant I didn't hear the noise of the crowd falling flat – unless it was away from home and we were quietening the home support.

I also combined the journalling and visualisation techniques in order to rehearse and learn the game sheet and the code words. The game sheet is a detailed set of instructions from the coach telling us what to do throughout the match. The code words are used by the captain or the number 10 for different options available to us in various parts of the pitch during the game. We had to memorise about 25 code words and be able to execute them the moment they were called, which meant they had to be as familiar as your own name. I'm not going to give away any of the code words or drills in case they are still in use, and I believe that some of them are. I did the journalling to aid my visualisation the day before the match, then repeated the same process on match day. I always re-read the game sheet on both days and worked my way through the code words and the line-out calls, memorising them and thinking through my part in them.

Let me give an example. I've kept all my diaries from over the years and in them I have all the play-sheets from many of the big games I played. From an Irish international in 2016, we had 23 individual plays to remember for when we were in possession of the ball, depending on the part of the pitch. There were all the different permutations when it came to a line-out, where the pack leader called a full or reduced numbers line-out, and full permutations for what to do if we were included in six-man, five-man and four-man line-outs or whether we had moved out to the backs. The play-sheets gave us four or five different exit plays from our own 22. For example, say we were defending a line-out on our own 5m line, you might call only four players for the line-out because your other forwards can be on the goal-line, 5m away, while their players are 10m away. Advantage to us immediately. I would position myself to allow for the hooker to take it fast, throwing it over the players in the line-out for me to run on to. If the opposition is not organised properly, I can move the ball forward quickly to set up a ruck, and then the scrum-half can either pass or kick the ball away. Everybody has to be alert and ready: the hooker to throw the ball to me, the scrum-half to follow quickly to clear the ball away swiftly from the ruck. It was a huge amount to remember, and all of it had to be recalled instantly in the pressure situation of a game. I visualised every scenario in detail the day before and the day of the game.

Once I had done my journalling on match day, I slept, unless it was a lunchtime kick-off. I've never had a problem with getting anxious about a game in advance of it. Never. I don't like an early kick-off because I like to chill out at home. I don't like being rushed in the morning. And who likes eating pasta at 7am to carb-load for a 1pm kick-off? I loved the evening kick-offs at 5pm and especially at 7pm. For home games with Leinster, once I'd had my match-day nap I'd eat about four and a half hours before the game, then chill, get my bag ready, put my tunes on, make my coffee and drive to the ground, seeing the waves of blue all around the stadium.

If it was an Ireland game, I would be with the players in the team hotel, but I settled into my routine as best I could, not missing out on the important bits. From late 2013 onwards I didn't even sleep in the team base, the Shelbourne Hotel, the night before games, preferring instead to stay at home and do my thing. When we had moved back to the Shelbourne one Thursday after a camp in Carton House to prepare for a Saturday match, once dinner and any team meetings were finished, I slipped away home to my own bed. I did the same again on the Friday evening. I needed a release from being full-on in advance of the games. I needed to have conversations that weren't about rugby. It was always on, on, on and that wasn't good. It made sense for me to have a good night's sleep in my own cot rather than sleeping in a strange bed. I didn't like the hotel rooms, always found them too hot. I left quietly, no fuss, and Mick Kearney knew where I was going in case the drug testers came along and I had to be called back. I never spoke to Joe Schmidt about it when he was Ireland coach, but I'm sure he must have known. I never spoke to other players about it, but I'm sure they knew too. I don't know what they thought about it, but it wasn't that I was looking for special treatment, it was just my way of making sure I was best prepared for the game. I was always back the following morning in good time for the team breakfast and whatever training drills were scheduled.

On match day, I aimed to be strapped up before I got to the grounds, but if not I'd ask the physios to do it immediately, get it out of the way. I would do the thumbs myself, something I'd done ever since a Leinster schools game as a teenager when I'd torn ligaments in a thumb after catching it in another player's shorts as I lifted him in a line-out. I strapped my left ankle because of a 2010 injury and my right shoulder was strapped from 2015 onwards to pin down my collarbone as

I have damaged my AC joint there – my shoulder now looks
like a coat-hanger in my post-rugby days – and finally my
ears.

Then I went and walked quickly around the pitch, getting
my bearings. I'd take off my flip-flops and walk on the grass
in bare feet, to get the feel of it. I'd be in my own world, with
my tunes on my headphones to help me focus. I'd come back
in and go through a stretching routine, first loosening, then
dynamic stretching and then a tiny bit of visualisation, just
close the eyes for one or two minutes, think about what's
going to happen in the game, what I want to happen. I just
chilled in the dressing-room, unless we were doing drills as
a forward unit. Early on in my career, I often lay down and
slept for a little while more, but as the years went on I tried
to get my nap at home before coming to the ground. It was
all about conserving energy, getting myself ready to explode
into life.

The use of headphones before a match is pretty
commonplace in sports now, but I got a lot of flak for it one
day when I was captaining Ireland because I walked out to the
coin toss with mine hanging around my neck. Some people,
mainly in the media, some on social media, seemed to take
enormous offence at this and made all sorts of assumptions
that it meant I wasn't focused or didn't care enough or was
doing it to fulfil some kind of sponsor obligation. It was
all nonsense. I wasn't paid by anybody and I hadn't done it
deliberately. I was doing my warm-up in the dressing-room
when Mick Kearney came over and told me it was time for
the coin toss. I just walked straight out without even thinking
that I needed to take the headphones off. When I later heard
about all the fuss, I thought it was pathetic.

I turned back to my journalling book in the last few

moments before we took to the pitch for the game. While others were putting on their jerseys or whatever, I opened the book and reminded myself of all the actions I wanted to perform by reading them. Then I'd put the book away and off we went.

CHAPTER 8

JOE WITH LEINSTER

reland didn't even come close to retaining the Six Nations in 2010. We started slowly, with a laboured 29-11 win against Italy at Croke Park, but when we went to Paris our long unbeaten run was ended by a 33-10 scoreline. It wasn't quite as poor a performance as those numbers might suggest because the official stats showed that we had roughly twice as much of the possession, passed the ball twice as much and forced France to make almost twice as many tackles. Unfortunately, we also had twice the error count because we couldn't cope with their rush defence and when they had their chances, they took them, whereas we didn't.

We responded with a proper performance next game up, enough to make us think that what had happened in Paris was a speed wobble rather than a derailment. We went to Twickenham two weeks later and Deccie told us that we had to play at full tilt and if we didn't, what happened to us in Paris would happen again. He stressed that we had to play to the limit in every game.

Wins at Twickenham came rarely enough, even if we had achieved a few over the previous decade, and this one was particularly sweet, not just because it came off the back of such a heavy defeat but because of the nature of the late strike to win it. Jonny Wilkinson had scored yet another of his drop goals nine minutes from time to give them a 16-13 lead they didn't really deserve, but we came back and with five minutes to go Tommy got a great try that Rog converted. We won 20-16, scoring three tries to their one. We were physically committed, focused and much cleverer, using the blindside and blindside wingers to vary our play. This time the stats were reversed compared to the French game, as they had more territory and possession and we had played the counterattacking game. We made 99 tackles in the game and missed just one and managed eight turnovers to their one. This was more like it.

We continued the good form at home to Wales two weeks later. There was a certain anxiety beforehand, notwithstanding the win in London. Wales were a coming team who had been unlucky in their games to date and they played with a high-tempo attacking style, scoring six tries in their first three games and making more line-breaks than any other side in the tournament. Having played with so many of them on the Lions tour the previous year, I knew how good they could be. But we mugged them. We stole six of their 18 line-outs and hit them on the counter, slowed them down when they had possession to the extent that they couldn't make any breaks or stretch us. We were just way better and easily good value for our 27-12 win.

The pressure was off now, which was an unusual thing for an Ireland team chasing a Triple Crown, something that was still very important to traditionalists because it had never been won easily and was a rare event. France had to beat England in Paris to win the Grand Slam. If they lost, a big victory for us over Scotland would give us an outside chance of pipping the French to the championship, although the points difference was loaded against us. We knew well enough that in international rugby you concentrate on winning the game first and then if you can run up a score, you do so, rather than disrespecting the opposition by working out how much you might be able to win by. So winning the Triple Crown was the main ambition.

There was a lot of talk about it being the last rugby international game that would ever be played at Croke Park before rugby returned to Lansdowne Road, now rebuilt as the Aviva Stadium. I suspect some fans wanted us to go out with a big bang. Instead, it was a complete anti-climax as we contrived to lose 23-20 when Dan Parks kicked their winning penalty in the last minute. We didn't deserve any better. Our scrum and line-out malfunctioned. We tried to do too much too soon, without having established a platform first. We tried running the ball from everywhere and got nowhere. We kept dropping the ball, making 14 errors in total during the game, and four handling errors in the first six minutes alone cost us two potential tries. We missed 10 tackles. They played territory better and their back-row, the so-called Killer Bs of Kelly Brown, Johnny Beattie and John Barclay, did a number on us. It knocked our confidence.

~

Leinster were looking at a year of change. Just before Christmas 2009, Michael Cheika had told us that he would be leaving at the end of the season for another job. It was a bit of a surprise, to put it mildly. It is part and parcel of the game when players leave, but when coaches go it is usually because something has gone wrong that he or the employers feel he is unable to rectify. Cheiks announced that he was leaving at a time when we felt we were going well and his stock with us and the fans was very high.

I wasn't part of the player leadership group at the time, so I wasn't involved in the process of researching and looking for a replacement for Cheiks. Leo Cullen led that on the playing side and Johnny was involved, too, even though he had been a starter for only a number of months. They met with Joe Schmidt, the Kiwi who was the assistant coach at Clermont, before Christmas to suss him out. They came back and endorsed him and the rest of us said, 'Fair enough'.

It's natural to be apprehensive when a new coach is coming in. I didn't know what Schmidt was likely to think of me, how he'd do things and what he'd see as my role in the team. New coaches often have their own players they like to bring in with them, their own systems and ways of playing. That said, the optimist in me always rules supreme and at this stage I was so well established in the team, I hoped I hadn't too much to worry about.

The season didn't go as well as it should have for reasons I can't really explain. It wasn't that we lacked in confidence and while I can't speak for others, I was as hungry as ever to win. We had come through the qualifying round of the Heineken Cup, as you would expect, although we had contrived to lose to London Irish at home in October and hadn't pulled up any trees with our performances to win the group. And, while we won an epic quarter-final at the RDS against Clermont, the game revealed plenty of flaws.

Johnny kicked a late penalty to give us a 29-28 lead over Clermont, but then Brock James missed a sitter of a drop goal in front of the posts with the last kick of the game, which would have won it for them. They had also missed 25 points from placed kicks earlier in the game. I was delighted to note that my incoming coach referenced me in his after-match comments, saying I'd had a big game carrying the ball and broken two or three tackles every time I carried. But as a team performance, it was worrying. Cheiks publicly castigated our discipline as abominable and not good enough to regain the trophy. It wasn't just that we gave away place-kicking chances, it was that we had no continuity in our play and couldn't impose ourselves on the game.

We had to go away to Toulouse for the semi-final, back to Le Stadium where we had famously triumphed four years earlier. For those of us who had been there that day it meant we had no fears. For the French, I suspect it gave them an even greater incentive to do whatever it took not to lose. They were exceptionally aggressive in getting to us quickly and hitting us as hard as possible. Only once that was done did they start to play rugby. We were experiencing all sorts of problems in the scrum, not helped by difficult underfoot conditions caused by pouring rain before the game began. Cheiks was ruthless enough in taking off Church after just 30 minutes to put CJ van der Linde in his place. We didn't have Johnny in the team either because of injury, but that wasn't the only reason we lost.

We were 9-9 early in the second-half and hopeful that we could snatch it. Then they hit us with two quick tries, Jauzion first and Skrela minutes later, both converted. I got a try in the 65th minute that brought us back within a converted try of catching them, but then Skrela kicked a penalty and they comfortably saw out a 26-16 win.

Toulouse went on to beat Biarritz in the final, but to this day I think that if we'd had a full team available to us, we could have won that semi-final and then the final. I still think we were good enough. It was disappointing for Cheiks, and there was more to come as we lost 17-12 to Ospreys in the RDS at the end of May in the first ever Magners League Grand Final. We hadn't won the title since 2008 and they hadn't won it since 2007, but we still fancied ourselves to win at home, even against a side featuring Tommy Bowe, Lee Byrne, James Hook, Mike Phillips, Alun Wyn Jones, Marty Holah, Dan Biggar and the former All Black Jerry Collins. Tommy got an early try and we were chasing the game all the way through, but apart from Johnny's penalties we weren't able to score.

After such a disappointing season, heading to the Southern Hemisphere for games against New Zealand and Australia was not exactly ideal. As it turned out, those games brought one of the worst moments of my career, in a place called New Plymouth.

It was a one-off test with the All Blacks, with another to follow against Australia the following week. Quite a few good players were unavailable to tour and the mood in the squad was just a bit off. I went into that game too highly charged emotionally. I play best when I'm relaxed and because I wasn't in a perfect state, I reacted to something early in the game instead of staying in the flow, as I tended to do. I can't explain why I was so worked up. It might have been to do with us being so short of regular forwards, with feeling that I had to compensate for that. Whatever the case, I did something that has remained with me ever since.

Before the game we had identified Richie McCaw, the All Blacks captain and number 7, as somebody we'd have to stop. He's a class player and blessed in the dark arts of stopping you from playing at the speed you want. He slows the pace at which the opposing team recycles the ball at a ruck and every second that he does that can be a huge benefit for defenders in organising themselves to defend better. If it takes a player a second to cover nearly 10m going forward, then the extra time that the ball is slowed gives the defender time to position properly, not be on the back foot but on the front foot instead, able to get forward off the line and make contact with the opposition on the other side of the gain-line. Otherwise the defender is passive, standing while absorbing the momentum of the oncoming player and almost certainly going backwards before the attacker recycles the ball and the process begins again.

McCaw's not a dirty player, he's not a cheater, he's a 7 and that's what 7s do. That's what all back-rows should be doing, getting into the mix at the rucks, trying to slow down the ball. It's good game management, if you can get away with it and not get penalised. I wouldn't call him a cheat because it's only cheating if you get caught and he never got caught. I did exactly the same when I could. It was up to the ref and his assistants to see it and stop it. That's the reality of what we have to do to win.

We knew he'd have no problem giving away a penalty very early in the game if we got close to the line because he'd reckon that he wouldn't be yellow-carded early on for such an infringement. So I had it in my head that if I saw him doing that, I'd deal with him in whatever way I had to, to line him up to make sure he didn't do it again and that we'd get the quick ball we'd need going forward.

In the 14th minute we were already 10 points down when we exploded into the game, got to their 22, making line-breaks, punching for a try. We were just short of the line and it happened. Richie came over the top and on to the ball to stop us scoring. I saw it and came in and tried to move him, but my first, legal attempt didn't get him off the ball. He was offside but referee Wayne Barnes hadn't done anything. I decided I'd ruck him.

You could do that then because the laws were different. You could use your feet to move a player out of the way if he was on the wrong side. You can't do it now. Admittedly, you couldn't do it then the way I did it. You couldn't just knee a player in the head. I thought, 'Sod this, I'm getting him off', so I just went, boom, I hit him with my knee. He didn't budge. I went for it a second time, and Church's leg got in the way. I hit Church's leg and the whistle went, long and loud, much longer in duration than normal, which signalled that the referee had seen something he regarded as very serious. And immediately I realised, 'Oh fuck'.

For some reason I kept thinking, 'I'll get a yellow, just a yellow.' That's all I remember thinking. But instead it was a red card and there was nothing I could do to change what I'd done or to persuade the referee to change his mind. As I walked off the pitch, what I'd done to the team hit me like a kick to the guts. Playing New Zealand with 15 players is tough enough; playing with 14 for the next 66 minutes, already 10 points down and with a scoring opportunity lost – because now the All Blacks had a penalty to clear their own lines – was going to be impossible. I knew the game was done. Everyone on my team was going to be firefighting while knowing the house was still going to burn down. They got a hiding and I was sitting there like a spare tool when the lads come off, absolutely bolloxed, and it was only half-time.

It ended up 66-28 at the end. I can't remember anyone saying anything in particular to me, calling me out for it, because straightaway after the game I stood up and said, 'Sorry, I've let everyone down here, it's not like me to do something like that, but I did and I'm sorry.' I don't remember if anyone said anything in response. I don't remember too much about the rest of the evening.

Deccie was pretty good to me about it. 'Look, it's done now,' was about all he said. I reckon he knew how badly I felt and that I understood how wrong my actions had been without needing to shout it at me. I went to the disciplinary hearing the next day and I owned it straightaway, not that I had much choice. I emphasised that it was out of character, that I was reacting to what I saw in front of me, but that I knew that wasn't an excuse and I was sorry. Wayne Barnes came in and described what he'd seen and, bizarrely, the optimist in me thought I was going to get off. I don't know why. I had a local Kiwi barrister arguing for me and they gave me an eight-week ban, with three weeks suspended for my previous good record. As it was summertime, the ban meant that I would miss the match with Australia the following weekend, but would be free to play again in September after my holidays were finished. It could have been a lot worse.

My first conversation with Joe Schmidt was on the phone, as I was sitting in Singapore Airport on my way back from New Zealand, on my own. He wanted me to take my holidays immediately and come back earlier to his first Leinster training camps in July, ahead of my Ireland team colleagues. I refused. 'I need a break,' I told him. And I did. I had started to realise that I was playing a lot of games compared to everyone else. It was a risk, I suppose, refusing my new coach, who I didn't know, but I was becoming more confident. I felt that I was on solid ground and that the stats backed me up. I needed to be selfish. He conceded ground on it. Some people think I'm cocky, and I genuinely try not to be. But I've no problem saying that I'd be confident about certain things in rugby, and being a good pro was one of them. The great thing about Joe, as I was to find out, was that he respected people who were upfront and honest with him. I was always upfront and honest with him.

Things started slowly enough under Joe, but we weren't playing at full strength because the Irish internationals who had been to the Southern Hemisphere came back into pre-season late. We lost our first three games under Joe, including one away to Treviso, 29-13, with lots of front-line players absent. Immediately, there were headlines about Joe losing the dressing-room and how he'd have to change his approach dramatically or he'd be out as quickly as he'd arrived. It was all nonsense. The players had bought into his ways from the first training session and wanted to double down instead of changing. We knew it was only a matter of time and it would all come good.

Then we played Munster at the Aviva in October and we won more comfortably than the 13-9 scoreline suggested. I remember finding that game relatively easy because Joe made it simple for us. He mapped it out exactly and his plan made sense. As time went on, we'd discover that he was constantly assessing how to be better pros, how to get fitter, how to use the information from all this GPS tracking we used. Cheika was the first coach to bring in that stuff, but Joe made it applicable to our training as well as to our playing. He brought our pre-season to another level in terms of fitness. He made you feel confident because you knew exactly what to do. He was always clear on the plan and that the plan would succeed, if we put in the work.

In one of Joe's first games, a Heineken Cup game against Bath, he hammered Darce in the after-match review. There was a penalty inside our 22 and instead of kicking to touch,

Johnny sent a cross-field kick to Isa, who made a line-break. We took off after the ball, but on the video review Joe paused it at the moment when Isa caught the ball. Darce was in front of Mike Ross. Joe pressed Play and showed us how Darce stood there while Mike Ross, a prop, took off and got to the ruck way ahead of Darce. Joe absolutely caned Darce for it in the team meeting: he hadn't met our values; he wasn't being relentless; he had switched off. Those were the kinds of lessons we got from Joe the whole time. It kept adding layers to our game. Darce became an even better player for what Joe told him and so did everybody else, and then the team was better. For years after that I ran those lines, straight upfield, and sometimes I didn't get return on it and sometimes I did. It may not have been to get the try and the personal glory, but it might have been to make the essential clean-out to allow somebody else to get the score. Didn't matter, as long as someone on the team scored.

Joe was tough but fair, I think, in the vast majority of cases. I think his style of dealing with people has probably changed over the years because of the slightly different environments of club and country and the level of his exposure to people. At international level he can't maintain the same level of control because he doesn't see the players as often and they also answer to their bosses at club level. That means he has to wait to get to them, but if he has seen them do things incorrectly, as he sees it, with their club, he'll emphasise that they can't do that for Ireland. And he misses nothing.

One of my first encounters with Joe happened in his first pre-season training with the team. I got the location for the session wrong. I thought we were meeting in the back fields in UCD, when we'd actually been moved to the other side of Belfield, where the GAA fields are. As a result, I turned up about 20 minutes late and they were well into the warm-up. I was always taught to own my mistakes straightaway, so I went to Joe and apologised. He wasn't happy, but we got on with it. Afterwards he told me that he'd spent the entire session waiting for me to mess up so he could jump on me. I didn't know that at the time. I was just training, and he was waiting. I didn't mess up.

I think that's what Joe discovered about me over time. I very rarely made a mistake, and I knew what I had to do and what my role was within the team and I did it. I might not always have been brilliant, but I did what was required. He got to see how I trained and how I approached a game, how I looked after myself so that I rarely got injured and was therefore available to train and play. As the years went on, I constantly reminded him that I was the cheapest player by minutes played and trained. I think that's why he left me be what I am, because he saw that it worked for me and for him. Whatever I did outside the game, he saw that I was a good pro.

I found that I was always able to talk to Joe about what we were doing. Johnny Sexton engaged with him a lot – because he had the knowledge to be able to do so – but for the rest of us if you challenged someone like Joe, who was always at the top of his game, always had things worked out, you'd better have your shit right and you'd better know exactly why you were saying something. I knew that I had to be able to back up any point I made because Joe would certainly be able to back up his.

∼

In fairness to Deccie, there was no question of my being punished for my summer indiscretion in New Zealand by being left out of the November series. I had done my time. We had four games ahead of us and we knew their importance in preparing ourselves for the World Cup, which was now just 10 months away.

The IRFU decided that South Africa, as reigning World Cup holders, would be fitting opponents for the first international in the rebuilt stadium. The Aviva had a capacity of 51,700, but for that first game it wasn't quite full. There had been a public controversy over the ticket prices, in the same month that the government had to seek an international rescue for the State finances, and the atmosphere wasn't quite as excited as we might have expected. It certainly didn't match the Leinster v Munster game from a few weeks earlier.

They may have been World Cup holders, but South Africa were coming off the back of a terrible Tri-Nations campaign, were without about 13 of their players due to injury and their coach, Peter de Villiers, was under pressure to hang on to the job. Just as we started and finished our four years at Croke Park with defeats, we managed to lose this one too. We nearly snatched a 23-23 draw when Rog's last kick, a conversion from the sideline, hit the post, but we knew we wouldn't have deserved it. Our performance was very poor and we were lucky with some of our scores.

We beat Samoa the following week before the big one, the arrival of New Zealand. The All Blacks were always the benchmark and, as Deccie wanted, we were getting to play them more regularly, to improve by going up against the best. The All Blacks beat us again, 38-18, and I got totally fed up at the almost patronising comments about how we'd given them a good game for about 60 minutes. We'd lost, so I didn't want any pats on the back for how entertaining it had been to watch. We didn't make as many mistakes as we might have in the past, but they still punished us for each and every one of them and that frustrated the hell out of me. But we knew going into the game that they would be clinical and precise and that we couldn't afford to make mistakes.

That game meant a reunion with McCaw – with whom I'd end up sitting at the after-match dinner, with his parents too. Ironically enough, after the game it was Fez who was publicly critical of how McCaw was allowed to offend again and again at the breakdown, with no referee seemingly willing to police one of the superstars of world rugby. It wasn't something we spoke about at dinner. I'd never complain to a rival about what he did on the pitch. I just tried to work out how to counteract it the next time I played him. Neither did he bring up what had happened when I kicked him in the previous game and got sent off. I had apologised to him afterwards, so that was over. I doubt if he cared, given that it had set them up for a big win that day.

I didn't necessarily feel any better about things when Les Kiss went public to defend our performance, putting his assessment of the statistics for the game into the public domain.

Our tackle count reached 183, huge for the time, of which 73 were made in the first 20 minutes alone. By the end of the first quarter we'd defended 42 rucks as against a mere five by New Zealand, those figures rising to 72-26 by half-time. We'd put in 122 tackles by half-time, as against 105 in the entire Samoa game the week before. I was well into double figures in terms of tackles made, as were three other forwards. It was a quick game, but very physical, and the contact zone at rucks was the toughest I'd played in at that stage of my career.

But then, we'd had to do all that because we'd failed to do some of the basics, such as accurately securing Dan Carter's restarts, which the defending team should be able to do. We failed to do this on five occasions and required about 40 extra tackles over the course of the game as a result of them regaining possession when they shouldn't have been able to do that, as well as two penalties that they kicked for six points.

Afterwards, in the video analysis in the team review, we were able to identify how every one of their scores in the first-half came as a result of mistakes we'd made when we were in possession first. No other team would have punished us as ruthlessly as they did, but that wasn't the point. We were told that it was the best we'd played in ages and yet we'd been beaten by 20 points at home. We'd lost the game on both sides of half-time, conceding three converted tries in just 10 minutes.

What I took from it was that their skill levels were way ahead of ours, in every part of the team, and that their pace and precision were jaw-dropping. There was this gap between us, despite the success of Leinster and Munster in Europe, the Grand Slam the previous year. They set wider targets at pace, came onto the ball from deep and used the full width of the pitch. And they weren't all muscle-bound either, not just big blokes looking to ram through us. They were athletes and footballers. They were streetwise and clinical and if we made a mistake, the next thing we'd find is that we were 5m from our own try-line, defending it, or they'd already scored.

I took more satisfaction out of beating Samoa while playing relatively poorly than being allegedly good value in losing to New Zealand. I was delighted that Deccie backed me up on that one. He agreed that taking consolation from rattling the All Blacks would be a regressive step to an era when ambitions were far lower.

Already in training, with
my friend Ronan Breen, the
Paddocks, Naas.

The Heaslip clan,
minus Dad, in
Israel, 1984.

My parents, who've been with me every step of the journey. If they're looking more nervous than usual here, it's with good reason: I'm about to get married.

Trinity College, home of Dublin University, the oldest club in world rugby, and where I plied my trade before making the step up to full-time rugby.

The U21 World Cup in 2004 was a massive learning experience. We had a great tournament, but the New Zealand system was lightyears ahead of our own. (©*INPHO/Morgan Treacy*)

Our rivalry with Munster was always a benchmark against which we could measure our progress – not just on the field, where the clashes were always intense, but off it, too. (©*INPHO/Lorraine O'Sullivan*)

Scrambling through for a try in our Heineken Cup final win against Leicester in 2009. Victory felt like a major breakthrough; we were on our way to carving out our own legacy. (©*INPHO/Graham Stuart*)

Celebrating en route to a try and victory over Scotland in 2009. The finger wagging wasn't always well received, but we were on our way to the Grand Slam. (©*INPHO/Billy Stickland*)

In the thick of it against England in 2011. (*©Peter Muhly/Stringer/Getty Images*)

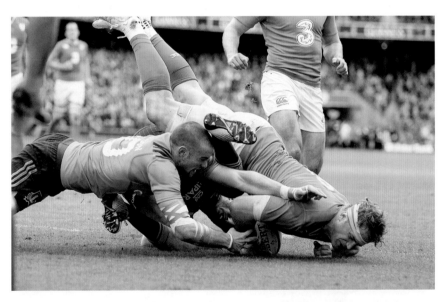

Applying the finishing touches to a great team move against Italy in 2016. It would later be voted World Rugby's Try of the Year. (*©INPHO/Dan Sheridan*)

At a Six Nations photo shoot with Church in 2014, a comrade in the Leinster and Ireland packs for most of my career. We managed to find a balance as roommates, too. (*Above ©INPHO/Billy Stickland*)

With Paulie (left) and Johnny (below), two immense personalities. (*Below ©INPHO/Cathal Noonan*)

His appointment came as a surprise to everyone, but Cheika kick-started the change at Leinster. (©*INPHO/James Crombie*)

With Eddie under pressure after our poor showing at the 2007 World Cup. I was one of several new faces drafted into the team. Months earlier, I'd missed out on selection for being 'too small'. (©*INPHO/Billy Stickland*)

Deccie brought new positivity to the Ireland set-up, as well as a sense of equal opportunity within the squad, which helped deliver one of Irish rugby's greatest achievements. (©INPHO/James Crombie)

Joe was, and is, the consummate professional, meticulous in his preparation and never one to let sentiment or emotion get in the way of the team's interests. It could feel inspiring or ruthless. (©INPHO/Dan Sheridan)

My first Lions tour, to South Africa in 2009, was an unforgettable experience, but fatigue, injuries, and a 55-metre penalty from Morne Steyn in the Second Test put paid to our hopes of victory. (©*INPHO/ Dan Sheridan*)

Going on tour with strangers can be odd, but it's a great bonding experience. Occasionally, Rala ended up as collateral damage.

The tour to Australia in 2013 ended in victory, but at the time it didn't feel like one I could call my own. I wasn't picked for the decisive test. (©*INPHO/Dan Sheridan*)

There's no escape from the physical demands of professional rugby; you have to be smart about how you train …

… and do everything you can to help your body recover. Over the years, I've tried all sorts, from cryo chambers and ice baths to sleeping in an altitude tent.

Jay-Z – social media presence, minor celebrity, dog – was a constant companion for most of my career.

In 2010, I saw red for a knee on Richie McCaw and felt like I'd let everyone down. Six years later, I was part of the team that ended Ireland's 111-year wait for victory against the All Blacks. An incredible feeling. (*Above ©INPHO/Billy Stickland*; *Below ©INPHO/Dan Sheridan*)

To say I've been fortunate is an understatement. As well as all the other stuff, rugby has given me a chance to travel the world, often alongside my other half, Sheena …

… and give back in ways that wouldn't have been possible otherwise. My trips with GOAL to India and Ethiopia have been life-changing.

Thirteen years, 229 appearances. Quite a journey. (©*INPHO/Billy Stickland*)

Eventually, we ended the month by beating Argentina 29-9 in Baltic conditions on a Sunday afternoon. We were happy with that, even if the performance wasn't great. Our ambition had been to win all four games that month, so winning only two felt like failure, no matter what positives we wanted to take, such as improving our patterns and seemingly being better able to adapt our play according to each different challenge presented to us. I was impatient about improvement because the World Cup wasn't far away. I knew that we had to start putting a run of victories behind us, to get into that habit, because to win a World Cup – and that was my ambition – we'd have to do it for seven weeks in a row.

I went back to Leinster for the Heineken Cup and home and away third and fourth matches in the group against Clermont, Joe's old team. That was when I got the first really serious injury of my professional career: syndesmosis in the left ankle. There's basically a ligament that holds together your tibia and fibula, where they join your ankle. It's effectively a high ankle sprain.

It happened in the first-half against Clermont in 2010, or rather it happened when Sean O'Brien (Seanie) fell on me. I couldn't turn on the pitch, but somehow continued to half-time and told the doctors then. It was damn sore, and I say that as someone with a high pain threshold. They taped it up and sent me out to see how I'd get on. Somebody went past me on the outside and I couldn't turn to go after him. Somebody else tackled him, thankfully, and the ball went out and I just walked over to the sideline going, 'I'm a liability,' but not taking the decision to put myself out of the game, wanting somebody else to do that for me. I knew there was something wrong but didn't know what it was. I was taken off, but I played again the following week at the Aviva against Clermont again.

That was a really cold day and I couldn't feel my ankle because they'd strapped it up so heavily. Somehow I got through a game in which I couldn't turn. I don't know how. I don't know if I did any further damage either, but it was never operated on, which probably should have happened the day after it first happened. It caused me problems for the rest of the season before I got a chance to rest it in the summer. I carried it into the 2011 Six Nations and I missed the first game in Italy because of it, which we won only because of a last-minute Rog drop goal.

We blew our Six Nations chances in the second game by losing at home to France, 25-22. It ended with us dropping the ball as we headed for the try-line. It was fitting. We'd been dropping the ball all day or kicking it away badly or taking the wrong decisions and giving away a bucketful of penalties that Morgan Parra just kept knocking over. And yet we did some things well and managed to go in 15-12 ahead at half-time because Fergus McFadden and Tomás got tries. But in the second-half Médard got a try that was converted and with more penalties added they moved to a 10-point lead. I got a try in the corner after a 26-phase battering of the French line and Rog converted it, and then Seanie had his chance but lost the ball when tackled.

We won the next game at Murrayfield 21-18, and I scored another try, but this wasn't good enough for the new breed of keyboard warriors who were emerging on social media. All sorts of abuse came our way, and one so-called fan even told Drico that he should retire from the game 'gracefully', something that Drico retweeted on Twitter. Church and myself engaged with the posters, defending ourselves and the team, but we got called in by Paul McNaughton, the manager at the time, and were told not to do so again in advance of any games or for at least 24 hours afterwards.

I wasn't happy about this degree of control being imposed on us. I don't believe you should ban people from saying something they sincerely believe. I was also careful enough in what I said. I can understand that the IRFU was probably concerned for us – that it might not be good to get involved in rows with the fans, that it might be taken up by the print and broadcast media out of context – but it was probably as concerned with how its sponsors viewed it, in the days before all the sponsors became obsessed with social media themselves. Not a lot of people understood how social media was developing at the time and those of us who were on it got a bit of a slagging from teammates. I see that some of them are now on it themselves and sometimes share things about their families as part of their own brand promotion.

It might have been a good thing that the social media ban was in place given what happened in Cardiff subsequently, because some of the lads might have cut loose, such was our frustration. We were leading Wales by 13-9 when Johnny came on as a sub for Rog in the 50th minute, and with his first touch of the ball kicked it out on the full, giving the Welsh a line-out. But the Welsh took a quick line-out with a different ball, handed to them by a ball-boy, something that is specifically not allowed in the laws of the game, and Mike Phillips raced about half the length of the pitch to score in the corner. Incredibly, the referee and his assistant gave the try, despite Drico and Paulie angrily pointing out the breach of the rules. It gave Wales a shot in the arm and they added a penalty, but it was a game we still should have won, irrespective of that gift of seven points to them. It only increased our frustration with how we were performing.

It all bubbled up in the next game, at home to England at a very wet Aviva, their first visit to our new stadium. England arrived looking to complete a Grand Slam, which is always the type of incentive an Ireland team likes. Johnny started at out-half instead of Rog and everyone raised their game and played properly despite the weather. We carried the game to them at a much higher tempo than we had in the Six Nations to date, running the ball unexpectedly, offloading in the tackle instead of going to ground, counterattacking instead of looking to put the ball into touch. We played what we saw in front of us instead of depending solely on pre-planned moves. We tackled like dervishes, too, didn't give away penalties and kept our handling errors to a minimum. It was what we had shown glimpses of during the November series but had been unable to execute consistently until this game, a more exciting, free-flowing game, opening up the opposition but not making mistakes to give possession back and using what territory we had to get scores. Tommy and Drico got tries and we won 24-8 and, in truth, the game was over by early in the second-half.

It's amazing what winning the last game of a Six Nations can do for you, especially in World Cup year and if you have played as well as we had. England ended up actually winning the championship because France beat Wales, and we came third because of an inferior points difference to France. We felt that we had shown what we could do once we got to the World Cup and we went back to our clubs in good spirits.

∽

Leinster had beaten Leicester 17-10 in the quarter-final at the Aviva, but it was nowhere near as close as that scoreline suggests as we only got the try with a minute to go. We had a big win in the semi-final, though, beating the holders Toulouse at the Aviva, the same team that had beaten us in France a year earlier. Some people outside the camp talked about it being a revenge mission, but I thought that was nonsense and showed a lack of understanding of what motivates teams and players. It was the desire to get to the final that drove us on, nothing else. We wanted to get to the final for its own sake and it just happened that Toulouse was the team in the way. The only thing that was relevant from the previous year was that we knew many of the aspects of how they liked to play, although we also had video analysis to tell us more than that.

It wasn't one of our best performances, but we did enough. We gave them a soft try in the first five minutes, failing to deal with a penalty that came down from the posts, but we didn't let that distract us and after that we made fewer mistakes, which is so often the key factor in a semi-final. Johnny kicked three penalties and converted my try to give us a 16-13 advantage at the break. It was an unusual try in that the referee had called for a knock-on against me when I burrowed my way under a pile of bodies to get the ball. We pleaded with Dave Pearson to go to the TMO and when he did, he gave us the try. They went ahead 20-13 early in the second-half, but Drico got a try to give us the impetus again and we went on to win 32-23. I was proud of the way we finished out the game, because while it had been fast and tiring, with high intensity throughout, we took it moment by moment, doing everything step by step, instead of worrying about how many minutes were left. We won because we made fewer mistakes and showed a real will to win, but it also meant we weren't going to be overconfident about the final.

The final at the Millennium Stadium against Northampton will always be remembered as Leinster's greatest day. As every Leinster fan knows, we were 22-6 down to Northampton at half-time, a seemingly insurmountable deficit. It was only afterwards we heard that the previous record second-half recovery had been by Bath in 1999, when they came from 15-6 down at half-time to beat Brive 19-18. What we achieved, to keep them scoreless for the entire second-half and to score 27 points ourselves, was remarkable by anyone's standards. Statistically there have been bigger second-half comebacks, but not many in games of this magnitude. It was not an exaggeration when people recalled France beating the All Blacks in a similar manner in the 1999 World Cup.

I've been asked many times about what happened at half-time, what was said that prompted that second-half performance and victory. To be honest, I don't remember too much about the half-time, not that much more than I would about most games. I remember us coming in, a couple of lads shouting and then we split into backs and forwards, the backs going mental on one side of the room, the forwards with Greg Feek, our scrum coach, talking calmly about how we could repair things, to stop them driving through and upwards against our front-row in the scrums. Then Jonno Gibbs spoke about the line-outs and rucking. It was fairly standard stuff. 'Right, we just have to fix one or two things and we're good, let's hold on to the ball, we're making line-breaks but we're just turning it over stupidly. Hold onto the ball,' and that was kind of it.

I genuinely don't remember the now legendary Johnny Sexton speech about Liverpool's comeback from 3-0 down at half-time in the Champions League final in Istanbul in 2005. I don't know if he did it in front of the team or just with the backs, but the reference would have been fairly lost on me anyway as I'm not into football. What I do remember was a sense of collective frustration that we weren't doing ourselves justice. We had made good line-breaks but then turned the ball over with knock-ons or stupid passes, or given away penalties at rucks we should have controlled.

In fairness to Northampton, they'd worked us into good positions, held on to the ball, brought us through phases and taken their scores very well. But we knew at half-time that they weren't better than us, that we'd gifted them a couple of things. 'Let's just hold on to the ball and go hard for ten minutes and see where we're at then,' was what we said to each other. 'We'll see if we get a better return doing that.'

Joe broke it down methodically for us, as Joe does. He encouraged us that we only needed to fix little things and then we would start to dominate. It was all about getting the method right and letting the outcome take care of itself. We weren't talking about winning the game during that half-time discussion, it was about getting into the game and letting things flow from there. We were turning over the ball too often, so we knew what the problem was and the solution was provided to us. Joe made it very clear what we had to do: own the ball. He also made a key change, bringing Shane Jennings (Jenno) on for Kevin McLaughlin in the back-row and moving Seanie from open side to number 6. It was tough on Kev, but it would give us the balance we needed. Jenno would give us more at the breakdown and in defence, while Seanie would have more opportunity to start running at tacklers and knocking them over like skittles. We went back out and hit the ground running.

We got lucky a few times in the second-half. For the first try we got there was a ruck around the middle of the park that I hit deep, probably taking out a guy past the ball, a bit further than would be allowed with modern refereeing. Drico picked up the ball and went straight because there was no one in front of him as I'd cleaned out the ruck so deep. He made a half break, I took off after him, got the ball, there was a ruck, and a couple of phases late it went to the left-hand side while I was hovering in the middle of the park. The ball came back with Johnny and I called out 'Billy', which meant Johnny was to give me the ball so that I could go up the gain-line and leave it up when I was tackled. But I wasn't stopped. I was able to continue running straight because there was no opposition in sight. Johnny had done one of his wraparounds, going behind me and to the other side of me and as their wing-forward Phil Dowson came towards me, I popped it to Johnny and blocked Dowson off. Johnny basically had a free run then, only having to brush off a weak tackle from the side. Dowson went absolutely ape at what he saw as my cheating, started shoving me, obviously wanted a fight, but I just turned away, refused to get involved with him and went straight back up the field to prepare for the restart.

The converted try left us nine points behind, but suddenly different moments started to go our way. We started holding on to the ball and going through them. Then there was a shoelace pick-up by Leo – amazing everyone that a tall second-row could get so low to pick a ball without knocking on – which kept possession for us, Seanie came into the game and made some good inroads, Nathan Hines scored a try, Johnny scored a great one in the corner and by the end of the third quarter we were ahead and rocking.

The real turning-point for me was a scrum around 40m out from their line, middle of the park. The ball came back to me at the base of the scrum. I could feel the scrum moving forward so I kept the ball in and the scrum moved forward and we got the penalty. It proved that everything we'd said at half-time that we were going to do, that we needed to fix, was happening. We were holding on to the ball, bringing them through phases, getting territory, keeping possession. Once all that was happening, we knew we'd get the scores. Johnny kicked the penalty and now we'd gone something like 20-odd points unanswered and were more than a try away from them touching us. There was no excessive emotion or adrenaline, we were in the perfect state of flow. It was all process allied to skill. We had the momentum. We had no down phases at all that in that half, only steady upward trajectory. Johnny got huge praise, and rightly so, for his enormous points tally, 28 in all, and for the way he controlled the game from number 10, but it was a team effort.

It was one of my favourite moments in a Leinster jersey. Winning was rarely as sweet. If you look at the pictures of how we celebrated, it was different from 2009. It was just the players in a huddle, no one holding the trophy, which was sitting in the middle of everyone, and we were just going absolutely mad. I can't imagine that anyone else at half-time outside of our dressing-room had real faith in the squad, but we were so calm, so collected. We knew exactly what we were able to do. We backed ourselves. And we did it.

After the match, Sheena told me that she and her mother, Sharon, had taken loads of abuse from Northampton fans in one of the boxes beside them throughout the first-half and half-time, mocking them, making derogatory comments about the Leinster players. It made the second-half all the sweeter for her, especially when they left with 15 minutes to go and she said nothing to them, just smiled at them as they walked away, chastened and voiceless.

I didn't get the chance to celebrate winning this Heineken Cup for as long as we had two years earlier. The Magners League was now decided by a final game and we had to go to Thomond Park to play a Munster team that had won 21 of its 24 games in the league but was still required to beat us again to be crowned champions. You can only imagine how fired up they were by the arrival of the new European champions. We were fatigued, though, and as Joe said later, they needed it more than we wanted it. But I did want it. I'm greedy and competitive when it comes to winning and I would have loved two pieces of silverware rather than one, so I wasn't happy when we lost 19-9.

That extra match also meant I now had only four weeks off before starting an early pre-season and preparations for one of the highlights of my career: a rugby World Cup.

~

But before that I did something completely different. I was in a position where, thanks to rugby, I had a certain degree of celebrity and I realised that I could use that to promote awareness of certain causes. I chose to focus on working with the ISPCC on an anti-bullying poster campaign and with GOAL on its international campaigns for people in poverty.

Sheena and I went to Kolkata in 2012 with Bob Casey, the former Leinster and Ireland second-row, who spent much of his career at London Irish and then was chief executive there for years before returning to Ireland to work in recruitment. We enjoyed nice hotels, but it was a shock to see the poverty on the streets outside and the way it was excused by defenders of the caste system, saying, 'Well, they obviously did something in a past life.'

We were brought around an orthopaedic centre in Kolkata and it was grim: the injuries that people had suffered and the lack of treatment, the contrast with what I knew was available at home. I wouldn't say it was an eye-opener for me because I'd seen plenty in the post-war zones I'd visited with my dad, but those things are easily enough forgotten if you don't have them put in front of your eyes again. There were so many people in that centre who needed surgery and wouldn't get it because they couldn't afford to pay for it, and this in a country where there was extreme wealth.

Bob, Sheena and I visited a slum and the atmosphere was putrid. We left our lovely air-conditioned hotel, drove 30 minutes and arrived in this place that in many respects resembled an actual refuse dump. It was roasting, really humid, the smell was terrible and we were looking at adults and children collecting junk, to be resold or recycled, but this was also where they actually lived.

What was crazy about it was how happy they seemed to be, particularly the children. Bob's an enormous man, but has this really friendly way to him that the children loved. We ended up playing cricket with them by the side of this rubbish dump and we had enormous fun. Of course, they don't yet know any better and their innocence is charming, but there was no escaping the appalling hardship. We went to a brothel area and it was deeply upsetting to see what went on there: the women with their male clients while their kids hid underneath the beds.

Later, I watched one guy washing in this lake and then I looked a little further away and another fellow was taking a shit in it, and you don't need to have a degree to know this is how illness spreads. GOAL works to provide basic clean water facilities and I got to see the tangible difference that something like €5,000 can make to an entire community, or indeed to generations.

I also visited Nepal with the Umbrella Foundation in Kathmandu because there was a link to what was going on in Kolkata. There is a trade in child slavery from Nepal to Kolkata. The charity in Kathmandu tries to rehome the children in Nepal, so they are not sent on to India. It was a much more relaxed atmosphere there and we played football with the kids who were being kept in their schools and houses. It wasn't life-changing, but it was a reminder of how fortunate I am in my own life.

CHAPTER 9

TAKING ON THE WORLD

had always regretted missing out on the 2007 World Cup experience, so New Zealand in 2011 was the chance to experience what I'd been denied then. It was exciting, and for all sorts of reasons. We hadn't delivered as we'd wanted to since the 2009 Grand Slam, but we still had a solid team that on its day could deliver big results. We had a good squad, with such a choice of players available that people like Lukie and Tomás couldn't get in, and we could cover for the loss of players such as David Wallace and Felix Jones to injuries they'd picked up in the August warm-up games. We felt that the group in which we'd been drawn gave us a good chance of reaching the quarter-finals stage. We still believed in our coaches. And it was the World Cup. If that doesn't excite a top international rugby player, then what will?

We knew that expectations outside the camp were lower than they had been in 2007: a run of four defeats in the August friendlies had achieved that. There was also a feeling that the euphoria of 2007 – and the bursting of that bubble – was not going to be allowed happen again. There was also the national mood at the time: the economy was in crisis, people were up to their eyes in debt, jobs were being lost everywhere and so many of our generation left the country to find work. That might be why so many ex-pats turned up in New Zealand. They were there already or living in Australia, but they hadn't given up on Ireland and supporting our games was their outlet.

That's one of the things I'll always remember from that tournament, the extraordinary support we received, the sea of green at our games, the noise that made it seem like we were back in Ireland, and the fun we had with people after the games. It was like a big carnival. If the game was on a Saturday, we'd get to the host city on Thursday and by Thursday afternoon/ Friday morning you'd see all these campervans rocking up, taking over these towns, drinking them dry, and the Irish fans having the time of their lives. At times you couldn't leave the hotel because of the crowds. It gave us a fantastic lift because we were so far away from home, we couldn't have been any further away bar going to the Antarctic, and yet they made it feel like home.

We gave them plenty to shout about too until, suddenly, it was over.

We started with a win over the USA, coached by Eddie O'Sullivan. There was no desire on my part to put one over on him. It was only about getting the win to start us off, which we did. It was a warm-up for the key game in the group, against Australia. If we beat Australia, we'd be on the other side of the draw to the hosts and the holders from the quarter-finals onwards, which would surely give us a better chance of progressing.

At the time Australia was the most successful country in the history of the World Cup. They'd won it twice, come second once and third once. They knew how to peak at the tournament, irrespective of what had happened to them in the four-year interim, and they were coming into this as Tri-Nations champions, the likely nearest challengers to the hosts. They always beat Ireland at world cups, even if Ireland had come close to them. I was only eight years old when they'd beaten Ireland in injury time at Lansdowne Road in the 1991 quarter-final, but I knew all about the history of that day: the Gordon Hamilton try that looked as if it had secured Ireland's biggest upset of all time, only for Michael Lynagh to score the winning try well into added time after Ireland had failed to clear to touch the kick-off from Hamilton's converted try. I had watched how close Ireland had been to beating them in the 2003 pool game before being hammered by the French in the quarter-final. I also knew that Ireland hadn't beaten Australia in the Southern Hemisphere since 1979.

We went into this encounter at Eden Park, home of All Blacks rugby, with the right game plan. Paulie always talks about the importance of achieving the perfect blend of game plan and process mixed with the correct emotional level/ mindset. We hit it that day. We played as well as we had when we blew England away in March. We did what we were capable of doing, if not consistently. This was what we had been building towards. And we had about 25,000 mad Irish fans to cheer us on, not in the least bit put out by the torrential rain before the game started.

Other things went our way in the run-up, too. We had known that David Pocock, probably their most important player, their Richie McCaw for what he was able to do at the breakdown, would be out injured, and then their captain and hooker Stephen Moore was ruled out at the last minute by the effects of a bug. But even without these two important players they would show themselves to be a top-class team, one of the best of the world. Except on this day, we were better.

It took us time to get on top, but we got the edge at the scrum and won more at the breakdown, forcing three turnovers in the first-half and recycling more and quicker ball than they managed to do. It was our best performance at the breakdown in a long time. We employed the 'choke tackle' to good effect, enveloping the runner higher and preventing him from getting to ground, gaining the scrum when the referee ended the maul. We didn't allow our own runners to become isolated because we attacked in pods, requiring one or two players to follow in quickly to support our tackled player by clearing out at speed with low body positions. But it was far from perfect at this stage. They kept the ball in play, which meant we couldn't use the line-out as a platform for set-play attacks, yet when we got two line-outs in the first-half we lost them both. We went in 6-6 at half-time despite all the effort.

In the second-half Darce went off with a hamstring injury, so Rog came in to out-half and Johnny moved to first-centre, which wasn't something we'd done before. It didn't matter, because we were getting on top and Rog took over the kicking, pushing us to 12-6 ahead with a couple of penalties. Young Conor Murray – sporting a Justin Bieber lookalike haircut in those days – came in at scrum-half and helped in the general harassment of their star number 9 Will Genia.

Everyone thinks of Fez at the back of the scrum, picking up Genia and driving him back like a rag doll, as one of the day's defining moments, and with good reason. But what I remember as one of the outstanding images was Church smashing Quade Cooper. Cooper was this hot emerging talent and there was Church, having none of it. Cooper tried to sidestep Church and our prop absolutely buried their star out-half, which summed it all up for me. It happened in the last 10 or 15 minutes of the game and it was massive, one of those moments that told me everything was going our way. We were in a perfect state of flow, every one of us, and we knew it was our day. They were trying everything but getting nowhere because we were just so on point. Rog kicked another penalty and even a converted try wouldn't be enough to save them now. They butchered one try-scoring chance and Seanie and Paulie both ended Aussie efforts, but Tommy nearly scored an 80m intercept try, only getting caught at the last second. Conor Murray had a try ruled out for offside. Nonetheless, at full-time it was 15-6.

We won because we deserved to win. It was regarded, rightly, as the single best performance and result of Ireland's World Cups since the competition started in 1987. But we saw it as only the starting-point. It was a group game and we now had to take advantage of this win to finish at the top of the group and get on the seemingly better side of the knock-out stages draw.

Next up was Russia. Beating them was easy and gave many members of the squad a chance to get on-the-pitch action. I was happy to play again, in a game where I had a little less grunt work to do but could run onto the ball and play a bit more football against what was an amateur-level team.

I was realising by this stage how the World Cup differed from everything else, even after my Lions experience of two years earlier. It was intense, playing from week to week, managing training, recovery and diet, not having the breaks you get in the Six Nations or Heineken Cup, just bang, bang, bang, go. Our video analysts and coaches had so much work to do so quickly, assembling the information for each game nearly from scratch and getting it to us in accessible form.

But there was one thing already becoming clear to me from looking at the competition in general. The teams thriving were the ones providing lightning-quick ruck ball for the scrum-half, giving it to him on a platter to keep the moves going at pace before defences could reset. It was the only way to find the space to attack and score.

All that was left to us in the group was to defeat Italy. We hadn't played well against them earlier in the year, in the game I'd missed due to injury, so that knocked any sense of complacency out of us. They had to win to stay in the tournament, at our expense, and while they would have had an inferior points difference on the same number of group points, they would have progressed on the basis that they had beaten us in the head-to-head. We didn't give them a sniff. We won 36-6, three tries to nil, with Rog at out-half. I was excited by what lay ahead.

By winning our group we had avoided the holders, South Africa, and went into the quarter-final against Wales in Wellington confident, even if we had lost to them in Cardiff the previous March. Our memory of that day was that we had lost to a try that was wrongly allowed because of a refereeing error. We were the better team but had left it behind us, and we wouldn't do that again. We had won 11 of the last 14 contests between the countries. We were a team full of players who had just won either the Heineken Cup or the Magners League that season – and loads of them over the previous five years – whereas the Welsh didn't even have a team that had reached the quarter-finals in the Heineken in 2011, let alone one that had ever won it. We had the more relevant experience of cup rugby. We were also on form in this tournament. We hadn't just beaten Australia and Italy, they hadn't scored any tries against us in our big pool games and we weren't conceding much by way of penalties either. I was part of a back-row that was going really well and getting plaudits well beyond the Irish fan base.

I swear we weren't thinking ahead to the semi-final, that we took nothing for granted. We were experienced enough not to do that. We did think that we would be better than Wales, but we knew that wasn't guaranteed. We respected their individual players, many of whom I knew to be very good from our time together on the Lions. Our entire focus was on giving everything we had. After that we'd worry about the next day.

And then we lost.

We started badly, conceding a try within the first three minutes, losing the ball in their half, whereupon they swept 60m down the pitch and Shane Williams went over the line. They converted and we were chasing the game. But that wasn't what threw us. Seanie, Fez and I discovered that they had a plan to deal with us as we carried the ball: the chop tackle. They went really low, taking us by the ankles to bring us to ground, gambling that we wouldn't get the offloads away as we fell. Ireland actually stole that approach not too long afterwards, but on that particular day we were surprised by it and it was utterly frustrating that we couldn't get up a head of steam with power running into contact. They kept cutting us down and without our main ball-carriers, the other favoured option was for us to kick. Normally we would have been happy to allow Rog to do just that, Munster cup rugby style, to play the corners, but Wales had planned for that, too. They were well positioned to receive the kicks and had very fast players to run the ball back.

And yet, we were only 10-3 down at half-time. I remember coming in and Gats was in the tunnel and he was shouting.

He was doing it to distract us as much as to benefit his own players. 'We're fitter than them, faster than them, stronger than them, we're fitter than them …' He shouted it over and over again, like literally on repeat, shouting it so every one of us would hear it. I still remember it to this day, which shows how it worked, how it got into my head. I wouldn't regard Gats as a great technical coach – from my time with him on Lions tours I had seen how he let others do much of the finer details – but he had his tactics spot-on and, more than that, he knew how to get guys into the right head space to play a game the way he wanted them to play it.

Five minutes into the second-half we got our try. Keith Earls (Earlsie) got in at the corner and Rog converted brilliantly. Now we were in a position to push on, but then we blew it. Just six minutes later we let Mike Phillips run down an unguarded blindside after a line-out we lost, in a channel just 2m wide, and he got the try.

It got worse. Not long afterwards, Jonathan Davies got their third try and again we weren't at the races defensively. After the conversion we were now 12 points behind. Given the way we were playing, it was too much.

When you lose a game, you tend to look back at what you've done wrong, rather than what they did right. In retrospect, the Welsh had more variety to their game than they were given credit for at the time. Yes, there was the bish-bosh of the big men Jamie Roberts and George North using their size and power to run through and over people, but there was also the elusiveness of Shane Williams. They won most of the collisions and Sam Warburton won too much at the breakdown or slowed our ruck ball. They made only four handling errors. They kicked better with the wind. They imposed themselves on us with their physicality but although they were pumped up, they were still precise in what they did.

So, it was probably right that they won as they were the better team on the day, but I still think that two of the tries we gave away were soft. We didn't take penalty shots at goal when maybe we should have, we were over the line twice but couldn't ground the ball for a try. We made 11 handling errors and we couldn't put all of those down to the wet conditions when it didn't seem to affect Wales. We were comfortable on our scrums and line-outs, but when they went wrong we conceded points. Wales had to make 141 tackles, but we made only 93. We spent 15 minutes inside their 22, but they had only six minutes in ours. We had 57% possession in the first-half and 60% territory and we went in behind at half-time. We were behind for all but eight minutes of the game.

In retrospect, the uncertainty as to who was our main man at number 10 – Rog or Johnny – didn't help us. In the Australia game, Johnny started as 10 but moved to 12 when Darce took a knock. After that, Deccie reverted to Rog being his first choice, even though Johnny had been first choice for more than a year and had shown his game-changing abilities in that Heineken Cup final. But then he hooked Rog early in the second-half and put Johnny in at a time when we were struggling.

That uncertainty on the part of the coach as to what his choice should be transmitted itself to the team. One of the things I liked about Joe, by contrast, was the certainty that he provided. He would say, 'If you don't train on a Tuesday, you are not available for selection for the weekend.' We always knew from Tuesday pretty much who was on the team. It meant that we knew what we had to do and what others had to do. For me, that gave me confidence that I would know my role and all my teammates would know theirs. When I didn't know who was being picked, I felt it created a degree of uncertainty and I didn't like that. I liked knowing; I'm quite process-driven.

In the World Cup, I think Deccie's indecision didn't help the squad. The number 10 position is like the quarterback in American football, it's one of the most important positions on the field. They call the shots, they direct the play, everything goes through the 10. It's fair to say that Rog and Johnny have very different styles of play. Johnny is probably more an aggressive, attacking 10. Rog had an amazing tactical brain in terms of kicking the ball around the field and a beautiful flat pass, right at the line. They were both great players, and Johnny remains so. But even great players need consistency to perform at their best level. And if you want consistency, it's nice to have that from a Tuesday rather than the team settling in on a Thursday, with only two days to prep. I'm sure at the time the back and forth wrecked Johnny and Rog's heads, although I wasn't too conscious of it if it did because I was more focused on myself and making sure I was in the best shape I could be. It was my first World Cup and I genuinely believed we could go the distance.

When we lost to Wales, I thought that might be that in terms of playing in World Cups. I remember saying to Rory Best (Besty), 'I think that's it, we'd be doing well if we're around for the next one,' and I think he was like, 'Yeah'. And he's still going, for his fourth. But while Paulie managed to get to 2015, despite some serious injuries in the meantime, it meant Drico had missed out on his great chance to get to a semi-final, at least.

It was a tough loss to take because when I look back on that game, I think how those two hours cost us the tournament, and they were hours that we could have controlled. It was made all the worse because there were so many Irish in Wellington, at the team hotel, all around the city, and the sense of general disappointment was crushing. We drowned our sorrows for pretty much the next two days.

The way the World Cup ends is pretty brutal. You play a game and you're either in or out, and if you're out, you leave the country a couple of days later, no longer of interest to anyone because the victor is the focus of attention, with their next game to play. It was a long flight home. You get back to your provinces and maybe have a week off. The last thing you want to do is hang around, so I left the country with my missus and when I came back, I went straight into Leinster mode.

It might be wrong to call it a grieving process, but losing and going out of the World Cup is a little bit different from getting beaten in the Six Nations. There's just so much time invested in the World Cup, from pretty much mid-June onwards. There are no games with Leinster in between internationals, no Pro14, no Europe. It was my focus from the end of the season in May, thinking about it during holidays, then getting into the work in June, July, August, September, into October. For five months, that's your whole focus. You're heavily invested in it and unless you've won the damn thing, your last meaningful game is a defeat. It's particularly tough if you didn't play well in the last game because that hangs over you.

The other thing is that you don't know if you're going to get another chance at the next World Cup. The coach may have different ideas for the next cycle, or he might not be there himself in four years' time. For me, getting back into the club environment quickly meant that I could draw a line under it and turn the page. Thankfully, European rugby quickly came on top of me again and I hopped gladly onto that rollercoaster and off I went again. Next ball.

CHAPTER 10

CAPTAIN

The 2012 Six Nations gave us an immediate opportunity to start afresh after our World Cup disappointment. In our opening match we lost 23-21 at home to Wales, and they scored three tries again. This was after having a 13-5 lead early in the second-half, even if we didn't really deserve it. Wales were down four of their first-choice pack and lost their captain, Sam Warburton, at half-time. Even so, they possessed the confidence, the skills and the sense of purpose to make up for all that, as well as a backline with a 9kg per man advantage who carried the ball into contact and recycled quickly. They clinched the game with a late winning penalty.

I wasn't interested in making excuses, even if others complained that the penalty that won it for them in the end – when Fez got pinged for a tip tackle – shouldn't have been given. I never saw any point in arguing about refereeing decisions. It was given, it was done and all you could do was try to make sure a game never again came down to something like that. The real issue, as far as I was concerned, was the concession of three tries. We gave them the ball too often. We were bullied physically on our own patch, our defence was passive and we offered little in attack. Losing to them again seemed to confirm that they were better us, which they probably were as they had now won three in a row against us for the first time since 1979.

It was the worst possible start for the weeks ahead. I remained optimistic nonetheless, as I always did. I took the results on the chin, dusted myself off and returned to training to get ready for the next game.

The next was against France in Paris, a late start on a Saturday evening, but it was postponed just minutes before kick-off because the pitch was frozen. It meant that we beat Italy at home before going back for the rescheduled game in Paris, which we drew, 17-17. This was really frustrating because we out-scored them by two tries to one. I had to do one of those immediate post-match TV interviews, which I reckon are fairly pointless for everyone, including the viewer, because there is little of value you can say immediately after the whistle. I remember the interviewer saying, 'You must be happy with that result', which clearly I wasn't. We were able to come here with Leinster and win Heineken Cup games, and the Munster lads had done it too, and yet we couldn't do it at international level. It was simple enough playing against French teams: you hold on to the ball, go through the phases and take your opportunities while giving them none. But we didn't do the second part of that properly, and so we lost the game.

Next, we beat Scotland at home, as we expected to do, but our campaign came to a catastrophic end at Twickenham when England beat us 30-9. It was humiliating. We were milled in the scrum and Owen Farrell had a field day with his kicking, scoring 20 points. We had plenty of good players, knew we should be doing better, and the mood in the squad about the direction we were getting from our coaches was changing.

At the same time, things were going well with Leinster under Joe. As defending champions, we cruised through the group stage of the Heineken Cup, winning five and drawing one, and then we hammered Cardiff 34-3 in the quarter-final. The semi-final was going to be something else entirely, though, as we faced our old foes, Clermont Auvergne, away in Bordeaux.

That semi-final turned out to be one of the hardest but best games of my entire career. If there was any other game to which it could be compared, it was the second Lions test in South Africa in 2009, it was that combative. It may have been our finest ever performance, to win against what was probably the best Clermont side ever, unbelievably talented and with most of their players in their prime. It was extraordinarily physical and aggressive. They set about disrupting our scrum and line-out and succeeded, to an extent, forcing us on to the defensive. Vern Cotter was their coach, but Joe's influence, less than two seasons after he had left the role of assistant coach, was still obvious in their level of organisation. They knew exactly how they wanted to play and executed the plan with confidence. Having lost to us in the quarter-final two years previously, and again in the group stage the previous season, and with the final in sight, it was obvious how much they wanted it and how far they were prepared to go to get it.

I had played in Bordeaux once before, in a warm-up game against France for the 2011 World Cup. The atmosphere in the stadium is electric. There is this massive long walk to get from the dressing-rooms to the pitch and you suck it all up on the way. I always try to ignore the crowd, but this lot, the noise they created, was incredible. There was a moment during the game when Leo Cullen half punched one of their guys and he gave a theatrical fall to the ground – and the reaction of the crowd, the pressure they put on referee Wayne Barnes to send Leo off was enormous. In fairness to Barnes, he took no nonsense that day and penalised them more than he did us, so they got no home advantage there.

The game itself was every bit as mad as the crowd. This was as fast and physical and pressurised as a test game for Ireland. It was high quality, few mistakes made, and when we did unlock them to score our try, which Church got, it was with a chess-piece move, a Joe creation. Then Rob got a monster drop goal left-footed from the left touch-line and Johnny a penalty and going into the final moments we had a 19-15 lead and we defended like our lives depended on it. They almost won it in the end, after the biggest of scares. Wesley Fofana lost control of the ball when he was reaching out for our try-line, after a tackle by Darce. It went to the TMO and ruled in our favour.

That game was fast, clinical, not an inch given and when I look back at it now, that was really the final. Everyone stood toe to toe, we threw our best at each other and no one conceded anything. There were large chunks of the game when the ball was in play and we were unparalleled, the systems Joe had in place for us working perfectly. I think we deserved to win, but I don't think anyone would have complained if we hadn't.

What stood out for me after the game was the generosity of the same Clermont fans who had spent the previous hour and a half baying for our blood and were so disappointed to have missed out yet again. Their supporters came over and congratulated us and wished us the best for the final. It meant a lot.

We deliberately didn't do a lap of honour, not just because the cup wasn't yet won but because of our amusement at the behaviour of the Ulster team the day before, when they beat

Edinburgh in their semi-final. They celebrated like crazy and did a lap of honour for their fans, which was fair enough, but then they posed for photos in front of the Twickenham 2012 sign and we all looked at them and said, 'Look at them, they're just happy to be in the final, they don't know what's coming.' Well, what was coming was that they were facing one of the best Leinster sides ever, and we hammered them. The game was done with 30 minutes to go. We brought on our entire bench and some of them added tries as we won 42-14. It was a great occasion for Irish and even European rugby, two Irish sides playing each other in the home of English rugby. Typically, though, the combined fans drank the bar dry before the game was even finished. The Heineken Cup final and they ran out of the sponsor's brew.

It wasn't anti-climactic to win so easily, it was actually more enjoyable. There was less tension. When we'd beaten Northampton the previous year, it was a 'how did we do this?' moment. This time was so different. I remember far more of the crowd and the atmosphere in that 2012 final because we were able to savour it a little bit more. I felt absolutely no sympathy for Ulster over the scoreline. None whatsoever. Why should I?

By this stage, the Leinster team was Joe's team. He had taken the solid foundations set by Cheika and built on them to create something that was a joy to play in, a team that was willing to attack from anywhere, could switch the points of attack almost at will and had Johnny confidently pulling all the strings. Plus we had a rock-solid defence because for all his willingness to let us engage in attacking play, Joe never let us forget our responsibilities in defence and insisted on our work rate. We had reached the stage where we trusted each other to do our jobs for the collective.

We failed to do the double, though, losing the Pro12 decider for the third year in a row. This was a particularly hard one to take as we led the Ospreys 17-9 at half-time in the final at the RDS and had a 30-21 advantage in the second-half. But Shane Williams got two tries, the second with 90 seconds to go, and Dan Biggar converted from the touch-line to win. It took a little bit of the shine off the club season. We should have finished it off as we'd wanted to.

But the season wasn't over because the IRFU had organised for Ireland to go back to New Zealand, this time to play three tests against the World Champions. I agreed with Deccie's philosophy that we should go up against these guys in a three-test series. He would say to us: 'If we want to win the World Cup or whatever, we've got to constantly go up against the best.' His view was that South Africa and Australia had beaten the All Blacks at crucial and unexpected moments because they were used to playing them and had less fear and more expectation as a result of that. He was right.

~

We arrived in Auckland at the start of June, with the first test on 9 June. We got well beaten in the first test, could have won the second and got absolutely hammered in the third.

We lost the first test at Eden Park 42-10, with Julian Savea running in a hat-trick of tries. And then we nearly got a result a week later in Christchurch, in a typical Irish backs-against-the-wall performance. It was my fiftieth cap and I was asked to lead the team out, which I regarded as a great honour. I remembered something Drico had said previously: 'A guy getting fifty caps, that's an established good international, like, fair play to him.' It made me feel like I'd proved myself.

We tried to put more of a shape on our play in that second game and had a better understanding of what structure we needed to compete with them. We actually led 10-9 at half-time after Conor Murray got a try that Johnny converted. Then they had their usual purple patch and went ahead, but we kept at it. Johnny put us level at 19-19 with 11 minutes to go, but unfortunately he missed a long-range penalty that might have won it for us, not that I would ever blame him or any other kicker for that. At that stage we would have been happy with the draw, that was our mindset.

It was level a minute into added time when Dan Carter missed a drop goal that would have won the game. Our joy lasted only seconds. Nigel Owens, as referee, decided that Rory Best had touched the ball in his effort to block the kick and awarded a 5m scrum. Carter had another drop-goal effort available to him once the ball came back from the scrum. I was one of the guys who chased out, trying to block it, but I failed and New Zealand won again. It was gut-wrenching. That could have been the perfect day. Yes, that's how we would have seen a draw.

I broke my finger in the last quarter of that game. I can't really remember how or who was responsible, it may have been at the bottom of a ruck or something, but I didn't realise until I put my hands up to try to block that Carter drop goal. The finger was sticking out in the wrong direction and I just looked at it and thought, 'That's not right' and automatically pulled on it to reset it myself. The adrenaline meant there was little or no pain, but it meant I didn't play the following weekend for the third test, in which they beat us 60-0 in Hamilton.

What happened after the second test shows you where we were at mentally. Most of the lads went on the absolute smash in Queenstown on the Sunday. Deccie asked me if I wanted to stay around or go home with Darce, who was also injured but wanted time at home to prepare for his wedding. He went, but I stayed, and I went on the piss for the week. There were guys, I won't say who they were, who were on the piss with me on the Monday and who played the following weekend. So it didn't really come as a surprise to me when I watched that game and it turned out to be an embarrassing defeat.

It's rare that Ireland fail to score. I was well oiled in the stands, in holiday mode, and maybe some of the lads had checked out too when we'd just lost the previous week. Maybe there was a sense that we'd had our chance and blown it and the season was over. As well as that, I think the players wondered what belief Deccie had in the squad he'd picked when he flew Paddy Wallace out from a beach in Spain as a replacement for Darce and then put him straight into the team. Whatever it was, the way we reacted to the second test compared to the way New Zealand reacted to it told us everything. New Zealand focused on making themselves better for the next day. We were a mix of feeling sorry for ourselves, with no sense that we could do better the next time out.

It was a very frustrating tour from start to finish, especially for those of us who'd had such success with Joe at Leinster and who felt that his coaching and planning were far superior to what we were getting with Ireland. I think the game had evolved beyond where Deccie was with his coaching. I had a lot of respect for what Deccie had achieved with us, bringing the team together, but that didn't quell the frustration of knowing we were getting better coaching from Joe at club level. Even some of the Munster players – who were loyal to Deccie because of what he'd achieved with them – were coming to doubt what we were doing.

In stark contrast, Joe had all these well-thought-out set-plays that we rehearsed until we were all certain about our roles. There was a very definite game plan. There was no real structure with Ireland, it was a case of play it as you see it. As a result, we kept going from side to side, trying to go around the corner. When we went up against the All Blacks, they had a way of playing and a system that just ripped us apart. We could last with them for so long during a game, but then they'd blow us away. Their system at the time was a 'wide to wide' game, using the full width of the pitch, keeping a hooker and a back-row in the 15m channel on one side and splitting the field. At the time it felt like we were running around, chasing shadows.

You're not really in the mood for too much analysis when you get to the end of a long season and you've been on the receiving end of a hiding like that. If I remember rightly, most of us just wanted our holidays, to return to our clubs for pre-season and then we'd deal with our issues on the national squad when we regrouped for the November series. Maybe some of us should have raised our concerns about coaching with Declan and his staff then, but we didn't. I know there would have been some conversations among the players in smaller groups, the Leinster players wondering why this was happening when we were back-to-back European champions, but it was more an undercurrent than the start of any kind of rebellion.

We regrouped at the end of October for the November series feeling more than a bit under pressure but promising ourselves that we'd never let anything like the horror of Hamilton happen again. We weren't helped by a long injury list, which left us without Drico, Paulie, Rob, Seanie, Fez and Rory. But this setback provided me with a personal opportunity: I would captain the team for the month.

The announcement that I was going to captain the team was a wonderfully proud moment. Deccie gave me the news over the phone. I was in Tesco doing the shopping when I got the call. The first thing I did was phone my dad and let him know. He said, 'Congratulations on your captaincy, but I'm still a colonel, so I pull rank', putting me right into my box straight off.

I felt I had served my time, having played 153 games for Leinster by that stage. I had also captained Leinster a few times, including an 18-6 win against Munster in Thomond Park in October, after which Joe had publicly complimented the way I went about the job. Deccie said he gave me the armband because I was 'the consummate professional', noting how prepared I was when I turned up for work. He said the captaincy had come to me as a result of my progression.

The game itself was a terrible anti-climax because after leading 12-3 at half-time, we didn't score again and lost 16-12. We had 60% possession and territory and yet we didn't look like scoring a try. We weren't helped by our failure to score in the 10 minutes when JP Pietersen was in the bin and by conceding 10 points in the 10 minutes I was yellow-carded. But while I maintained that my binning was harsh, for infringing at a line-out maul, and that JP was lucky he didn't get red for what was an assault on Chris Henry, charging into his chest with his shoulder as he went to catch a ball, I didn't use these things as an excuse. Nor did I use the fact that my old friend Wayne Barnes was in something of a mood that evening. When I complained to him that one Bok had dropped his knee into a prostrate-on-the-ground Johnny, I was told that my persistent complaints 'lacked credibility'. Nonetheless, I felt that by being binned I had failed to lead by example and I apologised afterwards.

The following week we played a non-test game against Fiji at Thomond Park and Deccie threw in lots of younger players, like Iain Henderson, to give them experience. We won 53-0 and it was a joy to see a young team embrace their roles and get the details right. I was more pleased with the zero points conceded than the number of tries scored because it is so difficult in international rugby to shut a team out and allow them no scores at all.

We still had one very important day ahead of us: Argentina at the Aviva on 24 November. This was an Argentine team that had enjoyed a good 2012, the first year they were admitted to the Rugby Championship, the expanded Tri-Nations, and we needed to beat them to guarantee our place among the second tier of seeds for the 2015 World Cup. The continuing absence of key players was a worry, but the seven-try pasting we gave Argentina suggested that we had put the ship back on course. Johnny and Tommy both got tries in our 46-24 win, and Craig Gilroy scored one on his debut. It was our first win in six test matches. The scoreline may have flattered us, but I wasn't complaining because it was one of those days when things clicked and we got the lucky bounces. I was delighted to be captain of a team that had shown great effort and professionalism, who had put in a proper shift.

Deccie asked me to come to his office at The Four Seasons, where he told me he was happy with how I'd performed as captain in the November series and asked me to stay on as captain. I was so thrilled that my first instinct was to jump across the table and hug him. I managed to restrain myself. It was a huge vote of confidence in me. Captaining your country at any time is important, but to do so in what is effectively the annual European championship of the sport is something else.

It became a big story in the media, not so much because I got the role but because a fit again Drico was not keeping the job. The problem for the commentators was that being captain of Ireland had in some ways defined Drico … and that was to become my problem. He had done so 83 times, more than any other player in any other country had ever achieved. He'd had more success than anyone else for Ireland, captaining us to three Triple Crowns (2004–2007) and to the 2009 Grand Slam. His leadership on the pitch in 2009 had been sensational, the way he'd dug in to get tries we needed when they didn't seem to be forthcoming in any other way. To many people he had come to represent what rugby in Ireland was. But his last run-out to lead Ireland had been that 60-0 defeat in New Zealand, so it was only natural that he wouldn't want that to be the note on which he bowed out.

I don't think Drico coped with it too well, although I could understand why. Once I knew he'd been made aware of the change, which wasn't public yet, I tried to contact him. We were both at Leinster the next day but I don't know if he saw me, so I went over to him and asked how he was. 'So you know?' he said. He told me that he didn't know that I'd been told that he'd been stepped down. He was obviously annoyed, although, he emphasised, not with me. It wasn't as if I'd made the decision, and I would have been stupid to have said, 'No, I don't want to be captain, it has to stay with Brian.'

For my part, I didn't feel guilty that I was taking his place and I didn't think that I didn't deserve it. I thought I was ready and I was incredibly excited about the opportunity. I knew Deccie was trying to change things up. Paulie was out injured for the foreseeable future and no one really knew how much longer Drico was going to continue playing. It was rumoured that he might retire at the end of the season.

So I imagine Deccie was probably thinking that Drico wasn't going to make it to the World Cup, given that he was now 34 years old, and with a young and upcoming squad he needed new leadership to see them through the challenges ahead. I also think Drico was a little bit distracted that season by the uncertainty as to whether this was his last season or not and whether he would be picked for the Lions tour as his swansong. He still hadn't made his decision (and eventually he bowed to the crowd chants of 'one more year' and played until the summer of 2014 because Joe persuaded him) and that featured in Deccie's thinking. But it wasn't up to me to say all of this to him. That was for Deccie to do, and I assumed he had done it.

The thing with Deccie was that he never explained to me what he saw me doing as captain. I think he just wanted me to continue doing what I had done in November. In my view, leadership in a team was about setting an example and backing it up with actions, not words. There were a lot of lads who talked a great game, who said all the right things beforehand so the right people would hear them say it, but there weren't enough guys who questioned the stuff they were being told to do. I was never going to be one of those captains who gave a crazy, massive emotional speech. I always tried to give clear direction in any messages I gave to the team.

It turned out to be a tough time in my career. The results went against us, there were lots of injuries, which meant the team kept changing, and we had a number of young players coming into a team that wasn't working well. In addition, I perceived, rightly or wrongly, that there were players who felt they should have been captain, not me. As a result, I don't think I got the necessary support from some of them, though I won't name names. But I think the results that season brought about the frustration, not my being captain.

Drico publicly supported me at a press conference during the campaign, saying the flak I'd been getting was totally unwarranted and pretty harsh and that I was doing a 'good job' and needed time to get better at it. I appreciated his words, but at the same time thought, what else could he have said? He was in an impossible situation when asked questions like that. He admitted that he'd been 'disappointed' to lose the captaincy – which I could understand – but that he'd 'parked it' and, as a senior player, was looking at the bigger picture and weighing in behind me. I appreciated that public support.

In retrospect, I may have been so excited at the opportunity that I was also a little naive. Drico had an easier transition when he became captain. Keith Wood was injured when Drico became captain for the first time, in 2002. When Woody came back, he returned as captain and did the job at the 2003 World Cup. Drico got the job on a full-time basis when Woody retired at the end of that tournament. At the time, Woody was as big a figure as Drico subsequently became and he acknowledged that it would have been difficult for him to be captain while Woody was on the pitch.

I faced into the Six Nations determined for Ireland to give the best performances possible and to win as many matches as possible. But it was a difficult campaign, and of course everyone – myself included – became more frustrated as we endured a string of poor games. When a team is losing, it's never easy, but it's particularly hard on the captain, as I was to discover. It's obviously easier to be captain of a team that keeps delivering. But history shows that good captains have their ups and downs. Ciaran Fitzgerald was a hero when Ireland won the Triple Crown in 1982 and the Five Nations in 1983, which led to him being made captain for the British

& Irish Lions that year. The test series was lost 4-0 and he took a ferocious battering from a hostile British media. The following year, Ireland lost every game and he was dropped. Was he suddenly a bad captain? No; he returned the next year and Ireland won the Triple Crown and the championship and were denied the Grand Slam by a draw in the second game against France. A captain can make a team better if he does his job properly, but there must be good and willing players in place first.

The Six Nations started so well. Given that we had lost our previous three games to Wales, starting in Cardiff was a tough call, but we blitzed them and led 30-3 early in the second-half. We ended up winning 30-22 because they came back at us with near abandon, perhaps because we kicked the ball too much to them and they ran it back at us, and we also lost two men to yellow cards for penalties conceded at the breakdown. But it was a great start for a young team; five of the 14 on the pitch at the end had just a dozen caps between them. Some noted that I was the only player to raise my arms aloft to celebrate on the whistle; nearly everyone else was too wrecked from the effort of protecting our lead. Subsequently, critics focused on the frantic defence to keep Wales out as a portent for the season, not the way we'd built our lead.

It went awry in our next game, against England at the Aviva, when they became the first English team to win a Six Nations game in Dublin since the Grand Slam team of 2003. The rain lashed down and we couldn't hold onto the ball. We had no accuracy in almost everything we tried to do. Simon Zebo broke his metatarsal and Johnny Sexton pulled his hamstring and both left the game before half-time. We went 6-0 down, levelled it, and then gave them two soft penalties to win it, even though they were down a man at the time. They kicked well, took us through the phases, were aggressive at the breakdown. They were just a little better.

It was a grim game, and personally one of my worst ever performances in an Irish jersey. I had a crap game, made a huge number of mistakes. It happens. Guys can just have a bad game, an annoying one-off that you put behind you. But when you have a particularly bad game playing for Ireland, the media piles in, a theme is set, it's on media rotation and everyone starts saying the same thing to you. I don't know why it happened that day. But some in the media were quick to tell me that it was the burden of being captain. All I could do was laugh at the people putting about those narratives because it was plucking at straws.

Then things got even worse. We went to Scotland and contrived to lose dismally. We had 80% possession and territorial dominance in the first-half but managed to take only a 3-0 lead to half-time. We blew about four good try-scoring opportunities. We were without Johnny at out-half and Deccie opted to start with Paddy Jackson instead of Rog. I passed on a couple of chances for Paddy to kick for goal, choosing to go for penalties to touch instead with the aim of scoring tries off the subsequent possession, but we got nothing from them and when I gave him his first kick he missed from the right, which was not his better side.

These decisions led to rows afterwards in the media, questioning whether I should have asked him to kick the earlier chances. There's no simple answer to when you should kick a penalty for points or go down the line to get a line-out from which you might manufacture a try. There's no guaranteed outcome, either way. But it's very easy for sideline critics and TV pundits to have a view, particularly when being wise after the event. My usual way of thinking, particularly in test matches, was to take whatever points were available by kicking. I admit that I got it wrong in that Scotland game. In the England game I went for the kick because of the rain and the physical battering we were taking. I reckoned that we needed points. I can't remember if we got them. That choice was wrong then, according to the pundits, and now this choice was wrong. I also got criticised for canvassing the views of some of my more senior players, but that is something that has carried on for years since under a variety of captains. Ultimately, I took the decision, but I wasn't running some kind of dictatorship.

In the second-half we got a try to go 8-0 up, but that didn't settle us. Now we started to give away penalties – Greig Laidlaw kicked three in 10 minutes – and we became more and more anxious. Paddy missed three of his four kicks, but our attacking line-outs were misfiring too. Rog replaced Paddy and miscued a cross-field kick so badly that it went way backwards and we gave away another three points from it. We lost 12-8 and the criticism was savage.

I felt that I had played well personally, certainly far better than in the England game, carrying the ball and getting through quite a bit of work. But as captain I had to think of the others and the outcome and I took the defeat far more personally than usual. It weighed on my shoulders. I felt a little bit more responsible.

We were without lots of our experienced and top players – Paulie, Fez, Tommy, Darce and Johnny, for example – and we had young players who were still learning their way at this level. I didn't use that as an excuse, though, as losing players to injury is part of rugby. It was the players on the pitch who didn't take the chances against Scotland. You just get on with things and don't linger on them.

Our next game was at home to France and the rain lashed down even harder than it had against England. We played much better, but again we blew it. We led 13-3 at half-time but allowed them to come back to draw, their dominance in the scrum bringing their scores. It was really flat in the dressing-room afterwards, one of those days when a draw leaves you feeling confused as to what your emotional state should be. I could have complained after the game that the referee, Steve Walsh, should have given us a late penalty, for Earlsie being barged as he chased a kick ahead, especially given what he had seen on the TMO, but I didn't, because it wouldn't have changed the outcome and I never used refereeing decisions as an excuse for our losses that season. Everybody remembers that season for the incredible injuries we had in the final game against Italy, but things were nearly as bad against France. Both our centres – Luke Marshall and Drico – got injured in the play that led to the French try, and Reddser came on as sub scrum-half and he broke his leg near the very end, which meant that Sean Cronin, a hooker, replaced him for the game's last play.

We had one game left in the Six Nations, but Deccie was already on the ropes. There were clearly moves afoot to get rid of him. While it was evident that his time had come, it was handled the wrong way. I had alickadoos and committee members coming up to me at the after-match function following the French game, hinting that they were going to do it, asking what I felt we should do next, with Deccie standing just 20m away from me. I felt in an impossible situation. I was torn between personal loyalty to him, because everybody liked him, and the best option for the team. But the decision had been made, and I know it was made even before the disaster of losing away to Italy in the last match.

The week of that game was dreadful. What we needed that week was a clear game plan, a clear process, clear assistance in how we were going to play this final match. It was a young squad, they needed specific instructions. Johnny was a brilliant at directing the play on the pitch, but we lost him on the morning of the match. He hadn't played since he'd left the pitch during the England game. We trained with him at out-half all week, but the morning of the match it was decided that his injury had not healed sufficiently. Paddy had to go back in again, with Ian Madigan (Mads)on the bench because Deccie had ditched Rog from the squad entirely.

There are times when you can't make your own luck. In a 13-minute period from the 25th minute, Keith Earls, then Luke Marshall and then Luke Fitzgerald, Earlsie's sub, all got injured. Drico got a yellow card for stamping, the first of three for the team. For a period, at 9-3 down, Paddy had a three-quarter line of Mads and Rob in the centre and Craig Gilroy and Peter O'Mahony, our 6, on the wings, with no full-back. In the circumstances we did very well and managed, through Paddy's kicking, to get back into the game just a point down at 16-15. But our discipline was poor. Donnacha Ryan and Conor Murray picked up yellow cards and we gave away 13 penalties as well as losing four of our own nine line-outs. We lost 22-15 and the critics were baying for blood.

I remember sitting in the dressing-room after the Italy game and saying, 'Look, this sucks, but this will stand to us, we'll learn from this, we'll learn how to get better, we'll learn what is expected of us.' A lot of those same players were part of the group that won the championship in 2014 and 2015. We had conceded just five tries during that Six Nations, which was bettered only by Wales. We had such bad luck with injuries that we ended up using 33 players during the tournament, an unheard-of number. But there was no getting away from the fact that we had avoided the Wooden Spoon only on points difference, because France couldn't beat Scotland by enough points. There was also no getting away from the fact that we had won only four of Deccie's last 16 games. We were sad on a personal level when he was let go very soon after the Italy game – he was a great person and brilliant at getting teams to bond and focus in the same direction – but at the same time there was an acceptance that things had to change.

I was well aware of the criticism I was taking, even if I consciously didn't read the newspapers or watch or listen to broadcast commentary and hadn't done so for years.

I know that people took issue with me when I said that I'd enjoyed every minute of that campaign, but I was proud of holding the position of captain and energised by it.

Sections of the media weren't exactly kind, but one of the toughest things about being captain was the speed with which I was expected to face the media, to meet their deadlines. I couldn't spend an hour after the game collecting my thoughts and relaxing in the shower because they needed immediate quotes. The after-match press conferences were tough, much more so than I'd expected. The emotions were raw, especially when we'd lost. I wore the wins and losses quite plainly. That failing of mine that others had already noted – of not having a poker face – came to the fore now. I may not have given the polished performances that the media demanded.

I admit that I did worry about maintaining my own level of performance because I was trying to set the tone in training and then in games. It was a tough balance because I don't think any player should try to do other players' jobs as well as their own. My approach was to try to set the standard for others to follow. Unfortunately, it didn't work out, as the results showed. It would become something of a millstone for me in the future.

After the Six Nations performance, I wasn't sure that I would be picked for the Lions tour and any dreams of being captain had evaporated. I went into the Italian dressing-room after the game to congratulate Sergio Parisse on their victory and to swap jerseys, and he said he'd see me in Hong Kong. I didn't know what he meant. 'Oh, I'm playing the Barbarians game and I'll see you in Hong Kong,' he said, referring to the warm-up match for the Lions on the way to Australia. I can remember saying to him, 'I don't know if I'll make that team. I don't know if I'll make the squad, we'll see, there's a lot of rugby to be played.' My hope was that in the remaining games of the season with Leinster I could put myself back in the mix.

In truth, though, things weren't going great for Leinster, either. We were eliminated from the Heineken Cup at the group stage, the first time that had happened to defending champions since Wasps in 2008. Clermont finally did for us, beating us home and away, and even though we got losing bonus points in each game and 20 points overall, it was Munster that pipped us to the last qualifying spot for the quarter-finals. That meant we had to take our place in the Amlin Challenge Cup instead, the secondary competition.

We beat Biarritz 44-16 in the semi-final and I got two tries after big runs, just the right thing to do with Gats and two other Lions coaches watching from the stands. Joe named me as captain for the final against Stade Français at the RDS, which was a huge boost in light of what had happened with Ireland during the season. It was proof that Joe rated me not just as a player but also, despite all the media coverage, as a leader. We won 34-13, even though we conceded possession and territory, because our defence was solid and our accuracy and cutting edge yielded the scores. It was an important win, both for Joe, who had been announced as the new Ireland head coach, and for the players, to reboot our confidence.

A week later we completed the double, beating Ulster 18-12 in the Pro12 final at the RDS. Finally, we were able to achieve domestic success the week after winning in Europe.

When I heard I was selected for my second Lions tour, it was as much a relief as anything. It didn't provoke quite the same excitement as being picked four years earlier, but I badly wanted to be included. Gats had been the assistant coach back then but now he was in charge and there was quite a lot of speculation as to whether he would be biased towards Welsh players. I was one of nine Irish players in the initial squad of 37, although more would join us as replacements for injured players.

I had known Gats for years, since I was a child. He and my brother Graham used to share lifts when Gats was coaching Connacht and Graham was a player there. I'd be in the back of the car, pestering him with questions. Graham told me that I gave Gats a kick in the shins once or twice, just to annoy him. It might not have been the smartest thing I'd ever done. By the time this tour was done, he'd have delivered me an uppercut.

We won the Pro12 final on the Saturday and flew out on Sunday 26 May after the rest of the tour, to face the Barbarians in Hong Kong. We went out on the smash before getting the flight. We were hungover as hell the next day, but we were sure none of us would be playing in the Wednesday game in Hong Kong because we'd just played that weekend and the rest of the squad had been in training for the previous two weeks. We got there on the Monday and didn't train and I went out for a few beers with the Leicester lads, who had also played that weekend. We had a great night, even though we knew we had training the following morning; we were following the 2009 protocols.

On Tuesday morning I was told that I'd be needed on the bench for Wednesday's game against the Barbarians because our captain, Sam Warburton, had pulled out injured. I was shocked. Gats could probably smell the beer off me as he told me and there I was, about to start the pitch session in the searing heat of Hong Kong, trying to learn all the moves and the rest of it while dealing with the heat and humidity, which reached 94%. I think my heart rate was just under 200, even though I only played the last 20 minutes. Everyone nearly died that day, whether we'd been out drinking or not.

But maybe that's what the Lions is about, why's it's different, that we care but don't really. We just roll up our sleeves and get the job done. I started against Western Force in Australia on the following Saturday. Just before half-time, a kick-off came my way, I caught it, took off, made a step, saw a gap and I was gone. I made a break down to the far 22 and I made another break in that game as well, and suddenly people were talking about what a good game I'd had. I think that just blew the hinges off, making people pay attention again to what I could do in an open, free game. I was bringing a side of my game I probably hadn't got to showcase in recent seasons with Leinster and Ireland. There wasn't as much structure to the Lions game because there wasn't time to develop it. It was more ad lib and that gave me space to play the way I loved to play. It happened in my next game, too, against Combined NSW-QSL Country, and that more or less set me up for the tour. I played the full game against the Brumbies the week before the first test, which was a good sign of where I stood in the pecking order. Play this game, have a week to prepare for the following Saturday.

I was delighted to get picked for the first test, retaining my place from the last test game of 2009, one of the few players who could say that. We won that game 23-21, but got very lucky towards the end when Kurtley Beale slipped while taking what surely would have been the match-winning penalty and then missed another long-range effort. The Wallabies missed loads of kicks, but we had Leigh Halfpenny kicking nearly everything. They had Israel Folau in freakishly good form on his debut, scoring two stunning tries, whereas we got one from George North, a brilliant solo effort, and one from Alex Cuthbert. We dug in well and Paulie and Alun Wyn Jones had big games in the second row. I remember it as a really tight game, with little between the sides, but I felt we were that little bit better, if not totally organised, and deserved the win.

We got beaten 16-15 in the second test. We made a lot of mistakes, for which they punished us. I was disappointed that I didn't get into the game as I wanted, didn't get a lot of moments on the ball to show the difference I could make as an attacking player. Paulie had broken his arm before the previous match and played on, but this time we missed him upfront, especially in the line-out. The scrums took ages to complete, killing the pace of the game, and they largely went Australia's way. Overall, the occasion seemed a bit flat. The difference in Australia's performance this time out was that they had a kicker for this game. Christian Lealiifano had been knocked out in the first minute of his debut the previous week, but he was back now to deliver a superlative goal-kicking performance. I was taken off in the 64th minute to let Seanie off the bench, just a couple of minutes before Sam Warburton did his hamstring and had to be replaced too. We were 15-9 up at the time, but then Adam Ashley Cooper got a try and Lealiifano converted it and Leigh missed a long-range penalty that would have stolen it for us at the death.

Immediately, I was looking forward to the third test, but it wasn't going to happen for me. The only one who gave me the heads-up on being dropped was our forwards coach, Graham Rowntree. I sat down with him to do a review of the previous tests on the Monday morning and he said, 'Look, you know, I don't think this week is going to go good for you.' My heart sank. With Warburton and Paulie out, I thought my experience would hold me in good stead.

The team was announced on the Tuesday and I wasn't in it, not even on the bench. Gats never said a word to me in advance. He offered me no explanation afterwards either. I'm not complaining about that. It was the last week of the tour, the series had to be won, he didn't need to take time explaining himself to me because he had other, more important things to do. He didn't need or have any interest in my complaints either. It wasn't as if he was going to change his mind.

Did I deserve to be dropped? Obviously, I'm going to say no. I'd been happy with my form that whole series. I thought I'd played well. I thought Gats was probably trying to hang the middle test defeat on a couple of players and I happened to be one of them. It was only afterwards that I learnt he had given a public explanation for my exclusion at a press conference. 'We just feel when the platform upfront is really good for Jamie, he can play a little bit looser, he carries well,' he said. 'Sometimes he needs to be prepared to play a little bit tighter in this game and hopefully Toby [Faletau] will give us that on Saturday.' There was nothing I could do about it, but I was pretty amazed to hear anyone question my ability or willingness to do the hard work in tight.

The fact that I was dropped for the final test received only a fraction of the attention that was focused on Drico being dropped. I had no problem with that element of it, only with the fact that I wasn't playing. When you're part of the same conversation as Drico, you're always going to be in the shadows. He was an icon of the game, had been the Lions captain in 2005, was on his fourth tour and, on form, should have been picked. His non-selection was a sensation. We were in our own worlds and we didn't talk to each other about it. I was thinking about myself. Who doesn't?

Toby Faletau, who got my place, was a great player, one I'd rate very highly. I wouldn't take away from him what he did when he got onto the pitch. He's a really good guy and we worked well with each other during the tour, trying to help each other. And I did it with him again in the sessions before the game that week. For all that, not being part of the team for the last test hurt. I went out on the absolute lash after my last training session on the Thursday, with all of the other players who weren't going to feature. As far I was concerned, I wasn't involved and my tour was done. There was no need for me to be at team meetings because there was nothing for me to do, other than be in the way. And on the day we won the third test, a little part of me felt that it wasn't mine.

When we won, it was almost like 'they' won, even though I'd been part of that team for the previous two tests. It was weird. I was happy because I was proud, delighted that we'd won the series, that I had played in two of the three games, but I also felt that I wasn't there when we actually won the series. It was the first time that had happened to me in my career and it was a tough thing to endure. It wasn't like all those days winning things with Leinster, the Grand Slam with Ireland, even the third test against South Africa when we won the last game but still lost the series. I just didn't feel really part of it. I remember Andy Farrell, the defence coach, saying to me, 'No, man, you're part of this,' and John Feehan, chief executive of the Lions, said the same thing, as did Graham Rowntree. But when everyone was celebrating in the dressing-room afterwards, I just felt like a spare tool, to be honest. I was subdued, a bit like a satellite to it all.

Looking back, the 2013 tour wasn't as much fun as South Africa in 2009. It was very serious and limited craic. On the one hand, there were lots of good things about it. We did stuff you wouldn't normally do even if you were on holiday there, stayed in amazing places, met wonderful people I wouldn't have met otherwise. I made good friends, particularly Owen Farrell and Adam Jones, and it has always been good to see them since. On the other hand, I think we had the wrong captain, and that is nothing against Sam Warburton, who is a really good guy and was a brilliant player. But in my view, Paulie should have been captain because he is simply on a higher level to almost everyone I've met. The Lions requires a coach who gets what the Lions is all about and Geech was brilliant at that, but Gats, being perhaps more results-focused, wasn't quite as good in that regard. That meant the demands on the captain were greater, requiring someone who could easily understand the vibe of the players and what they needed as a group. In that regard, I think Paulie would have been just that bit stronger than Sam.

That said, I still wanted to be part of the 2017 Lions squad in New Zealand. A third tour would have been a cool personal achievement, to play against the team who, at that stage, would be double World Cup-holders. I don't know if I'd have been picked had I been available, despite an excellent 2016. Gats came to Irish squad training at Carton House during the 2017 Six Nations, to get a sense from Joe how players were going. When he saw me his greeting was, 'Hey, old man, do they still have you hanging around the place?' It may have been a joke, but I wasn't too happy about it. Was he telling me in a backhanded way that he was ruling me out of the forthcoming Lions tour on age grounds, no matter what I did during the Six Nations? Or was he putting it up to me to lift my performances to get in? I wouldn't get a chance to find out what he had been really thinking.

CHAPTER 11

JOE WITH IRELAND

Joe Schmidt took over the Ireland job during the summer of 2013, inheriting a team that was deflated, in disarray and with far lower expectations of what it could achieve than we'd held a few seasons earlier.

The guys who hadn't played with Joe before were a bit worried, but I told them it was quite simple: 'Just know your stuff, know your systems and you'll be grand.' But not all of them were ready for his level of intensity, which was such a step up from what had been the norm. Joe has high levels of expectation. He expects you to be a really good pro and part of that is having really good DEXA scores, which measure how much fat and muscle is being carried on the body. He does these assessments in the open, in front of everyone. Straight from the moment he got the job, he started putting our details up on the projector screen during meetings, calling people out for failing to meet the standards set for them. If people didn't like the approach, they could lump it. In Joe's camp, there was no place for snowflakes.

At the start, Joe definitely leaned on Leinster players to show the others what they needed to match. He had to do that in order to establish standards. We already knew what to expect, but he had to get the others to buy in so that they would have an equal chance and not play second fiddle to the Leinster guys. The others did get on board quickly, encouraged, I think, by the way Joe and Paulie, as a Munster icon, hit it off right from the start.

What we got from Joe, and what we hadn't been getting from Deccie, was decisiveness. He might not always have been right, but at least he was certain. When Joe made a decision, it was firm and he told you straight up, 'This is the way we're going.' Everyone knew where the bus was going and players had to decide whether they were getting on or not. Joe delivered his points quickly, very rarely holding meetings that lasted more than 15 minutes, 20 minutes tops. He's a teacher at heart. He distilled the information clearly and concisely and provided the action points. It was a world away from the methods employed by Deccie who, despite also being a teacher at heart, tried too hard to please everyone, aching not to cause offence.

Some players found it difficult to play in such a controlled system, but Joe very quickly got us up to speed. A lot of guys reacted really well to it, though, and were fully engaged with it for those first November internationals. Many of the set-piece moves with Ireland at the start were the same as they had been in Leinster, just called by different names. Once we knew the whole language that Joe was using, the framework, it was really easy for us to understand what he wanted to do. For those outside of Leinster it was probably more difficult to adapt, but he wasn't waiting around.

When he took over Joe held a summer camp for us in August over a couple of days. He went through all the moves he expected us to memorise. Once he had shown us those moves, the following day he expected everybody on the training field to be able to execute them perfectly. If you messed up in training, he wouldn't forgive you for it. He came down hard on the players. 'It's your job to know,' he insisted. If you continued to mess up, he got someone else in to do the job instead. Joe created a pressure environment in training because that's what it was like in a game. He set the pace and you moved up to it or fell by the wayside.

Our first game of the November series was against Samoa, a game we won 40-9. The issue as to who would be captain remained a live one until the week before that game. We knew it wouldn't be Drico because while he had agreed to give it 'one more year', he wasn't going to the World Cup in 2015 and a new captain had to be picked with that in mind. Paulie seemed an obvious choice, but there were some who wondered if he'd get it because of an incident in a Munster v Leinster game in which he'd kicked Dave Kearney in the head and Joe had gone nuts about it, even though Paulie insisted it was an accident. Privately, I had a hope that I might be chosen because I was a Lions test player, had captained Leinster under Joe at the end of the previous season and he knew me to be a good professional. However, there was also a chance Joe would want to be seen to choose someone from outside his Leinster set as captain, to emphasise that this was a national team, not a Leinster one in green. His decision was announced five days before the game and he went for Paulie. I honestly didn't have a problem with that choice, given the respect I had for Paulie, but I was a bit confused by the way Joe told me.

We'd already done a week's training at Carton House and for some reason Joe was dragging the arse out of it, not making any decision or public announcement. There was an area just outside the team room where there was a dartboard. I was walking out of there and Joe just happened to be going by and I asked if he could have a minute. He said, 'Oh yeah, Jamie, just one quick thing. I'm going to go with Paulie as captain.' 'Okay,' I said, not surprised, even if I was a bit disappointed. Then he said, 'Look, a couple of different reasons but I just think Paulie, now that he's back in, he's the right man for the job. I want you to stay on as vice-captain'.

Paulie was 100% the right choice, but I think Joe was aware how it might look for him if he appointed one of his former Leinster players. He has always been conscious of how he's portrayed in the media, knows everything written or said about him, and I suppose he was wary of the optics of choosing me or any Leinster player.

I said nothing more and just got on with it. Paulie was the best captain I'd ever played under – I knew that from the Lions tour – and it was brilliant for Ireland to have him at the helm. I went straight to him and told him I was delighted for him and would be 100% supportive of him. And he went out of his way to keep me involved as vice-captain.

As things turned out, Paulie wasn't fit to lead us in the first game of the Joe era due to injury, so I was the one who wore the captain's armband in our win over Samoa. Paulie was back the following week for the game against Australia, which went horribly wrong. We got thumped 32-15. They were better than us at everything, most especially at the scrum. They scored four tries to nil despite playing 17 minutes of the game with only 14 men. We defended poorly, too passively and things really went askew when Johnny had to leave the pitch injured. We didn't look like a Joe team that day.

The Australia game has since been forgotten by most people because of what happened the following week, against New Zealand. That All Blacks team, World Champions, winner of every game they had played in 2013, was special. You had to be ruthless to beat them, precise, no mistakes. Even though they played at an incredible pace, they were still able to see a mistake and exploit it in a way that other teams couldn't. Against other teams, you made a mistake and you had a chance to gather yourself and recover within a couple of phases. Make a mistake against the All Blacks and they immediately spotted the chink in the armour and just poured in, cracking everything wide open.

Yet I talked up our prospects in the week before the game, declaring that they weren't untouchable. I admitted that they were smart, accurate, with good players and all sorts of strengths, but I also claimed they had small chinks, too, and that it was up to us to come with a game plan to exploit them. I emphasised that we needed belief to back up the motivation to win, belief in each other and in what we were doing, and to do that from moment to moment in order to get the right outcome.

We went into that 2013 game more confident than I'd ever seen us against the All Blacks for one simple reason: we had a really clear picture of what we had do. I can't remember what the exact game plan was, but I know that Joe had spent months analysing the All Blacks. He had a real insight into how to beat these guys and gave us definite instructions as to how to do it. There was absolute clarity in the moves he wanted us to execute. 'Don't worry about the outcome of this, worry on the process,' he told us. He didn't talk about winning or losing the game. 'The outcome will take care of itself,' he said, as long as we did what we were told in every aspect of the game: defending kick-offs, scrums, line-outs, everyone knew exactly what we had to do.

I don't know if we really had the belief that we could win the game, though, because as every Irish rugby fan knows it was a case of 'close, but no cigar'. I don't think any of the fans at the Aviva that day gave us a chance. The All Blacks were the team that were going from having won a World Cup in 2011 to winning again in 2015. We were a team that had had a dismal Six Nations and just two warm-up games under Joe, one of which was a hammering. What Joe had achieved at Leinster didn't seem to count for a whole lot at this level, at least not yet.

Were we surprised when we went 19-0 up as we exploited their mistakes in a frantic first 20 minutes? Did it change the way we were thinking? I don't think so. We laid down the pace, fast and frantic, and we cranked up the pressure so they made mistakes, and we were ruthless in punishing them. That was us doing what we wanted. Everything to plan. We knew we were in a good place, but we continued to focus. Next ball. We knew that we hadn't been put under a whole lot of pressure. We knew they would get a purple patch and when they did, we creaked a little bit and let them get back into the game. We started making errors and compounded them. We had set the pace so hard that we couldn't maintain it.

We had a chance to get more than a score clear of them about six minutes before the end. When Johnny missed the penalty, I didn't blame him or think our chances of winning were blown. I know everyone said that had he got it, they would have needed two scores in the time that was left and that was most unlikely. That wasn't the point, though. Next ball. Focus. Concentrate. Do what we've practised. Make sure it doesn't matter. We're defending a 22 drop-out now. Get on with the job.

In that last phase, when they scored the try to save themselves, they went the guts of five minutes recycling the ball. That's the maximum length of time to which we've since trained in real-time scenarios. Up until then, we'd done three-minute drills, constantly attacking or defending, constant game play to prepare us for that, sucking all the energy out of us, but now we had to go for even longer. And they did this to us when most of us were exhausted because of our work rate in the previous 80 minutes.

The four and a half minutes they hung on to the ball and worked their way up the pitch was hell mentally as well as physically. The focus shifted from the process to 'don't mess up'. We were all so concentrated on not missing a tackle that we were conceding ground, not getting off the line aggressively, far too passive. Les Kiss's (Kissy's) defensive system tended to be an up and out system, which probably played a little to their strengths, their use of the pod in the middle to make space to go wide, but we got passive because individuals didn't want to make mistakes and be blamed for it. It was a mental tiredness as much as a physical one. I don't think history – that Ireland had never beaten the All Blacks – was relevant. I don't think there was a collective fear of defeat, just individuals who didn't want to be the one who gave away the penalty that let them kick down the field and have a line-out to attack our line. Instead, we let them make their way up the pitch, metre by metre, by being too passive.

The patience they showed and belief in themselves, their trust in the process, the system, the players was extraordinary. Their subs were major players in this. We compounded two system errors on the right-hand side and next thing, Crotty is in at the corner. Then we have another system error on the conversion by charging too early on a kick he missed, and he got to take it again, getting the score that won a game that would otherwise have been drawn.

Unlike 2012, I don't think a draw would have been good enough. Not after the way we had started that game. In any case, a draw wouldn't have done us any good because it would have allowed us to paper over a lot of cracks and pretend they weren't there. In the long run, we were better off losing that day because we learnt some genuine lessons: we needed to be able to maintain the pace we started at, to be fit enough to maintain execution and efficiency for 80 minutes. Our big takeaway was that our bench wasn't as good as theirs, and I don't know if that would have been highlighted so clearly if we had drawn the game. Joe realised – and the players did – that it's a 23-player machine. On any day, we needed 23 players who were able to start or finish anywhere on the pitch.

After the close defeat, I politely took all the compliments about how well we'd performed and how unlucky we'd been to lose, but inside I was seething. What could be so bloody amazing about being sat in the dressing-room with another defeat? The positive from it was that it made us believe we were good enough, which helped us to prepare properly for the 2014 Six Nations. It filled the squad with confidence in Joe's system. Anyone who hadn't bought in before was doing so now. Nobody was saying that the Leinster boys were talking shite about Joe's supposed magic. People like Paulie were always looking to get better and now they were confident that what Joe was doing was going to make us better. We were all on the bus now.

～

There was an unfortunate occurrence during the 2013 November internationals that put me at loggerheads with the management of the Irish team. It concerned how they handled the theft of two valuable watches from my room in the Shelbourne Hotel. I felt that nobody cared, that I was being told to be quiet and suck it up, even though it was a huge loss for me.

We received our watches from the 2013 Lions tour. They were sold to us at a deeply discounted price and were engraved, which for Breitling is unusual. The only other group for which it does engravings is the Special Bolt Service arm of the SAS; our security guys on the Lions trip were ex-SBS guys, which is how it got teed up. I ordered two watches, one for myself and another that I would give to my dad or auction to raise funds for GOAL. We moved from Carton House to the Shelbourne and I decided to bring one of the watches to a jeweller to change the strap. I wore one and put the other – which was actually from the 2009 tour – in the box for the new watch. Then I put a TAG Heuer watch and the other new one in the safe in my room.

On the Sunday I took them out of the safe and put them on the bed, but forgot to take them. When I remembered, I went back upstairs. They were gone. I reported it to the Gardaí and they were interested in publicising it on *Crimecall.* I mentioned this to the hotel management and was immediately told that if this happened, I'd be sued for slander. I was furious. I wanted to know if they had CCTV coverage to show who had gone into my room, but they wouldn't help. It was my word that my watches had been stolen against theirs, their implication being that I was making it up. I had a big row with Mick Kearney because I felt he wasn't backing me and the IRFU gave me very little support as the row went on. A few years later a guy posted the inscribed Breitling watch on Instagram, but as soon as we got to him he said he'd sold it again and wouldn't give a reasonable answer as to how he got it in the first place.

~

Joe's departure to the Ireland job resulted in Matt O'Connor arriving as our new head coach at Leinster. He was a former centre who had played just once for Australia during his career – against Ireland in 1994 – but he had established a good reputation as a coach with Leicester, first looking after the backs and then as head coach for four years. He won the English premiership with Leicester in 2013, just before he came over to join Leinster on a three-year contract. He was sacked after two years.

I felt for Matt because I was his captain for much of the tail-end of his first season and the second of those years and I really liked him as a person. We had some success with him in charge but not enough of it. We won the Pro12 in his first year, the 2013/2014 season, but we lost the Heineken Cup quarter-final away to Toulon. There was no disgrace in that because they were an incredible side at the time and won the cup that year. The following year we won our group and our home quarter-final against Bath, but we came up against Toulon again in the semi-final and it didn't go as planned. But failing to make the play-offs of the Pro12 did for Matt as coach, as well as a widespread perception that we weren't playing the style of rugby the fans wanted. My view was that winning rugby would have sorted those complaints. Plus, it didn't help him that those were the two years when Johnny was playing his rugby with Racing 92 in Paris.

Matt's biggest problem, though, was that he wasn't Joe Schmidt. When Joe was the guy in charge, he'd had the bandwidth to be able to do so much, to be in total control. Joe wasn't just our coach, training and managing the first team squad, he also dealt with the media, oversaw the development of younger players at the Academy, looked for new players from outside the club, created a successful culture across the entire club and built the senior team into something special. He took on so much that any coach following him had to be mindful that he mightn't be able to do the same and therefore should get help with elements of it. These myriad demands hadn't been placed on Matt at Leicester, and I don't think he had realised that this job required a more extensive set of skills. That would have been the case for almost anyone coming in to fill Joe's shoes, but Matt failed to appreciate it and do the necessary delegation of tasks.

Matt was also coming from a different system in England, where the clubs tended to play their top players a lot more and not rotate the personnel in the squad as much. When we weren't having as much success as we wanted, and when the pressure came on as a result, he relied on picking the same team week after week. He didn't bring through new talent, which is the Leinster way – a constant reinvigoration brought about by young players from the Academy. It also brought him into some conflict with Joe, who wanted certain players rested to keep them fresh for international duty. When Matt complained publicly that he didn't have his top players available, he got a very pointed slap-down in return: he didn't use them properly when he did have them.

The players, rightly or wrongly, didn't get the sense that he was managing the team according to the same values they were trying to live by, probably because he hadn't been involved in establishing them, and this resulted in a disconnect. When it comes to culture, you need buy-in at every level and then both enforcement and accountability from the top down. If the top level doesn't live by the values that they're preaching, the bottom disengages. You have to walk the talk.

At training, for example, I'd sometimes say to him, 'Look, Matt, you know we're recording the sessions? We can look back on it later, we don't need to labour a point on the field during training.' If someone made a mistake, we were used to focusing on the next task instead of bickering about what had gone wrong. Under Matt, when a mistake was made there'd be a five-minute talk about it on the pitch. Training at times ended up lasting more than 90 minutes, which often had a knock-on effect with injuries and fatigue. He wasn't being sufficiently disciplined in the timeframe we had constructed for doing our work. I'd ask, 'Why are we doing this?' And he'd go, 'Okay, yeah, I understand, you're right,' and promise that it would change. But it was in one ear and out the other because the next day the same thing would happen again. Everyone became very frustrated.

It was a real pity because Matt also had some really good ideas about ways of playing, but he didn't provide us with the level of detail Joe had. He didn't pull us up enough on the things we were doing wrong. As a result, some players stopped bothering to do what they should have been required to do, even the basics. It was a vicious circle.

Matt could be quite confrontational with the media, too. I remember one day he had a go at Rúaidhrí O'Connor of the *Irish Independent* and I was sitting there saying to myself, 'Oh God, here we go'. Rúaidhrí often annoys players and coaches with some of his commentary, but that's the game he has to play and he has to ask questions. I reckon he was loving the fact that he was stoking the fire between the national set-up and the club, but I remember saying, 'Don't bite, Matt, don't bite.' Matt went after him, providing Rúaidhrí with exactly the type of quotes he must have wanted. Before one Champions Cup game in the 2015/2016 season, Matt decided to confront the media about our playing form. 'Just a question for you blokes, how do you categorise form? Is it winning games? Is it scoring tries? We've scored the most tries in the League. I'm asking the question. What's form to you blokes? Because you ask about it a lot.' He may have had a point at the time, but it wasn't the way to go about it and when people haven't warmed to you, then you have little support when things get even tougher. It didn't help either when we lost that game to Harlequins just a few days later.

We won the Pro12 in 2014, which was a good end to Matt's first season, beating Ulster in the semi-final 13-9 at the RDS, and then we hammered Glasgow 34-12 in the final. It was Drico's last Leinster game, but he went off injured after just eight minutes. It didn't unsettle us and lads like Jimmy Gopperth and Zane Kirchner, who had struggled to replace Johnny and Isa, who was retired at this point, did well for us. I captained the side that night because Leo was on the bench. When Leo retired after that game I was promoted to permanent captain. Some people wondered if it was the right decision, to give it to somebody who would be away with Ireland a lot, but I had played 18 full 80-minute games for Leinster that season and hadn't missed a minute of Ireland's internationals either. After what had happened with my Ireland captaincy, I was delighted with the recognition and responsibility of taking on the Leinster captain's role. Leo stepped up to be forwards coach, but we lost Johnno Gibbs, who had taken a job with Clermont. He would be badly missed.

The following season was far more difficult and we took an awful beating from Munster when they came to the Aviva in October, losing 34-23, ending a run of seven straight defeats to us in games in Dublin. It was our third defeat in the first five games of the League and we dropped to sixth place. It was a game I took very badly because we didn't reach our standards at all. It was one of those games after which I couldn't sleep. Jay-Z, my dog, ended up getting a good walk on Sandymount Strand at 5am as I replayed what went wrong and tried to work it out of my system. Eventually, I watched it back and that settled me, because I saw the things I could work on.

We continued to struggle as a team. We got through our pool in the Champions Cup, but our performances were error-strewn and while I worked my socks off in our games, what the fans were noticing was how the levels weren't matching what we'd achieved under Joe. Publicly, I dismissed the notion of pressure. 'The best way to describe it is noise,' I said at a press conference, but the questions hit a nerve. We weren't actually that far off scoring the number of tries we had under Joe, but we were conceding way more.

We got through the pool stage in the 2014/2015 season when we drew 20-20 away to Wasps in our final game. Then we drew Bath at home for the quarter-final in the first weekend of April. We won that game with a pretty lame performance, but went into the semi-final against the defending champions Toulon – a team packed with expensively purchased players – confident that we could pull something out of the fire.

We almost did. We gave it everything in that semi-final in Marseilles, drawing 12-12 after 80 minutes and going to extra time. It was an ugly game in the rain, the kind of slugfest you often get at this stage of the competition, with both sides making loads of handling errors despite trying to make as few mistakes as possible. The conditions made running with the ball almost impossible, so a lot of the game was spent kicking it. We almost won it at the end of normal time, but Jimmy Gopperth's drop-goal effort didn't make it. Then we managed to literally throw it away in the first 10 minutes of extra time. They had a man in the bin in the last minute of the first period of extra time when Ian Madigan (Mads) threw a long skip pass on a three-on-one overlap that Bryan Habana intercepted. The converted try and two penalties they'd scored already saw them take a 25-15 lead. Had we got the try, we would have been ahead with those 10 minutes to play. We scored a try off a line-out maul in the second period, but Jimmy's conversion kick hit the upright and we missed penalties and drop goals and the final score was 25-20 against us.

We had put in the effort, there was no doubting that, and we defended really well, but we were inaccurate at the wrong times and didn't turn pressure into points. There was nothing between the sides but when we made mistakes, they punished us. It was utterly deflating, but we had another problem to face. Our Pro12 campaign had been so poor that we were at risk of not qualifying for the semi-finals. When we didn't, it meant the worst league season for Leinster in 11 years and the end of the line for Matt. It's easier to fire the coach than change 40 players.

Sheena and I took Matt and his wife out to dinner before he left Ireland, along with our masseur Mike Thompson and his wife. It was an interesting conversation, to say the least, and its contents will remain confidential. He has informative things to say about people and structures at Leinster and insights to offer and I took them on board. I've occasionally kept in touch with him via WhatsApp since. He was sacked by Leicester, after he went back there, and more brutally than Leinster had done it.

I felt I had made the effort for Matt – he had been highly complementary in his public comments about my professionalism around the team environment, how I rarely missed a game, trained every session, and that was noted by others when I was shortlisted for the European Player of the Year Award. But while I appreciated that, it was of little consolation because I wanted to win with Leinster and was used to winning. Leo Cullen took over from Matt, but he found out that turning a tanker around, even one that has slowed down, is a time-consuming and difficult job.

CHAPTER 12

CONTINUOUS DEVELOPMENT

Rugby is physical combat, it's high intensity, incredibly demanding and the standard of the modern game just keeps rising higher. At both Leinster and Ireland, Joe did a great job of improving our skills, preparation and mindset so that we wouldn't rely on emotional one-off performances based on an underdog mentality. He made us more technical in our approach to delivering a performance, to allow us to be the favourites to win going into games and not be burdened by that, and to be able to back up performances with long unbeaten runs of matches.

Joe's approach was all about structure. His game plan was very much based on set-plays, moves off scrums and line-outs and restarts. So much of what happens on the pitch is planned, much in the way of American football. There are multiple set-plays for each scrum and line-out scenario – depending on the part of the pitch you are in – and we used code words to communicate those to each other. The set-plays are planned multiple phases ahead, for when players are stopped by the opposition. What was really good about Joe's training when it came to set-plays was that we rehearsed them so often, they became automatic. When the code word was shouted out, everyone knew their role. Joe put us under so much pressure through constant repetition in training that nobody dared to fail to do their part. Much of this was achieved by training in the same way as we played. In training he recreated the high-pressure scenario of a game, so that on the day our reactions were immediate, no thinking required. Joe said we had to 'control the controllables', so that's what we did.

We were all fit and could run long distances, but the thing that breaks most players in rugby is the time that the ball is in play. A long phase of a game now might be four and a half minutes before the ball goes out of play, or is dropped, or there is a score, but in that time you're not just running, you're also tackling, hitting rucks, getting up, turning, going again without a break to catch a breath, moving into new positions, being aware of what you are supposed to be doing, what your teammates are doing, some of which might be wrong, and of course what the opposition is doing. The higher the standard, the faster the pace all this happens. It sucks your energy. Your brain actually consumes the most energy of all the parts of your body.

I would take just one deep breath between plays, in a game or in training, to re-centre myself. Just one. I can bring my heart rate down quickly and not just in training but in games, too. I don't know how or why I'm able to do that, but my heart rate can come down swiftly and the monitors I've worn in training have proved that. When there is a stoppage in play, I'm conscious of getting that breath. There have been studies on how deep breaths can slow everything down for the body, get you back to equilibrium. I used it as a reset in games, especially if I'd made a mistake or there had been a score.

Whenever I made a mistake on the pitch, I liked to do something physical to rebuild my momentum again, such as hitting a ruck or making a tackle. If I could do it almost immediately after committing the error, that would put me back in a good frame of mind. Resetting is an important thing to do. I did it after doing something well just as often as after doing something badly. It allowed me to develop momentum. Reset, refocus, go on to the next job.

Joe framed the training sessions this way. When mistakes were made, we didn't gather around and chat about them, it was literally straight on to the next play. That didn't mean the mistake was forgotten about. Joe noticed and logged everything and you got slammed in the post-training review for every error. We didn't just review games, we also critically assessed our performance in training sessions, which were video-recorded to allow us to do this.

In most professions there is a compulsory process of continuous professional development (CPD). Many players measured their development simply by whether they got picked for a team or not. I didn't. I wanted far more detail that would allow me to work out how I had improved and could improve as a player. Some feedback was delivered privately, especially if it required more detail than there was time for in a normal review. But it was never personal, it was for the good of the team. I don't think Joe ever had an issue with people making mistakes as long as they didn't repeat them. He was more forgiving if he could see that a person was working to correct those errors.

Did I have a great game every time I stepped on the field? No, I made mistakes in most games that I played, but I learnt from them. I didn't try to do this on the pitch, there's no time. The learning happened afterwards, when I reviewed the game carefully and slowly. When reviewing my performance, I watched the game twice: straight afterwards and again the next day. The second viewing was less emotional, less connected to the score-line, and often delivered a different perspective as a result.

If I'd had a bad game, it wouldn't have been for lack of effort. But a couple of little errors could have become, in my mind, a bad game – that's where the review was really helpful, to show me the reality of it and interpret my performance correctly. I always avoided reading match reports. I understood what the newspapers were doing, it was their job to sell a story, but they were not looking at it the same way we were, therefore their views weren't relevant to how I did my job.

A team review was usually carried out the Monday after a game. For that, each player could use one of the team laptops, which carried a video of the game taken from four different angles. We could review any game or any training session like this. It doesn't take 80 minutes to watch a game, only about 30 minutes when it's edited to what we need. But it's part of the job. I would have watched every game at least twice before arriving into work for the team review. I had a hard-drive and I purchased Sportscode so I could do the work at home on my own laptop.

I watched the match before the team viewing so that I was prepared for Joe's reviews, which were ruthless, albeit done with the right intentions. He wanted us to improve in every little thing we did. I knew that if I'd made an error in a match over the weekend, it would be shown to everyone on Monday morning and I would have to suck it up. You could argue that we were in fear of him, but I would say that we understood his method and bought into his values.

I don't think Joe has confidence in people who don't put the work in, who just rely on their natural talent and aren't disciplined in their processes. If I was called out in training, I didn't mind because everyone else was called out too and it was for the good of the team. You can go have your battle with Joe about his assessment, but he is a really tough opponent. Joe remembers everything, has the examples to back it up and you're left floundering. I only once saw anyone beat him in a rugby argument. No surprise that was Johnny, because Johnny has an encyclopaedic rugby brain, very similar to Joe. I can't remember what it was about, but that wasn't the point. It was the only time in a team setting where I saw Joe take a slight step back.

Most coaches I've worked under have wanted to play fast but haven't necessarily been able to achieve that. Joe insisted on it. If everyone wasn't in place and it showed up in the review, he'd give us hell about not being in position, ready to go. Everybody has different jobs that aren't necessarily obvious to viewers. Every time Johnny has to make a decision on what he's doing with a penalty, for example, the wingers have already hared out to the edges to give him the option of kicking towards them if they find space. If it's on, he wants to be able to go for it. You can't slow down for anyone.

There's a whole lot of donkey work players do in a game that doesn't get seen by spectators who are just watching the ball. I might run lines that the public or media don't pick up on, but in review Joe would note those things that don't need skill but demonstrate your willingness to work. It's all about things like running a line down the middle of the field to support a line-break on the edge – the ball might never come back to you, but it was still the right thing to do. Or how quickly you get back into the defensive line after the opponents break your line and you have to reset. If one of your teammates breaks the line or makes a half-break, who is there to support him? That kind of stuff doesn't necessarily get noticed, it doesn't make good TV watching a guy make a run that doesn't get him the ball, but it might be the action of a smart and hard-working player. A good coach sees that.

At the top level, the ability to review and assess a game becomes something of an art. Everyone has their own biases as to how they and others performed. While we're all teammates, we're also protecting our own patch. The first instinct, in most cases, is not to blame yourself if something goes wrong. It's not necessarily a case of finding someone else to blame but of finding a way that the blame doesn't land squarely on yourself. That's only natural. Then you start to realise that it can't be someone else's mistake the whole time. You develop the confidence to look at yourself a bit harder, looking for patterns of mistakes and asking yourself if and how they can be fixed. Is it the technique? A mental thing? If I'm making the same kind of mistakes regularly, why is that? Do I not know what I'm meant to be doing? Am I practising my drills regularly enough? Am I doing the extras? If I'm told, if I know the right way, will I do the wrong thing again?

I constantly looked for feedback. At the end of each year at Leinster, Joe brought us individually to his office. He handed you a sheet, detailing the different things he felt you should have done better during the season. He asked what you thought you should have done better, then gave his opinion. I loved this conversation and decided to bring it further.

At the end of every season, I examined what I had learnt and decided what I needed to work on during the summer break. I made it a habit to ask other people to do the same for me, people I respected. I wouldn't ask my current teammates, but I went to former players, after they had retired, like Isa, the first time he retired, Paulie and Brad Thorn. Also people from way back, like Colin McEntee, my coach in Academy days and a former back-row himself who had known me since I was fifteen and watched my game develop but was outside the bubble and could see things clearly. I emailed them and said: 'Give me three things to continue, three things I need to improve.' I didn't specify any area, nothing was off-limits. They came back with their feedback and I studied it carefully. Sometimes I heard things I might not have wanted to hear, but it worked for me because every pre-season from about 2012 on I came back leaner, fitter, better prepared. Everything was going in the right direction.

One piece of feedback that was constant throughout my career, from every quarter, was that I needed to be less obvious in showing my emotions and my opinions. In team meetings if someone said something that I thought was rubbish, you could read it all over my face. I couldn't hide my disappointment with people who I felt didn't know what they were talking about or who weren't professional enough. I had no poker face. I would be annoyed with someone who didn't seem like they were looking after themselves properly. It might be their nutrition, their recovery, not knowing what they were supposed to know, constantly going on the piss at the weekend and missing things the following week as a result. I'd be straight out, 'What the hell are you doing?' I wouldn't be afraid to pull them aside and say it, or be short with them. It probably made me tough to deal with at times, and I concede that it may have made me unpopular with some players. It is something I had to work on constantly. But I was of the view that we were a team and if players didn't pull their weight, the team would fail and the work I and others were doing would be undermined by their failure to do their jobs.

There were players I didn't get along with. I don't think that's unusual, happens in every work environment. I wasn't friendly with everyone I worked with, but who is? There were even a couple of lads I'd have loved to thump the head off, but I didn't. And I'm sure there were lads who felt like that about me. You put aside those feelings for the common goal. It didn't matter because we shared a common set of values. I didn't have to like people to work with them. Whatever we thought of each other personally, the main thing was that we were all pulling in the same direction. I never held grudges. I never fell out with someone so badly that we wouldn't speak to each other now. When it blew up, you got it out of the way, shook on it, that was it. If I had a personality issue with someone, I stayed clear. The whole focus was the team; that superseded any of the personal stuff.

The whole approach to feedback, that it's delivered in front of everyone and is continual, marks rugby apart from most workplaces. I think a lot of companies talk about honest feedback but no one actually gives it because they're afraid of hurting people's feelings. The key is how you deliver feedback. When people set aside their egos, they learn how to communicate their views properly – not making it personal but attaching it to the common values of the team. Getting everyone at Leinster, and then Ireland, to buy into that may have been one of Joe's greatest achievements, which then brought its rewards on the pitch.

This whole approach required humility and discipline, virtues that Joe demanded of all his players. His focus, and therefore our focus, on that was relentless. These were our values and we displayed them in training as much as in games.

We lived them. It wasn't always easy for players coming into this environment. Leinster has a justifiable reputation for producing new players, many of whom have established themselves over the years. But others didn't, sometimes because of injury, but sometimes because they simply didn't work hard enough to match the standards. Every year you hear a story, 'This guy's going to be class', 'This under-20 lad is going to be unbelievable', big reports about the standout players at an age grade. But it can be very different when there isn't an age limit. Up until then, someone might be able to get by on their athletic gifts, their natural talent. It could be footballing talent, being the quickest on the field or just the biggest or strongest in that age group. But once a player moves into senior rugby, that might not be enough. It takes a certain character to then push on and become a regular for one of the professional club teams. Consistent performance requires a good and solid mindset. The most talented don't always make it. It's the ones who apply themselves with unwavering dedication and are the most professional who have the best chance. It's the same again moving up to international rugby. A higher standard demands even more.

In order to keep my place on the team, I worked continuously on my skills. I could see more and more bigger and stronger guys arriving into the Academy from schools and felt I had to stay ahead of the competition by improving all the time. We were lucky at Leinster, and later at Ireland, that for a period our s&c coach was an ex-sprinter and he worked with us on running technique. Mick Winkleman came from exos, an amazing training facility in America. He's one of the best in the business when it comes to coaching queuing and drilling movement patterns. But I would have liked more coaching over my career on how to run properly, to develop speed efficiency. We did blocks of running every so often, but because the season was so busy, the bulk of the speed training was done in the summer and then once the season kicked off, there often wasn't time to come back to it.

I maintained pretty good defensive stats because I worked on it every Thursday. It was all based on movement patterns. I'd start off very slowly, getting my technique right, my approach to the tackle, getting my feet position right and slowly practising how I would enter the tackle. Then I practised with someone running at me. If his left hand came out to fend me off, my technique was to snap out with my right hand to push down his left hand as I hit him with my left shoulder, and then my arm followed in. I drilled that in slow motion and then on the other side, still slow motion, and then I'd do it in real time. It might sound boring, it might sound like overkill to practise something I already knew how to do, but I did it every week without fail to keep me sharp.

I practised scenarios where I had to react, where my back was to the play and I'd hear the shout, 'Break', and I turned and reacted to what way the opposition was going, getting my footwork right as quickly as possible and entering the tackle. In training it was never a big smash hit tackle, it was about working on getting the technique right. Then I ramped up the pace, doing it faster, recreating scenarios where the opposition was coming at me at increasing pace. Defensively, if you're going backwards, it is much harder because if you come off the line, you have to turn and get back and get around the other side of the ruck when it's coming back behind you and you're on the back foot. The momentum is naturally with the attacking side, particularly if they get a quick ruck ball. The flip side, obviously, is that if you hit them back over the gain-line when you're defending, then you've taken the front foot and you get your own defensive line set. Then you're able to go, go, go, while they're resetting, they're running backwards to get ready to go. In that scenario we might not have the ball, but our defence has become offensive.

We did a really short drill to get our footwork right coming into the tackle, other drills where we couldn't use our arms to get our body positions right, where we weren't hitting anyone hard and the person we were tackling was carrying a protective pad. That was about learning to get head and shoulder into the correct positions, getting the footwork right and then driving through the tackle. It was all about being in a strong position to wrap up your opponent in the tackle.

At those Thursday sessions I also practised poaching techniques. Rehearsing how I would win the ball at a ruck was one of the most important parts of my game as a number 8, getting my body position right, bearing the weight on my legs correctly. The laws on this aspect of the game changed a number of times during my career. It was up to me to know those laws so that I wasn't penalised and was able to poach the ball correctly, even if I had already been running around like crazy for a few minutes.

Many of my duties as a player were defensive, but I also had to practise carrying the ball into contact and into space, offloading and passing, and bringing the ball to ground. I felt that one of my strengths was an ability to read the game very well, to pick the best option each time. It's way easier to run on to the ball than it is to reset and take it standing, so I always tried to time my runs correctly to match what other players were doing. I was comfortable passing off both hands, and at pace, even though I never really had to pass the ball over long distances, but again I worked at that.

For the forwards, as a unit there was little emphasis on practising individual skills, the concentration being on the things we did together, in set pieces, rucking and mauling. So it was left to us to do personal skills much in our own time. Joe did specific work with the backs, basic kicking, catching, passing, but forwards did scrums and line-outs, essential skills for us. We did drills around how to lift, maul techniques, scrum techniques. We probably had to be a bit more conscious that if we wanted to do more passing and catching, we had to go and do them ourselves. At that stage in our career, we had to take a certain amount of responsibility on ourselves to practise certain skills, but not everyone did that. There may have been a presumption that once players reached a certain level, they didn't need to improve, or even maintain.

There were a lot of things I'd have liked to have been better at, such as kicking, getting under high balls, fielding and being a much more impactful tackler. I was a very good defender, but I would have liked to have scored far more impact tackles, to have been more offensive in driving opponents back. I would have liked to have been a better footballer with ball in hand. I didn't see these as deficits, I viewed them as challenges, areas to work on and improve. I looked to see who was 'best in class' in the aspects of the game I wanted to be the best at myself. I'd look how they did it, to glean knowledge from them.

As a footballer, I'd have liked to have had the playmaking ability of someone like Johnny, his vision, to be able to go hard to the line but then have that ability to hit the front-door pass or flip it out the back. He has really quick hands, which would have been a good skill to possess as a number 8. I'd have loved to have done more offloading, but I wasn't encouraged to do it because of the way we played under Joe.

On Joe's watch, the type of game I played changed. I did more and more of the dirty work in the trenches, instead of galloping into wide open spaces as I had in the early days of my career, particularly up to 2009. I still did my share of carrying the ball, but my job required me not to be turned over in possession, never to miss a clear-out or a tackle, to make the right decisions as to what to do with or without the ball. I didn't mind because under Joe's system, I was doing it for the team. I was doing it to win.

CHAPTER 13

ANOTHER WORLD CUP

The defeat against New Zealand in November 2013 was treated appropriately: instead of deflating us, it gave us confidence and clarity. We knew how good we could be, but we were also clear on the aspects where we weren't good enough. The Six Nations in 2014 was going to be about working on those elements and bringing our whole game up to a higher level.

Before we got into the Six Nations preparation in earnest, there was the Christmas break.

The Leinster players were having a Christmas party night, but I was reluctant to go because I had been seriously considering a contract offer in France and there had been a lot of publicity about it. Leo was captain at the time and he rang me and told me to stop dicking about and join my teammates. He was right. My problem was that it was a fancy-dress party. What would I wear? Sheena was working with Leinster at the time and she organised many of the players' charity appearances, such as the annual Blue Santa visit to Our Lady's Children's Hospital in Crumlin. She had the outfit in the car. I stuck it on and, as Blue Santa, headed off to the pub to meet the team.

Sheena collected me later that night. At the time we were living in Rathmines, on Richmond Hill. As we turned the corner from Lower Rathmines Road, our way was blocked by a taxi. One of its doors was standing open and this guy was lying on the road with his head on the footrest of the driver's door. I had a few on me, but there was clearly something wrong. The adrenalin kicked in and I told Sheena to pull over and call the Gardaí while I staggered over to take a closer look.

The guy lying down was moaning for help. He was foreign, black and blood was coming out of his mouth. I told him that help was on the way. We were just around the corner from the Blackbird pub, which was hopping with the Christmas crowd. Someone must have spotted us because people started coming out to have a look. What do they see only this big guy in a blue Santa suit standing over a black taxi driver who's on the ground. Next thing, this guy came out of nowhere and jumped on my back, but I wasn't his target. He was actually trying to get me out of his way to get to the taxi driver. I shrugged him off and then held him off with my arm, but now a woman was on the other side of the taxi screaming at me that 'he bit my fella's fingers off, he bit them off'. To say I was confused is an understatement. 'Who?', I asked, looking for a bloke with missing fingers. And then a couple of moments later, this guy comes over with the top of his thumb in a pint glass of ice. At this stage, I was beginning to wonder if this was a beer-induced dream.

Sheena came over to tell me that the Gardaí were on their way, but in the meantime there's all this shouting going on and I was still standing over the driver, to protect him. And now I could hear people coming out of the pub going, 'What

the fuck is Jamie Heaslip doing there in a blue Santa suit?'
It must have looked like I was the one who put this guy on
the ground.

Thankfully, the Gardaí arrived pretty quickly. I pleaded
with them to let me go home. I was worried that people
would start taking pictures with their camera phones. I said
to them, 'I don't need this, lads. This is not mine. I live over
there. Come over when you're finished here and I'll give you
a statement.' The Gardaí came to my house later, but I still
had to go to the station the following day to give a statement.
I felt like such an eejit when I had to answer questions such as,
'What were you wearing?' I had to explain why I was wearing
a blue Santa suit and the Garda wrote it all down slowly.

The case ended up in court, first the District Court and
then the Circuit Court, but fortunately I didn't have to give
evidence as the taxi driver pleaded guilty. It turned out that
he had become involved in a row with his customers because
they'd been slagging his name, and he hit the girl. As the fight
developed, he bit the fingers off her boyfriend. It was all very
surreal, but I put it behind me as we headed into the new year
and a renewed focus on the Six Nations.

The first game of the tournament, Scotland at the Aviva,
had the potential to be a good start for us, but we were thrown
early in the day when we were told that Paulie wouldn't be able
to play because he'd developed a chest infection overnight.
It was a bit of shock because he'd overseen our line-out
session on the Saturday evening and there was nothing wrong
with him, but he ended up with the doctor at about 4.30am
and out he went. Dan Tuohy replaced him and I was
nominated as captain, which meant I was captaining the
team for the sixth Six Nations game in a row. After what had
happened against Italy the previous March, I grabbed the
opportunity.

It was a poor enough game: scrums re-set, endless box-kicking, plenty of lateral back play and rows at ruck time. But we pulled ahead just before half-time and after that we were never going to be caught. Despite all the fuss the previous year about my not taking points on offer for penalties, I did opt for one penalty kick to touch early in the second-half and I got the try off the resulting maul. We ended up winning 28-6, but we knew it was only a start. Joe let us know that a tough video review was coming on Monday, to show us all the things we did incorrectly or could have done better. Standards were being set.

Paulie was back the following week when we thumped Wales. This was Ireland playing more like Joe's Leinster – not exactly the same style of play but in terms of our preparation and execution of instructions. Joe dictated a game plan that the Welsh did not expect and we implemented it for the full 80 minutes. Peter O'Mahony and Chris Henry were alongside me in the back-row and we did a number on our Welsh rivals. We put the ball in the air a lot, either from Conor or Johnny or long touch-finders to the corners. Gats criticised it afterwards, noting that we had 'kicked the leather off the ball'. It surprised some observers that the way Ireland was developing under Joe was with a more conservative style than he had employed at Leinster, but Joe did whatever was necessary to win at the level he was at. Yes, it was lower-risk rugby, but it meant that we retained possession, especially at the rucks. In the Wales game, this meant we dominated the line-outs and used the maul as a weapon, from which we scored two tries.

Unfortunately, we couldn't keep the run going at Twickenham, which meant the Triple Crown and Grand Slam were both gone halfway through the campaign. We lost 13-10 in a game that was decided more or less 25 minutes from full-time when England got the try and conversion that put them in front. We lost 10 points in a matter of minutes. After Farrell scored a penalty to bring it to 6-10, the restart went straight to touch and they scored their try from the scrum in the middle of the pitch. We felt that we had let the game get away from us because we had actually played with more adventure in the backs – albeit from set-plays – than we had against Scotland and Wales. And while we had defended very well, we had also made too many passing and handling mistakes, kicked badly at times and missed 21 tackles. A few more players felt the full intensity of Joe's post-match video review.

The championship was still there to be won, with Italy at home and France away still to come. The Italy match had a strange subtext because it became all about Drico's final appearance at Lansdowne Road for Ireland. It was also his 140th international cap, giving him the world record. We were all aware of the significance of the day, but there was far less talk of it among the players than among fans and the media. In fairness, Drico delivered a great performance for us. He played like a dervish, utterly sharp and focused and was involved in three of our seven tries in a 46-7 win. He left to a standing ovation and an after-match on-pitch reception of a kind few internationals have ever received or are ever likely to get. The big score was important because it helped our points difference enormously (the current system of bonus points had not been introduced at this stage).

All we had to do in Paris was win, something that Ireland had not achieved in my time with the team or since Brian's famous hat-trick in 2000. England had beaten Italy in Rome 52-11, but that wasn't enough to change things: any win for us would mean that our points difference was better than theirs. It meant that we only had to focus on one thing, winning, not on winning by any particular amount. The experience of Leinster and Munster teams in winning club games in France finally stood to us – as did the confidence Joe gave us in the game plan he dictated.

We went in 13-12 down at half-time after Johnny missed a penalty, but that in no way fazed us. In fact, Johnny had a terrific game, scoring tries in each half, the second one started by his colossal hit on Mathieu Bastareaud, which led to one of the best counterattacks by an Irish team I'd ever been involved in, during which Paulie cleared out a ruck on their line, arriving to it faster than any of us back-rows. When Johnny converted that try and added a penalty, we were 22-13 ahead with the victory line in sight.

France came after us, wave after wave. Szarzewski got in for a try after a passage of play resulting from an over-hit box-kick by Conor, but it looked as if he had knocked-on in touching the ball off the base of the post. Steve Walsh, the ref, decided not to consult the TMO and the try stood. We had 17 minutes left to hang on. Not long after, Johnny was knocked out cold by a forearm smash by Bastareaud on the run. Mads came on for his first Six Nations appearance with just 10 minutes left. France missed a very kickable penalty to go a point in front and then almost scored a winning try, only for Papé's final pass to Chouly to be ruled as forward. Then they turned over our scrum, but we won the ball back to end the game.

We were Six Nations champions for the first time since 2009 and for only the second time this century. France were better in this game than at any time during the season – utterly physical upfront but attacking with panache from the back – but we were even better. We outscored them on tries by three to two and we defended better, using the choke tackle to great effect to stop offloads and turn around possession. Our breakdown work slowed them down all day. Joe had added another dimension to our game, instructing us to go wide and play blind inside passes, trusting that teammates would be there to receive them.

After the misery of the previous year I was delighted to have done my bit, to have played every minute of the campaign and done everything I could to win. It was so satisfying to have done it in France, given how many Irish teams had failed there and with less at stake. It was a real 'monkey off the back' outcome. We cut loose and enjoyed ourselves afterwards with family and friends in the hotel, and then a group of us stayed up all night and started what we called 'The Breakfast Club' – myself, Church, Pete, Jordi and others – which carried on until we arrived back in Dublin. The only time I didn't have a bottle of beer in my hand was coming through passport control. I was determined to enjoy it, otherwise what's the point?

After the season ended, we headed off on tour to Argentina. It was no jolly. We had only one day off in the fortnight, had to take eight domestic flights and made 26 coach journeys, alongside full training and extensive video analysis. And we played two matches. It was intense, and even Joe said that he found it tough going. I was asked in one press conference what I'd seen of Argentina and I replied honestly, 'The hotels and training grounds.' It was annoying because it was a country I wanted to see, but we were working.

I didn't start the first test, coming on from the bench as an impact sub with 22 minutes to go. I wasn't used to not starting and found it difficult to join a game where the tempo had already been set. I knew what Joe was doing – I had played 26 games that season and not missed a minute of any of them, so he was resting me somewhat. But it gave me a deeper appreciation of what it was like for players who have to fill that substitute role regularly, and who I expected to meet the set standards the moment they hit the pitch. Joe was also deepening the squad, allowing more players to gain international experience. We won the first game 29-17 and the second 23-17, which showed that we never let our focus drop, no matter how demanding the trip was. We came back from Argentina feeling that our improvement was continuing, that more players now knew what Joe expected of them.

We had an excellent start to the November series, beating South Africa at the Aviva 29-15. It was our first win over them since 2009 and we were the first Six Nations team to beat them in four years. They had beaten the All Blacks in their previous game and were ranked number two in the world. We dug in to achieve it, our work rate, application and resilience – the emerging features of this Joe team – allowing us to overcome a physically dominant team. We tackled and harried them, slowed them down and showed great speed in defence. Rhys Ruddock had a terrific game in difficult circumstances. He was on the subs bench but ended up starting because on the morning of the game Chris Henry suffered a mini-stroke in their hotel room. Rhys realised immediately that it was serious – Chris wasn't able to speak – and he sprinted, wearing nothing but his boxer shorts, into the breakfast room in the Shelbourne Hotel to fetch the team doctors. Chris had had a transient ischaemic attack, which meant that a previously undetected hole in his heart had led to a blocked blood vessel in his brain, causing a mini-stroke. Fortunately, the quick response by Rhys and the doctors ensured a full recovery and Chris was back in the squad by March and played in the World Cup. On the day, we were told that he had a virus. We were focused on the match and accepted that but were a bit shocked afterwards when we realised what had really happened.

The heavy rain stopped before the game kicked off, but the pitch was still very wet and it led to lots of handling errors and turnovers as everyone crashed into each other. But winning against such a big, physical team, being able to match that aggression and then be smarter in finding space to play, meant a lot to us. We were adding new elements to our game – for example, being able to stop the powerful South African maul was down to the work John Plumtree, our new forwards coach, was doing with us and we were able to execute it perfectly because we had rehearsed it extensively in training. That game was also notable because it was our first home international, 80 games going back to 1999, in which neither Drico nor Darce played. It was a reminder that you borrow the jersey, you don't own it and you have to relinquish it.

The month got even better when we beat Australia 26-23. We had an incredible start, scoring 17 points in the first 17 minutes, with Simon Zebo (Zeebs) and Tommy getting tries from the wings. Then the Wallabies started throwing the ball around, scored three tries and went 20-17 up before half-time. We made all sorts of mistakes, the kinds Joe hates, and we went in level at half-time, 20-20, then came out and scored two penalties to one in the second-half to win the game. We had to hang in, though, through a pounding, stuck in our own 22, making tackle after tackle for what seemed an age. But it wasn't going to be like New Zealand a year earlier because we were better prepared. We won a penalty on a defensive scrum near the end and the Aussies knocked-on twice in the closing minutes as they chased the elusive winning score.

We had come a long way since taking a 17-point hammering from Australia just a year earlier. Now we had beaten two of the best Southern Hemisphere countries, won the Six Nations and become Europe's top-ranked country. But I knew Joe wouldn't be happy. In the post-match interview, I said, 'There's a lot to improve on again. Whatever confidence we have, Joe will surely take it apart a little bit come the Christmas camp.' It wasn't that Joe sought to undermine us, it was that he stopped even the smallest bit of complacency from working its way in. We had to strive to be better. I loved that.

Incredibly, some pundits were critical of the style of play that was winning for us. It was pointed out that we'd had the fewest offloads during the Six Nations, just 27, but Joe responded that we were the leading try-scorers, with 16. He said that if any player had 'an opportunity and they want to make the most of it, then they know they have the licence to play'. It's interesting for me to look back at what he was saying then. He went on to say: 'It's just a case of what the leaders, the guys on the pitch, feel is necessary at any given time. That allows them to be relatively autonomous on the pitch and to make, in the most part, really good decisions. It's an important part of us keeping tempo in the game, keeping our opponents guessing and I think, to a degree, it encourages players' enjoyment of the game. They're risk-takers, they like to get out and try to match up, see what they can do to be inventive and to encourage a game, that's something they enjoy.'

That was true, but only to a point. Joe's systems were not up for debate, and that was fair enough because when a team does what he says, more often than not they will win. Joe is so smart on how to break down other teams that you have no option but to follow his plan. Each player knew exactly what he had to do and knew the risk of being replaced if he didn't deliver what Joe demanded. I was doing the job he wanted done, not what the fans or media wanted. I probably didn't get as many carries on the ball as I would have liked and I sacrificed elements of my own game, the open-field running, for example, that I was known for in my early seasons, in order to concentrate on my role within the team. I implemented the game plan that he devised for each game and I did it because I was convinced it was the best way for the team to win.

A team is about balance. So when I played alongside Seanie, I knew what type of work he would do, that he would carry much more, therefore my job was different. Early in my career there weren't as many ball-carrying forwards, but as more and more came into the game it was left to others to make sure the grunt work was done. I couldn't have cared less how we did it or who got the plaudits. I just wanted to stay on a winning team.

~

The 2015 Six Nations was more testing personally. I missed the first game, the 26-3 away win to Italy, because of a shoulder injury I had picked up with Leinster. It was frustrating not to be involved in the start of our defence of the title, but I was confident that I would get back into the team once fit again, no matter how well Ireland played. I felt that Joe had that confidence in me to do what he wanted.

As predicted, I was back for the next game, at Lansdowne Road against France. We won 18-11. This was yet another brutal, physical contest that had Wayne Barnes blowing his whistle regularly. It ended for me after an assault by their second-row, Pascal Papé, who drove his knee into my back when I was in a standing position in a maul. I felt the impact immediately and turned and roared at Barnes as I went to the ground. Barnes went to the TMO to watch the replay and then called Papé across, told him he considered the action 'deliberate' and gave him a yellow card when it should have been a red.

I received treatment and stood up again, thinking I'd run it off, but it was painful when I lifted at the next line-out and when we went to the maul on retaking possession, I couldn't get myself into a good position. The game went a couple of phases before another line-out, a five-man one that I didn't enter. The ball came over the tail and I should have dived on it, but I couldn't even bend over. Besty grabbed the ball instead, but at the next break in play I immediately put my hand up for help. I was taken off and once I stopped running, my back started to tighten up.

It was 15-6 at this stage, but I didn't get to see the end of the game. I was brought straight down to St Vincent's Hospital for a CT scan, with a second the following morning. Eanna Falvey, our team doctor and a brilliant guy, was on top of it with the physios. They were hopeful that if I followed instructions, and given that they knew me to be a good healer, I would be fit to play again within four weeks, missing the England game but playing against Wales.

The IRFU did something then that greatly angered me and led to a row with Mick Kearney and Joe. There were all sorts of questions from the media as to the extent of the injury – especially as Papé had been cited and was facing a lengthy ban – and how long it would take me to recover. I wanted the details kept private, believing my medical condition should not be for public display. Joe was of the view that when injuries happened, 'the press need to know, we need to give them a story or else they'll go off with another narrative.' I didn't agree. I felt strongly that my medical information belonged to me, not to the public. I understood why the media wanted to know, but I believed no personal information should be released without my permission. Technically, I could ask my doctor not to give my coach details about medical diagnosis and treatment. If a non-playing employee in the IRFU had a medical issue, the IRFU was not allowed to disclose that fact.

Mick and Joe insisted on putting out a statement to stem the speculation. I agreed reluctantly, something I regretted afterwards. The statement was far too detailed. It said that the scan had 'revealed fractures of the transverse process of three vertebrae' and that 'although this injury causes a good deal of discomfort, it does not impact on the structural integrity of the spine, and once healed should pose no long-term issues … Typically this injury is treated akin to a soft tissue injury; according to symptoms. Jamie is already feeling more comfortable and it is hoped that he will be available to play again in approximately four weeks.'

It was one of the most animated rows I ever had with Joe. I'm a pretty laidback guy, so I don't lose my temper often, but I've no problem voicing my opinion, especially when I disagree with something. This was one of those times. I didn't agree that the media had some divine right to use my private information to sell newspapers.

Notwithstanding the row, I stayed with the team in camp to help them prepare for the England game and to have ready access to the doctors and physios. There was a lot riding on the England game: victory would let us equal the all-time

Irish record of 10 wins in a row, achieved in 2002 and 2003 under Eddie O'Sullivan. We had lost our previous three Six Nations encounters with England, so nothing could be taken for granted. Jordi Murphy took my place and we had a good 19-9 win, with Robbie Henshaw scoring a try and Johnny kicking the rest of the points.

I was recalled for the Wales game, but unfortunately we lost our Grand Slam opportunity in a 23-16 defeat. It was a strange game. We were 12 points down within 13 minutes as Wayne Barnes gave a succession of penalties against us – for not rolling away from the ruck, not releasing the tackled player (my fault) or slowing ruck ball – all of which Leigh Halfpenny kicked. We had more ball and more territory, but because of that start we were always chasing the game. In the pursuit, we made too many handling errors and mistakes at key moments. Wales just soaked it all up, defending as if they were chasing the Grand Slam, which they weren't. They flung themselves into tackles, knocked our carriers behind the gain-line and slowed down our ruck ball. For probably the first time under Joe, our aerial game malfunctioned. I also got some of the blame for coming in to tackle Dan Biggar on one of their moves, and that created the space for replacement centre Scott Williams to go through a gap and score. We got back to 20-16 with a penalty try 12 minutes from the end, but I was replaced by Jordi, probably because Joe feared I wouldn't last the pace after my injury-enforced time out. I had to watch as we couldn't get out of our own half and conceded another penalty, which they kicked. We went looking for a draw, but our line-out maul near the end was held up and Wales won a penalty off the turnover scrum and that was it. I felt that I had made a good contribution – 18 carries with the ball – and that my fitness after injury had not been an issue.

Our championship hopes were still alive, however. We did a short video review of the Wales game, highlighting our faults, but spent more time looking for Scottish weaknesses to exploit in our final game, at Murrayfield. Unlike our final game the previous year – when winning was enough – we needed to win by a big margin to establish a large enough points difference advantage before England played France. We also had to watch what Wales scored against Italy in the game that was on before us. But for all that, we knew that we had to focus primarily on beating the Scots. We were aware that the bulk of our scores against them at home in 2014 had come very late in the game. We had to show them respect.

The day turned out to be possibly the most remarkable in Six Nations history, a thriller for the fans, a rollercoaster for the players. Wales beat Italy first, scoring seven second-half tries for a 61-20 win. That immediately put the pressure on us: we now had to win by 21 points to go ahead of Wales, and even that might not be enough if England beat France by a wide margin. It was an unusual position in which to go into a Six Nations game but, looking back, it may have worked in our favour. Had we not needed to beat that big target, we might not have set a big enough one for England to beat.

We started well, Paulie getting a try that Johnny converted and then another penalty from him gave us a 10-point lead inside 10 minutes. They got a penalty, but then we got another try. Seanie took a long throw to the tail of the line-out on the home 22 and he only had to fend off a couple of weak challenges to get in for a try that Johnny again converted. Then Finn Russell got a try, which he converted, and Johnny kicked another penalty for us. We went in 20-10 ahead at half-time.

In the second-half, Johnny kicked another penalty and Jared Payne got a try that Johnny converted. We knew the victory was assured at 30-10, but now we needed to add extra points. Johnny missed two penalties before a third effort was successful and we had bettered Wales's points difference. Seanie got over for another try, Johnny got another penalty, and Mads missed a late one. The final score was 40-10.

However, there was another crucial moment. With four minutes left on the clock, Stuart Hogg stepped inside Tommy Bowe and across the try-line. I chased him back and hit him as he dived in to place the ball for the try, dislodging the ball. The TMO checked and confirmed that it was not a try. Had he scored and had it been converted, England's target would have been a 19-point victory against France, rather than 26 points. I can't claim that I knew at that moment that I needed to do it for the points difference tally. The only thing I can remember about it was thinking that I would be killed by Joe in the review if I gave up on it and didn't make the effort to get back. To Joe, it doesn't matter what minute of the game it is or what the score is, you do the right thing.

It paid off. Our 40-10 win was exciting, but what happened afterwards at Twickenham was insane. England started with a converted try, then France came back to lead 15-7 after 18 minutes. We were having our beers, starting to celebrate, when England suddenly went to town, scoring tries all over the place in one of the most remarkable games I've ever watched – or partly watched, because I kept turning away and turning back again, wanting to see and not wanting to see. There was no getting away from the end of the game, though. With minutes to go, England led by 55-35 and needed just one converted try to pip us to the title. The French had an opportunity to kick it out but, bizarrely, opted to take the risk of running it from near their own goal-line. Eventually, Rory Kockott kicked it out. It was still 55-35. They had fallen a converted try short. Our celebrations began.

We were the first Irish team to win the Championship outright in successive years since 1948 and 1949, an indication of how difficult that job can be for Ireland. We were presented with a replica trophy on the pitch at Murrayfield – the real one was at Twickenham because the organisers had clearly expected England to win – in front of the remaining Irish fans, to a soundtrack of u2's 'A Beautiful Day', 'The Irish Rover' and, perhaps apt given the day we'd had, Bon Jovi's 'Livin' on a Prayer'. How we partied that night.

The stats were telling a really good story for the future of Irish rugby. We conceded just 49 points in the Six Nations campaign of 2014 and just 56 in 2015. That latter figure was 37 fewer than Wales and 44 fewer than England, the largest difference between the best and second-best defence since the Six Nations began in 2000. Over a two-championship stretch, only the World Cup-winning English team of 2002 and 2003 conceded fewer points than in Joe's first 10 Six Nations games. Only the Welsh side of 2012 and 2013, on the back of being World Cup semi-finalists in 2011, had conceded fewer tries. The season also marked the sixth successive championship won by the team with the tightest defence. That gave us good reason to be confident about the World Cup.

There were other elements to our game that gave us great hope. We had the most attacking rucks among the Six Nations teams by a big margin and we were the best at retaining ruck ball and the quickest at recycling it: an average of 2.9 seconds per ruck, just under the important three-second mark generally accepted as signifying 'quick ball'. We also had the highest ratio of activity per ruck arrival, with our backs being particularly good at this. That said, we had the fewest offloads. We played a low-risk game, but it was highly efficient and effective, started by two half-backs in Johnny and Conor who played a fantastic kicking game to win territory. Once we gained ground, we tended to keep it. Now all we had to do was keep it going at the 2015 Rugby World Cup.

∾

The venue for the World Cup was England and Wales and there were 20 teams competing across four pools, the top two in each going into the quarter-finals. We started with a handy win against Canada, 50-7, at the Millennium Stadium in Cardiff. We scored seven tries and the bonus point for four tries was achieved five minutes before half-time. We showed a bit of variety in our play, but there were errors that meant we left a few tries behind and gave away too many penalties. What was noticeable to us was the level of support we enjoyed, both in the streets outside and in the stadium itself. It was like four years earlier, carnival time. We moved to London next and Romania at Wembley, in front of a record crowd for a World Cup fixture. It was another party atmosphere as Joe chose to use many of the squad players, with me on the pitch as captain for the first 60 minutes. We won comfortably, 44-10, but our attention was already focused on the next game against Italy, which was effectively the qualifier for the quarter-finals as France had already beaten them in the group stage.

We went to the Olympic Stadium, now the West Ham football ground, to play Italy. We laboured through it, strangely lethargic, unable to get an attacking game going. We had gone up 10-3 in the first quarter, Earlsie getting a try that Johnny converted, but we didn't kick on from there and were only 10-6 at half-time and then 10-9 early in the second-half. We ended up winning 16-9, but it didn't make for a pleasant review with Joe.

A week later we blitzed France in what will be remembered as one of the great Irish World Cup performances. We won 24-9, but the scoreline tells only a fraction of the story. We lost Johnny to a groin injury after Picamoles thumped him, but we didn't realise until afterwards that Johnny had vomited on the sideline before heading down the tunnel. Mads came in to replace him and we trusted him to do his job. Then we lost Paulie in the last play of the first-half to an injury that would end not just his World Cup but his playing career. I didn't realise how badly injured he was until after the game, but I should have. In the dressing-room at half-time he was on oxygen and taking heavy painkillers, but I was so focused on what I had to do that it just didn't register with me. Then Joe told me that Paulie was gone and I was captain for the rest of the game. The result, winning, was all I cared about at the time. Doing the job. It was a calm dressing-room. Everyone was concentrating on their roles and on problem-solving. Then we went out to take action.

Early in the second-half Peter O'Mahony wrecked his knee, an injury that would keep him out for nearly a year. We were missing our key players and the French were relentlessly physical. There was much at stake because both teams wanted to avoid losing and thereby meeting New Zealand in the quarter-final, so that increased the intensity. But this game was a war of attrition, like many of the big games we'd had with Leinster in France, and with every blow we took, we dug in deeper.

We took the initiative quickly in the second-half. The ball went wide to Rob, who had players outside him, but when he saw Michalak in front of him, he knew he could run over him. Mads missed the conversion to Rob's try, but being more than one score ahead at 14-6 gave us great confidence. Parra pulled back a penalty, but then Conor got in for another try, which Mads converted, and then he kicked a penalty. It was 24-9 at full-time. We were deserving winners.

Afterwards, people suggested that we had become overly emotional about the outcome. The atmosphere pretty much surpassed any other game in which I'd played, but I don't think we treated it as winning our World Cup. We saw it as a stepping-stone. Some people chose to make an issue of the pictures of Mads in tears after the game, suggesting that we had lost the plot. I think that photo of Mads wasn't related to what the squad was feeling, that it was based on his personal experience and did not sum up the emotional state of the rest of us. He had been playing second fiddle to Johnny, had come on in a massive game with questions hanging over him – 'Is he good enough to take over from Johnny?' – and he had stepped up to the plate, played really well and answered those questions emphatically. He had controlled the game. We knew all about his footwork and his speed, but against France he had controlled the game as the quarterback. He was entitled to feel that he had made it.

We were physically drained afterwards, and we did end up counting the cost of winning. There were the injuries, but then there was also a possible suspension for Seanie for an alleged swing at Papé, who had been holding him back. Papé made a meal of it, but unfortunately Seanie got a one-match ban at a disciplinary hearing later that week. Jared Payne, our key defender at outside centre, was also ruled out with a fractured foot, so we went into the quarter-final against Argentina more than a bit under-strength. We painted it internally as an opportunity for others to step up and take their places, to play with the hand we'd been dealt and not to make excuses in advance of the game. Paulie and Pete stayed with the squad, to encourage them, while Johnny kept rehabbing in an effort to make the game. The importance of the game meant that Joe's 'if you don't train on Tuesday, you don't play at the weekend' rule went out the window as far as Johnny was concerned. 'It's not ideal, but it is what it is,' I told one of the pre-match press conferences, and I emphasised the strength of the collective. The reality was that those missing were all very big players in pivotal positions with lots of experience. Glass half-full type of guy that I am, I was saying, 'We can do a job here.' I wasn't on my own in thinking that. We still had lots of very good players.

Throughout the week we tried to maintain confidence in the team and it didn't waver. We were aware of how good Argentina had become since we'd won our games on tour there in 2014, especially the way they had played in their pool game against the All Blacks before eventually losing to them. One thing that went wrong in our preparation for that game, and that would prove decisive, was that the pitch we trained on during the week was tiny in comparison to the Millennium Stadium. We probably thought we were looking really sharp defensively during the week, but then it was game day and Argentina did this wide-to-wide pattern, using the full width of the pitch to attack us quickly as runners came from deep. Our defensive method was to go up and out, instead of coming aggressively to the line, and they were stealing 10m/15m/20m every time they went to the edge. It worked for them. They scored two tries in the first quarter to give them a 17-0 lead.

In truth, our defensive system hadn't really moved on as much as it might have from what had served us so well in the previous years. Other teams had spotted the weaknesses in our wide pattern. Les Kiss was the defensive coach at the time, but it would be unfair to put it on just one person because there were many different coaches contributing to the decisions made as to how we executed defence. Joe had a lot of responsibility there, too. He didn't just let Kissy do his own thing, it was all done under Joe's instruction.

On the day, Argentina did almost everything better. They cleared out their own rucks and counter-rucked far more efficiently. They scrummaged hard. They linked better – and more speedily – between backs and forwards. They got to the gain-line quickly and danced around us or kicked ahead. They had pace and footwork. By contrast, we were far behind the gain-line, ponderous and dropping the ball or not protecting it in the tackles.

Despite all that, we still managed to creep back into the game. Luke Fitzgerald, on as a sub, scored a try, as did Jordi, and when Mads kicked a penalty in the 53rd minute we were just three points down. Mads had another kick to draw us level at 23-23, but he missed. That was a big moment. Definitely. If he had hit the target, I think we would have broken them. If we'd received the kick-off, we'd have kicked it down and put pressure on them. Instead, the moment that broke our spirit was an Argentina try after the missed penalty. We had the right mentality, even after our penalty miss, that we would get it next opportunity. Instead, next time they got the ball, they scored. I think they went the length of the field to score it and that really breaks the spirit. As leader, I'm saying, 'Right, lads, we've still got time to get back into this.' Then they got another try. The team was exhausted and there was little time left and I was left saying, 'Right, lads, we're playing for fucking pride now.' We did, but we lost 43-20.

Sometimes nonsense gets put around by the media, like the idea that teams don't like playing at certain grounds. I don't know whether some of the questions put to players come from ignorance or an attempt to get a rise out of us. I've had that question, asking if Ireland don't like playing at the Millennium Stadium in Cardiff. How many great days have the Irish provinces or national team had there? Some of the same people who quoted the Argentina defeat in the 2015 Rugby World Cup at me seemed to have forgotten that we beat France there only a week earlier. Professionals don't care where the game is played.

The final score was a big blow to suffer, not so much the scoreline but the outcome. Argentina played a very expansive game, they stretched us, took their scores when they got the opportunities, and we didn't take all of ours. And we didn't have enough depth off the bench to change things. The reality was that they were much better than us on the day. That might all sound like excuses, but I think it is a genuine explanation. Sometimes you come up against a team that is better, when all you have done isn't enough. It didn't diminish my confidence in what Joe was doing for us. When we'd had a setback at Leinster under him, we'd bounced back better. I felt we would do the same now.

It took time to rationalise it all like that, though. Losing in 2015 felt a bit worse than losing in 2011, maybe because I was older and knew I might not get to another World Cup. Perhaps the expectation coming from outside the camp, that we would beat Argentina and get into the semi-final, got to us. The number of people coming over to see the games was insane, the hype and interest were intense. Joe's a master at playing down expectations, but people got carried away. I came home and booked a trip straightaway, went off to New York with Sheena, and parked it. I had to. I couldn't change what had happened. Next ball.

CHAPTER 14

CHICAGO

Whenever things were challenging with Ireland, Leinster was usually my refuge. I could go back there and feel the joy of working within a properly functioning machine. But after the World Cup, things weren't going as well as I would have liked at the club. Leo Cullen was settling in as head coach, having taken up the role during the summer after Matt was let go, but it wasn't exactly a smooth transition, especially as he was short all of the Leinster players involved with the World Cup until late October.

We ended up having a disastrous Champions Cup campaign in 2015/2016, finishing bottom of our group with Wasps, Toulon and Bath, not even qualifying for the secondary tournament that we'd won in 2013. The Pro12 League didn't finish well for us either. We won against Ulster in the semi-final, 30-18, leading many people to believe that we'd turned things around. But Connacht did a number on us in the final in Edinburgh, beating us 20-10 and deservedly so. We used 56 players during the season, including 10 from the Academy, and I remained confident that we were improving and would have success. Bringing new players into a team that isn't doing well is a challenge, but Leo was doing an excellent job in laying the foundations for the future, bringing in promising young players at the right times.

Leinster suffered a very heavy defeat to Wasps, 33-6, in a November Champions Cup game at the RDS and as captain I had to face the media in the post-match press conference. Several of them criticised my demeanour, claiming that I wasn't sufficiently humble and created a sour atmosphere. Admitting that I was disappointed by the result wasn't good enough for them. Apparently, I had missed an opportunity to pass a message to Leinster supporters. That disapproval was a taster of what lay ahead prior to Joe announcing who would be Ireland captain for the Six Nations 2016, to replace Paulie. All sorts of critical analysis pieces appeared in January 2016, acknowledging that I could do the job on the pitch, but alleging that I lacked the necessary humility for their off-field requirements. Their main gripe seemed to be that I didn't want to be their friend but that it was a necessary part of the job.

I realised I had a problem in my relationship with the media and that I contributed to that, and I couldn't just blame individual reporters or the media in general for not giving me a fair shake. As with everything, I decided to get advice from an expert, so I went to Joanne Byrne, an experienced public relations consultant who deals regularly with the media. She was blunt in telling me at our first meeting that sections of the media had issues with me, that some of them simply didn't like me. And I had to concede that.

Joanne is great for clear and concise feedback. She monitored my interviews and public engagements and the articles that appeared, and encouraged me to see things from their side. On occasion I may have had a tendency to be confrontational, to be prickly in defending myself, to quickly go on the attack. She encouraged me to open up, show more of who I am, be authentic and engage with them. I agreed; I had to respect their jobs and their importance to the promotion of the game. I realised that even if I disagreed with their opinions or take on the game, they held the microphones or had the laptops and were in a position to lead the narrative. Other players had been better at fostering their interactions with the media over the years and I tried to address the issue. I'm sure I still had the odd bad day but everyone does.

I think some in the media had constructed a narrative about me because I didn't play the game as they wanted. At one stage, the Irish communications officer advised me that I shouldn't bring an apple with me into the media room post-match because some journalists had complained that eating an apple was disrespectful to them. I was facilitating them, by going straight to them after a game to help with their deadlines, but I needed food. 'Are you really telling me that eating an apple is showing disrespect to these people?' I said to him, gobsmacked. 'Are they serious adults? How is eating something after playing a game of such intensity disrespectful? Do they actually understand what's physically involved in a game of rugby, the calories lost, the need to replenish?'

I trusted that Joe would take no notice of this, even though I was aware that he read the media avidly and was very protective of how he was portrayed and very interested in maintaining good relations with leading figures in the media. Looking back, I should have suspected that he wouldn't want to spend time defending his choice to the media and being on the back foot, but at the time I was confident that I had done more than enough to warrant selection. After all, I was vice-captain at the World Cup and took the armband in the second-half against France and in the game against Argentina.

I thought I had learned a lot and developed a lot as a leader over the previous two years under Paulie's stewardship. I felt I was ready for it again.

I was captain of Leinster, but a major reason for continuing to play in Ireland was my hope of captaining the Irish team again. I felt that Joe liked me because over the years he had learnt that I very rarely made a mistake. That's not to say I was amazing every time I went out there, it just meant I knew what I had to do, what my role was within the team, and I did it. When Joe looked at how I trained and how I approached games, and the fact that I looked after myself and was very rarely injured or missed a training session, he would have to admit that it made me useful to him. There may have been things outside rugby he didn't like, because he may have preferred my total attention on rugby, but I felt he understood that rugby didn't define me and that my outside interests didn't conflict with me being a good pro. As far as I was concerned, they helped make me a better balanced person and player. I had never had any major clashes with him – other than releasing information about my injuries – or major mistakes on the field. All of that was on the plus side. But now I can see that we didn't have a relationship beyond the basic stuff. Joe rarely called me on the phone, and it was usually about something like my contract or the captaincy. I hadn't considered that developing some kind of deeper personal relationship was necessary or warranted. It was work, after all.

One of those rare calls came in January 2016 when Joe asked to meet me at The Greenery in Donnybrook. I went expecting to hear good news, but I didn't get it. 'Yeah, you know, I think I'm going to go with Besty,' he said. I'm not going to lie, I was really disappointed. I knew I couldn't change his mind, but that didn't mean I was happy about it and, although I can't remember exactly what I said, I let him know that. His reaction was a bit weird. He didn't agree or disagree with me. Normally, when you put something to Joe about rugby, he responded immediately and decisively, his position laid out perfectly, his thoughts marshalled. This time, there was nothing. Even so, I knew that was the end of it and I wasn't getting the armband.

I was unhappy with the decision for me, but it didn't affect my working relationship with Joe or my performances for Ireland. It was done and I got over it. I still liked Joe and did what he wanted, but it was a professional relationship. I realise that I owe a lot of what I got out of my career to Joe. I don't for a moment think I did it all by myself. He played a huge role in showing me what it meant to be a good pro and how to prepare and look after myself. He showed me the bigger picture, which allowed me to then bring those skills into other parts of my life. Joe was tough but fair, in the majority of cases. He's excellent at understanding people and their motivations, what makes them tick. He knew what made the group dynamic work, as well, and how each individual contributed to it. You always knew exactly where you stood with Joe, and I always appreciated that. There's a scene in *Moneyball*, the baseball film, when Billy Beane (played by Brad Pitt), tells his young assistant Peter Brand (Jonah Hill) how to cut a player from the roster: 'They're professional ball players. Just be straight with them. No fluff. Just facts.' He calls in a player and says bluntly, 'Pete, I gotta let you go. Jack's office will handle the details.' Beane then turns to Brand and says, 'Would you rather a bullet to the head or fire to the chest and bleed to death?' Well, I understood that. I'd always choose a bullet to the head, and that's what Joe always delivered.

Not getting the Irish captaincy was the second such blow I'd taken in just a matter of months. I'd lost the Leinster job not long after coming back from the 2015 World Cup. Leo had said nothing while I was away with Ireland, but for the first Champions Cup game in November he suddenly announced that Isa was the new club captain for the season, with Johnny and me his co-vice-captains. I was surprised, to say the least, and in retrospect was probably more upset by that than by Joe's decision for Ireland. Isa is one of the greatest ever Leinster players, but I felt he'd taken two years out and now was being rewarded for his absence. I didn't see Isa on the day it was announced and I felt badly about that in case he felt I was avoiding him. I managed to contact him by phone, apologised for not seeing him in person and promised to back him 100% in anything he wanted or needed. I can't remember exactly how Leo explained his decision to me, but I know he wanted someone who wasn't going to be dragged away with the Irish squad and I understood why he wanted consistency. He would get that with Isa, who didn't play international rugby. I rationalised it a bit by expecting to get the Irish job. The disappointment of not being Leinster captain hit in a bit more when Joe overlooked me for that.

Ireland had a frustrating start to the 2016 Six Nations. We threw away a 13-point lead against Wales in the opening match to end with a 16-16 draw, then got beaten 10-9 by France. Two weeks later, we had to go to Twickenham.

My record against England wasn't great. In six previous visits, I'd only been on the winning team once. Eddie Jones tried to wind it up beforehand, saying we were just a kicking team, and Drico commented publicly that we were afraid to offload. I laughed it off at a press conference: 'I wouldn't agree completely with Brian's comment. But he's obviously entitled to his opinion. And as a pundit, he has to offer up an opinion and that was his.'

What else could I say? If I had said, 'Yes, Brian's right,' I would have been issuing a public criticism of my coach and everyone would have seized upon it and attacked me for my disloyalty. In some ways it shows how many of these press conferences are sham, where everybody takes the easy PR option in their answers. There is little authenticity because the consequences of going off-script are terrible. As a pundit, Brian was perfectly entitled to offer his opinion and in retrospect it was an informed one, but it didn't really matter. All that mattered was what the coach and team thought. You can also be sure that Joe had given plenty of consideration to our offloading game before Brian, or anyone else, said anything about it publicly.

In the end, English power led to a 21-10 defeat for us. It left us in a difficult position, playing almost for pride in the rest of the Six Nations, which is something that shouldn't happen to a professional. But I took the view that any day I wore the Irish jersey, irrespective of the circumstances or opposition, I did my very best and so did everyone else. I always loved the moment when I came into the dressing-room and saw my jersey hanging there, waiting for me. And I loved turning the jersey around to see my name stitched across it. Each time I said to myself, 'This is my jersey for the day, I have got to do it right.'

We won our last two games, against Italy and Scotland, both at home. We beat Scotland 35-25 and I had a very enjoyable day, getting my hands on the ball often and in the outside channels, rather than just in the trenches. The Italy game was a big win, best remembered for my try, which won the 2016 Try of The Year at the World Rugby Awards. It started from a ruck just outside our 22m line. I was the first man in that ruck, generating fast ball. The ball spun wide to the right and as Zeebs created an overlap out wide, I looked for where I would be most useful. Of the seven forwards on their feet, I was the only one who decided to disregard the direction of the ball and make a beeline directly up the pitch. I sprinted nearly 80m and linked with Fergus McFadden as he came across the park and I carried two defenders over the line with me to score the try. Joe said afterwards that that one phase of play probably summed me up as a player. Much of what I did for that try wasn't seen in the television coverage, but whenever I saw a situation like that, I always ran up the pitch while the defenders were being dragged over to where the ball was. If the ball came back to my side, then I was in business; if it didn't, I had to work hard to get back into position. In the Monday morning review, Joe caned a couple of players for their roles, or non-roles, in that score. He pointed out that others, on their feet from the ruck faster than me, had just stood looking around. 'Why aren't you reading the play? Why aren't you moving, reacting to what's going on?' he demanded. He was not happy, even though we had won 58-15 that day and scored nine tries, of which I bagged two.

It was an odd Six Nations, but Joe used it to bring in new players, with five new caps added. We scored almost twice as many tries as the previous season – 15 to 8 – and made the most clean breaks, the fewest handling errors and had the highest percentage of returns from rucks. It was only the offloads that let us down in attack, but our defence was a problem, as the hangover from the World Cup continued and we leaked seven tries in our last three games.

I wasn't despondent, though, far from it. The new players had done well and, as I saw it, the margins were very fine.

We'd won matches in the Six Nations in 2014 and 2015 by the same margins we'd lost them that year. It showed the new players, preparing for a fresh World Cup cycle, how much hard work had to be put in to get ourselves into a situation where the outcome would fall in our favour. And it wouldn't be hard work for a week before a big game. It would demand solid hard work over the entire season.

∼

The summer tour to South Africa restarted the Joe project with Ireland. He had made a superb addition to his coaching staff, introducing Andy Farrell, the former England assistant coach, to replace Les Kiss as defence coach. I was delighted with that, having worked with Andy on the British & Irish Lions tour. I had no problem that he was associated with England's failure at the previous World Cup.

We kicked off the tour with one of the best Irish wins of the professional era, beating South Africa 26-20 at the Newlands Stadium in Cape Town, despite CJ Stander getting sent off in the 23rd minute when he jumped and collided with a kicker as he tried to block the ball. We were even down to 13 men for 10 minutes when Robbie Henshaw was sin-binned, but it didn't matter. Our defence was top-notch, we attacked with verve and you'd have been hard pressed to see that we were playing with reduced numbers, apart from the time Andrew Trimble had pack down as wing-forward at a scrum. We never panicked. No Irish team had ever won in South Africa before. They were shocked.

The team learned so much from that day, particularly that the team that makes the least amount of mistakes is usually the one that gets the right outcome. When we were down to 13 players we actually outscored them 3 to nil in that period. We dealt with each challenge in a methodical fashion and kept control of our set-pieces. We never panicked, even though there were lots of inexperienced players on the pitch. It was utter professionalism against a top-quality side.

We lost 32-26 the following week in the altitude of Ellis Park in Johannesburg with an even more inexperienced side, as Joe chose to give more players top-level experience. In fact, we were 26-10 ahead after an hour and I scored one of the tries, throwing a dummy pass in a rolling maul that confused the opposition, but not the officials, who knew it was within the laws. The performance may have been even more impressive than that the week before, for 60 minutes at least, but then we got blitzed in the last 20 minutes by the furiously strong, and bullying, Boks, who clearly couldn't face the embarrassment of losing a test series at home to a country like Ireland. We started to miss tackles and shipped three tries, meaning the series would be decided in Port Elizabeth the following week.

We allowed the game the following week to get away from us, too, losing 19-13 after missing plenty of chances to build a score and failing to get over the line for a try at the death. We took the game to them, despite having a very inexperienced line-up of Paddy Jackson, Stuart Olding and Luke Marshall at 10, 12 and 13. We had 68% of the possession and 73% of the territory and really felt at the end that we had thrown it away. However, the true benefit of that summer tour was really felt in our brilliant November series.

That was one trip we all wanted to get on: going to Chicago to play the All Blacks in a one-off international. It was exciting. It was exotic, even. We didn't do big games in places like that. It was a unique opportunity and I couldn't wait to be part of it.

It was November in Chicago, but the weather was great, sun belting down all week. We were staying in Trump International Hotel & Tower, looking down over the river, and the city was in major celebration mode because the Cubs had won the baseball World Series for the first time since 1929. We heard that about 5 million people would be in the city for the celebrations. There were so many people milling around on Saturday morning that we had to leave before 9am to get to the stadium to do our captain's run, taking all the back streets. And there was Soldier Field itself, one of the great NFL stadiums, wonderfully old-fashioned on the exterior in its 1920s art deco-influenced architectural glory but modern in its interior rebuild. The pitch was surrounded by 12ft high walls with the seats above them, creating the ultimate gladiatorial atmosphere. This was the Colosseum. How could we not be excited?

Joe set the tone pretty early, ramping up the pressure in training that week because I think he was afraid we'd treat it as a holiday. He had warned us during the summer tour that when we regrouped for the All Blacks game, we would go straight into game week. We were given all the information about how he wanted us to play, how they played, how we would defend against them by getting off the line and not allowing them any width in their game. We'd be kicking a lot, but with a defined purpose. He emphasised getting our setpieces in order and putting them into their own half with those kicks. Everything just felt so sharp, all week. The training ground we used wasn't exactly ideal because of its dimensions, but Joe didn't accept that as an excuse for any dropped balls or forgotten plays or not being at the right place at the right time.

Joe cranked up the pressure on Monday, Tuesday,

Wednesday and then he came right off it on Thursday, just eased off completely. There was a lot of confidence in the squad. We were prepared. When we saw the Irish crowd on the day itself, an ocean of green waving through Soldier Field, tens of thousands of them and certainly the majority of the 62,300 people there, we were lifted further. Those things aren't supposed to matter, but sometimes they do.

As the All Blacks got ready to do their Haka, we got ready for our symbolic gesture. Just a few weeks earlier, Anthony Foley, the Munster head coach, had died suddenly and far too young on the morning of a Munster game in Paris. I hadn't known him too well – although I had rated highly the work he had done as defensive coach for Ireland in my 2013 season when we conceded few tries despite the defeats – but I had played against him and was one of his successors in the number 8 Ireland jersey. Somebody, I can't remember who, had the idea of us forming in a figure eight to meet the Haka challenge. It felt perfect, a fitting tribute, and we worked on it in the days beforehand, making sure that everybody knew exactly where to stand, so that nobody would ruin what would rightly become an iconic image.

We built a big lead in the first-half, as we had in 2013, but not quite in the same way. They scored first, and too easily, but the 5-0 lead they had within five minutes was the only time that day they would be in front. Joe Moody got yellow-carded for a tip tackle on Robbie and we scored 15 points while he was in the bin. Jordi and CJ got tries – Jordi burrowing over from a maul, CJ getting in after Rob produced great footwork. Johnny converted one and kicked a penalty. We were 18-8 up when we lost Jordi. He suffered a horrific injury to his knee and it took a long time to treat him on the pitch. He was given the morphine pen on the field, his pain was so bad. But our concentration didn't waver. We noticed, we hoped he was alright, but we were cold about it because there was a job to be done. Josh van der Flier came in to replace him and we refocused. Next ball.

The try that really rattled the All Blacks came six minutes before half-time when a great Johnny garryowen was reclaimed by Conor, who a couple of phases later exposed weak defence on the side of the ruck, threw a dummy and ran in to score from 20m. When converted, that gave us a 25-8 lead.

We had 66% possession and territory in that first-half, which was remarkable. We had the All Blacks in trouble everywhere. They conceded twice as many penalties as us in the first-half and won just a little bit more than half their line-outs, whereas we won all of ours. We won double the turnovers – eight to four – and we weren't falling off our tackles like we had in previous encounters. Our kicking game, into space, was excellent and executed just as Joe had planned and demanded. The only question was whether or not we could keep it going.

When we came in at half-time somebody, I can't remember who, said, 'Look, they're going to get their purple patch, they're a great team and they're going to get back, but that doesn't mean we have to panic.' We had to 'trust what we're doing, trust our process'. We had a couple of points we decided we needed to fix, although I can't remember what they were, but we told each other, 'Stick to our processes, play in the right areas, we don't have to overplay.' That was an interesting place to be, maybe even an unusual one, to have everyone trying to calm each other down instead of geeing each other up for greater effort. In the past, it probably would have been a case of telling ourselves we had to do more, try harder and we'd have ended up forcing the game. In the past the purple patch would have hit and we'd have panicked a little, 'Shit, here comes the wave, oh no,' and then we'd have been washed over. Not this day.

It was important we got the first score of the second-half. We did that when Zeebs went in at the corner after concerted forward pressure. At 30-8 up with 30 minutes to play, we were in better shape than we had been three years earlier, but then they came at us. TJ Perenara, on as a sub, got their first try, and then Beauden Barrett somehow gave an under-arm, one-handed offload for Ben Smith to score by the corner flag, and then Barrett converted that. Thankfully, we kicked the next penalty, and it was Conor who had to do it because Johnny was cramping. But then Scott Barrett got a try that his brother converted, and suddenly we had only a four-point advantage at 33-29. Then we lost Johnny to injury.

He was replaced by Joey Carbery, who'd had his 21st birthday party in Chicago the previous Tuesday evening. I had a fleeting thought that it was bad news when I realised that Johnny was going off, but just as quickly I felt certain that Joey was here because he was good enough. We were confident that Joe had him ready. We had seen Joey quite a bit in Leinster and we knew his talent. He didn't have to do anything amazing, we weren't asking for that. Joe had put him under a lot of pressure during the week, to fit in and do exactly what was required of him in the system. Nothing beyond that. Do the job. In any case, I was too busy concentrating on doing my own job to worry about how somebody else was doing his.

We didn't panic when they scored their tries. We fixed it on the field. We said we were going to hold on to the ball, stick to our system, look for opportunities to get more scores, and we did. We were trying to draw their wingers up, to create space behind them and when we did, Joey had space to kick into. As did Zeebs. We weren't passive. We were aggressive. That probably defined the difference between that match and 2013. We weren't panicked but we were edgy, in the right way. In 2013, everyone was afraid of being the player who made the mistake. In 2016 we were proactive, not reactive: 'Let's stick to what we're doing, go down there and call a set-play.' They had their turn, we'd have ours again. Nothing was going to stop us. It was one of those days where we just hit that flow state where it all clicked.

There were some big moments that gave us the advantage, however. Andrew Trimble made a massive hit on Squire to force a turnover and the crowd went mad. No matter how much in the zone we were, we couldn't help but hear it. Conor fed the scrum, we attacked wide, Zeebs put in a gorgeous kick behind their defence and when Savea grabbed it, Conor was there to force him into touch in goal.

We called a play off the scrum for Robbie's try. We knew that if we ran at the 10 who was on for Barrett, Aaron Cruden, Savea at 7 would chase me hard and that would give space for Robbie to run into, running against the angle. I started in the scrum in channel two and then switched to channel one, picked and went hard. Joe had been rehearsing that move with us since the summer. He had ID-ed how their system was set up defensively in those situations. I ran diagonally, drew the defenders, then popped a reverse ball to Robbie, who was coming on to my outside shoulder like a bull. He held off three tackles before reaching and touching down to win it. I got some slagging for my celebration, standing there like a fool with my two arms raised to the sky, as everyone piled onto Robbie.

I don't remember thinking, 'That's it, we've won', that there was no time left for them to get the two scores they needed. As Joey was landing the conversion to give us an 11-point lead, we got back to the huddle and as captain – Besty had been replaced by Sean Cronin – I remember going, 'These guys are still going to play, so let's stick to our systems, stick to our process, let's play down there.' Basic stuff, but it had to be said. 'Trust the game plan and trust in yourself.' Minutes later, it was over.

It was such a sweet thing to beat them, 40-29. It was pretty emotional for me, and it's rare I get emotional after games. I walked around the pitch, carrying the tricolour, milking every moment of it. Even though I had believed we could do it, I couldn't believe we had done it. If we'd lost the lead we'd had at that point, we'd have had our excuses had we wanted them. It had been a bugbear of mine for a while, this idea that the golden generation was gone and the next bunch of players wasn't going to be good enough to achieve what they had. Of course they were brilliant players, but their time had passed. That's life.

I remember saying to Mick Kearney afterwards that New Zealand had been such a challenge for us throughout the years, and why this win meant so much. I had been on the receiving end of some hidings and young Joey was taking the piss out of me, talking about how his first cap was beating the All Blacks. 'Joey, don't say that to me. I can't talk to you right now,' I said, but I was laughing. I knew Ireland's ambition had to be to win a World Cup, but that's a big ask for a country of our size with many people playing other sports. So I wasn't going to downplay the importance of beating New Zealand in a one-off game, no matter what the critics might say.

After the game, the New Zealand players were very humble about their loss. They said we were the better team on the day and were quite respectful. There was no post-match dinner, just a brief drinks reception, a few quick speeches and that was it. I wasn't playing the following week, so I celebrated that night. My wife was over, with her mum, and I had drinks with them. There's a photo I love of Church and myself on a balcony in Trump Towers, overlooking the river, having cigars and whiskey, our little ritual for special occasions. This was one of the most special. It was a pretty cool moment.

~

The intensity of the return game against the All Blacks in Dublin two weeks later was mental. It was like a modern-day equivalent of a Rocky Balboa movie, where we basically stood there toe-to-toe and just took lumps out of each other. It was more than just a good game of rugby. Both teams attacked hard and at incredible pace, there was excellent defence on both sides and even if they got three converted tries and we got only three penalties, we still should have won it. We missed chances for tries that we should have nailed. It was deeply frustrating.

I tore into them from the start. My first intervention was to get into Aaron Smith's face for his first box-kick. He kicked badly. I nearly got in for a try from off the back of a scrum, but two of them managed to stop me. A little later I recovered ball we were in danger of losing from a line-out and I hit Seanie as he came on a brilliant line, but he didn't get over for a try either because he dropped the ball. Later I got Devin Toner (Dev) through a similar gap in midfield. I was getting on the ball, making things happen. It was one of my best days, as I did all my usual grunt work, making the hard yards with short bursts, but I also got on the ball in open play. I changed angles on my runs, got momentum into attacks. I won line-outs, both in attack and defence, and took pressure off my second-rows as the All Blacks, smarting from what had happened in Chicago, targeted them.

The All Blacks conceded 14 penalties that day, but still won. We conceded only four, the same as in Chicago. We were in contention all the way up to the last 10 minutes. Our discipline meant that we didn't give easy access points. That said, if not giving penalties away is key, there are times when you have to do it, to prevent tries being scored if you prefer to take the hit of three points instead of seven and are confident that even if you lose a man to the bin, you'll be able to organise to cover his loss for 10 minutes and not concede further.

We were so disappointed that we didn't win that game. That was where we were at mentally and in terms of confidence. It was no longer about turning up and seeing how it would pan out. Now we went out expecting to win every game. It was an immensely physical game and they deserved to win, but even in defeat it gave us confidence for the future. I was looking forward to playing them again. The fear was gone. Things had changed because of the Chicago win. We were now their peers, at their level. It was so different from a decade earlier when I'd come into the team. And it was different from 2012 or 2013, when we were thrilled to get close to them as one-offs. In 2016, we were as good as them.

The All Blacks had always been my benchmark, the standard-setter, how I measured my progress and Ireland's. They evolved a lot quicker than other teams. When they came to Dublin for that return game, they'd already tweaked the way they were playing. They went hard after our rucks, wouldn't let us play fast. New Zealand don't have to play in such a structured manner as we do because they have freakish talent. They have a really good system for developing talent from a young age and from what I've heard of the coaching methods, they spend an equal amount of time on unstructured playing, working on how they put a system around unstructured play, as they do on setpieces. As a result, they score a lot of tries from counterattack and in-game play as opposed to structured play.

Some people claimed that the All Blacks went too far that day when it came to the physical stuff. Two of our lads suffered head injuries, two All Blacks were cited after the game. The match citing commissioner reviewed 12 incidents in total, 11 by the All Blacks. Two high tackles by Sam Cane and Malakai Fekitoa, on Robbie and Zeebs respectively, required disciplinary hearings. I just shrugged it off. We could have blamed our defeat on losing Robbie and CJ to injury, but we'd lost players to injury in Chicago. It was knocking-on the ball when in scoring positions that cost us. We didn't take the scoring opportunities we had. We got to their line but couldn't get over. We had line-breaks but didn't capitalise on them. That's why we lost.

Players don't complain about the violent nature of the game because if we did, we might be scared of it. You enter each game knowing there's a risk, that it's a contact sport, that people get hurt. You're running straight into someone, after all. Physics dictates there's going to be impact, there's going to be force and sometimes lads get banged up. A lad falls on you. You get a knee in the head. All sorts of things can happen. It happened a lot in that game. Complaining about the All Blacks' behaviour wasn't going to change the result, and it might have diluted the focus we had to apply to our next game, against Australia. You have to trust referees to spot and deal with foul play and not worry about it because if you do, you won't play to the best of your ability.

We finished off a brilliant year by beating Australia at home 27-24. It meant that we became only the second team to complete a hat-trick of wins over New Zealand, South Africa and Australia in the same calendar year, emulating England in 2003 when they won the World Cup. Even better, we held out against Australia despite a spate of injuries that kept men off the team in the first place – Johnny, Seanie and Rob included – and saw player after player taken off injured during the game. I was proud to see the character developing in the team. We did almost everything right in the Australia game and there was a great sense of camaraderie born out of these tough battles. I was ambitious and excited for the next World Cup, even if it was still a long way off.

I'd had a good Six Nations and summer tour to South Africa, but I think my performance in the first All Blacks game was the clincher for getting shortlisted for the World Player of the Award for the second time, but the first since 2009. I came up against All Blacks duo Beauden Barrett and Dane Coles and England's Owen Farrell, Maro Itoje and Billy Vunipola. I didn't win. Barrett got it. Although we won the Try of the Year Award for my score against Italy. Nonetheless, the nomination was confirmation to me that my professionalism was being recognised and rewarded and I felt I was well placed for selection on the 2017 Lions tour to South Africa.

~

I had thoroughly enjoyed the November series, but I looked forward to returning to Leinster to work more with Stuart

Lancaster. The former England coach – sacked after the 2015 World Cup – had been brought in by Leo as head coach in September 2016 in a move that surprised everyone. He had an immediate impact and it was clear to me that his hiring would turn out to be as beneficial to the team as the arrival of Joe seven years earlier. Personally, it gave me an incredible lift. His coaching was superb. Even the couple of months I'd had with Stuart that season so far had encouraged me to expand my game with Ireland, without sacrificing my duties as set down by Joe. I was really enjoying that blend of trying to figure out the moments within Joe's very structured game where I could bring creativity into my evolving role on the field.

Joe and Stuart are easily the two best coaches I've played under, but their philosophies are very different. Joe's emphasis was very much on controlling the controllables. By contrast, Stuart was comfortable in chaos. Despite that key difference, they both coach in very similar ways. Stuart's style is an evolution of Joe's style. Stuart couldn't have done what he's done with Leinster if he hadn't inherited the system and set-ups from Joe, who in turn couldn't have done what he did unless Cheiks had been there before him, laying down the foundations.

Joe made me a better pro, but I believe that Stuart, even in the short time I worked with him, made me a better player. What Stuart did really well, by contrast to Joe, was to construct and replicate chaotic environments, how we would respond if the ball went loose, if we faced a structured play we hadn't seen before. He wanted decision-making cut down in such situations so that the player's response was automatic. In that he was very similar to Joe, but he was asking us to do it for things we'd hadn't planned for, whereas with Joe you had your own structured plays and you defended against the opposition and then reset to play your own game. Stuart was making us ready to react to the unexpected, to counterattack better. You're on automatic because you've seen that scenario a billion times. I'm not going to say it's the 10,000-hour rule, but it's the equivalent of that. You've been exposed to it so often that you can just do it. The minute you stand still, though, stop doing the work, you lose it. It has to be constant effort.

The Leinster players called Tuesdays 'Stuesdays' because that was the day Stuart went to town on us in training. We trained in short bursts, hard and fast, replicating the time the ball is in play during a game, which means phases of up to five minutes. Training was never much longer because players did enough cardio work during the week to keep them aerobically fit. What we did with Stuart concentrated on our anaerobic fitness – strength, speed and power in those bursts – and recovering from that. The coaches knew what metres per minute the players have to hit and the high-speed metres to perform best in a game. They knew all the statistics and Stuart tailored training to mimic that. It was a long way from running up and down Killiney Hill. The game has changed so much in little more than a decade. The pace the players are now playing and training at means they can't be massively big anymore, unless they can still get around the field at that pace.

When Stuart joined Leinster, I think he was a bit annoyed with the basic skillset of the group, but it has now improved dramatically. He placed a strong emphasis on ball-handling skills and I think that's why Leinster's passing can be really slick and accurate. He did a lot of very basic skills and then evolved them as the guys got better. Stuart didn't have as many launch plays for Leinster as Joe had for Ireland. I think that's why Leinster got back to the top, because of the time spent on in-game unstructured play, set-up and how to play – as opposed to Ireland, where a lot of time is spent on structured set-ups. I believe that Ireland need to play a little bit more like Leinster do under Stuart. Ireland need to know how to react quickly when the opposition makes a mistake or is stopped, the way the All Blacks do. I don't think enough time is spent on that unstructured set-up with Ireland. I wonder if Andy Farrell, given his time with Stuart previously, will do more of that when he takes over from Joe with Ireland?

~

Our high hopes for the 2017 Six Nations were legitimate, but we blew up on the first day, losing to Scotland at Murrayfield 27-22. Joe got a lot of stick afterwards for mentioning that the bus bringing us to the game had been badly delayed and that it upset our preparation, but that wasn't the reason we lost and it was a pity Joe said it because it led to a bit of mockery in sections of the media and seemed disrespectful to Scotland. All of our good form, our dynamism from November, suddenly disappeared in the first-half, which ended up going 21-5 against us. We recovered to take the lead, but then contrived to lose it again, which was unforgivable. I know games have ebbs and flows, but to come from that far back and then not see it out was criminal. The Grand Slam and Triple Crown hopes, which were high because we had drawn France and England at home, were gone in one game and the pressure was on.

Some of our old failings returned, with Scotland attacking us out wide as if they were Argentina. Their defence pushed up hard in a line, they made far more tackles, even if they missed more than us too, and while we did carry and clear out and recycle the ball, we went nowhere with it. We made a dozen line-breaks to their six, but it was our fourth game running in which we conceded three tries. Questions came from the media as to whether the system was working and Andy Farrell's methods were all they'd been cracked up to be, something that would be answered in good time. The Scots seemed to have our number, physically and mentally. We led with 18 minutes to go, but two late Laidlaw penalties did for us.

Besty was unwell for the next game, away to Italy, so I captained Ireland for what would be the final time. We won 63-10 in Rome, with CJ Stander and Craig Gilroy both scoring three tries. It was so different from the last time I'd been captain there. The previous week, our narrow defeat at Murrayfield had given us the tournament's first ever losing bonus point under the new points system, and now we got the first ever bonus point for scoring four tries, something we had managed by the 35th minute. I had a very enjoyable day, carrying 16 times for 48m and offloading successfully four times. I was bringing my Stuart-inspired game to the green jersey and I enjoyed being captain.

We followed this with a 19-9 home victory over France in the rain at the Aviva. We deserved it in a game that was as tough and physical as any of the recent games with France. Conor scored our only try, Johnny kicked the rest, but we kept the defence solid and recycled possession with discipline and care. We won out on the penalty count again, were perfect at line-outs and survived the scrum pressure. We were now in contention to win the championship, although England were flying.

It all went wrong again in Cardiff. We tried hard, made few enough mistakes, even though I had a couple of knock-ons, but they made fewer. The Welsh defence withstood all we threw at them, reading all our moves and tackling aggressively, and all our scores came from penalties. By contrast, we were too predictable. There wasn't constant ball movement, there was no offloading, it was all sledgehammer stuff, but they stood up to it. They also took their chances. Yet again we conceded three tries. We were still in it with three minutes to go, six points down, but instead they got the last try, converted it and we lost 22-9.

I wasn't to know it would be my last time taking to the pitch to play international rugby, so it is only in retrospect that I regard it as a bad way to go out. Instead, I went into full preparation for the final game of the season, against England. And you know how that went.

CHAPTER 15

NO SECOND CHANCE

After the game against England, I went to the post-match meal instead of to the hospital. I thought there might be some formal acknowledgement because I'd won my 100th cap the previous week. I was a bit annoyed when that didn't happen, probably more than I should have been because of the confusion I was feeling about the injury. I ended up sitting beside Owen Farrell, who I knew from the Lions tour and who is a good lad, and I told him my leg was dead and that it felt weird, but I was thinking there was nothing I could do about it.

I went home, slept for the night, better than usual because I hadn't played, and when I woke up the next morning nothing had changed. Still no pain, but also no improvement, just the numbness and no power which, in my head, made it worse. So I went to the hospital for an MRI scan and there it was on the screen: a left-sided disc protrusion, my L5S1 disc. As I remember it being explained to me, as someone who didn't know all the medical terminology at the time but understands a lot more of it now, the problem was right down at the bottom of my spine in the lumbar region: the disc was impinging on a nerve and that was blocking the signals going down to my leg, which was why it had lost power.

On Monday I went to see the specialist medical consultant, Ashley Poynton, at the Mater Private Hospital. He confirmed a disc herniation, caused by the impact of hitting the tackle bag with considerable force. He didn't pull any punches: 'It's not good. This is the protocol, I'll give you an epidural and steroidal injection, basically to settle it, and if it doesn't settle down we'll have to do surgery.' He wanted to avoid surgery and so did I.

It was a relief to know what was wrong, that there was a real physical issue and that I wasn't going mad and imagining it. The consultant said we'd look at it again in ten days. I was fine with that. We always had the week off after the Six Nations and Sheena and I were booked into the Cliff House Hotel in Ardmore for a short break. I had the epidural and was told not to drive, so Sheena did that. I was supposed to rest up and wait for the second check-up, but we only stayed there a couple of days and came back to Dublin and, for some reason, some sixth sense, I decided to go into Leinster on the Thursday and have the medical staff take a look at it again.

I had thought, the optimist in me, injection, problem sorted, return to playing again for the quarter-finals of the Champions Cup, have a good run of games for Leinster and hopefully be back in the mix for selection for the Lions tour to New Zealand. That was the plan. But things changed in an instant when Gareth Farrell, the head physio, examined me and said I had to see the doctor, that this was something beyond physio intervention. The doctor came in and asked me when I'd had the epidural. We tried to do the heel test again but I couldn't. I could feel the atmosphere in the room changing. They told me they didn't think the epidural was working. The nerve damage was going on a little bit too long. They'd seen the likes of this before and knew how long it could take for a player to recover if it wasn't dealt with quickly. 'You need to see the specialist again and not next week,' I was told. 'Now.'

I've wondered since if I hadn't gone back in then, just how much more damage would have been caused. That was Thursday morning and by that evening I was back in the Mater, preparing for surgery. Poynton was away so Marcus Timlin was the surgeon who made the recommendation and who would do the surgery. I made the decision quickly once he spelt out the dangers of not doing anything. That swift choice was probably the influence of both Dad and Joe. They'd both always preached 'do what needs to be done' – it was always about honestly assessing problems and identifying solutions. There are obviously potential pitfalls with every surgery, but it was a chance I had to take if I was going to play again. So I rang Sheena and my folks and I made light of it, and on Friday at 6.30am the operation took place.

The doctors told me afterwards that they found a lot of damage to the disc once they'd gone in. Discs are a bit like doughnuts and there's a jelly inside them, and basically the thing had exploded and the jelly had oozed out and done a load of damage, impinging massively on a nerve. From what I'm told, they basically discarded all the stuff that had oozed out and sealed it up again. Job done. Or so I'd hoped.

Apparently, when I woke up after the surgery, I was asking questions about rehab and when I could start it because I had a lot of rugby I wanted to play. I was told that people usually get back to work after about six weeks. I was doing the maths and going, 'Yeah, that gives me a chance to play before the Lions tour.' The surgeon said, 'Well, the six weeks is what I tell people who are going to sit in an office.' Everybody in rugby sort of played along with me for the first couple of days after surgery. Then I was taken aside and gently told, 'Look, your season is over.' Slowly, I realised it was.

Bizarrely, there was still no pain, just a type of restriction, a stiffness. I was given a lot of OxyNorm after the surgery and more to bring home with me. I took some, but I didn't like it because it put me in a weird haze and, in any case, I didn't need it. That was one thing I got lucky with, I suppose.

I still had it in my head that I'd be back for the following season and that while I'd miss not being part of the Lions, I'd make the most of the time off I now had. I wasn't going on a rugby tour, so I could plan summer holidays with Sheena, the first time we could do that properly without looking for a last-minute trip in whatever small window was left open to us. I decided to do other things so I wouldn't feel sorry for myself, but I also planned to do all the rehab that would make a fully active professional rugby player again.

And then it all got worse.

After the surgery I had spent a long time lying on my back, as instructed, with as little movement as possible. I was extremely disciplined in how I approached my rehab. I wasn't allowed to leave the house for the first two weeks. I wasn't allowed to get in a car for four weeks. I wasn't allowed to train for six weeks. I don't think I'd gone six weeks without training since my first summer as a pro. I had never not trained. I may have varied the intensity, but I never missed training.

My only issue was with headaches. I would get them every time I stood up for more than a few minutes. At first I thought it might be the medication but they continued even after I came off it. They hadn't affected me when I was lying down, but they did their damage once I was standing for a longer period of time. I endured some savage headaches. I drink a lot of coffee and apparently that had helped dull the headaches that would otherwise have been made worse by even brief periods of standing.

The initial decision was to wait and see if it resolved itself, as can happen, without further medical intervention. It did seem to settle down, for a while at least, and in time, I went back into training. But when I got back to heavy running and training, the headaches started coming on again. It was a dull headache that went away once I lay down at home and rested, but then it would kick off again the next day when I went back training. I underwent another scan and they found a massive pool of fluid at the bottom of my spine. This is called a pseudomeningocele. It was decided that I should undergo a procedure called a blood patch, an injection that uses autologous (my own) blood to close the holes in the dura mater of the spinal cord – a bit like fixing a puncture on a bicycle tube – once all the fluid had been drained. That did the trick.

However, other problems continued with my recovery. As my training and rehab intensified, it also became clear that my range of motion was very limited, painful and, if anything, was disimproving. I tried desperately to avoid a second surgery, and so did the doctors, all of us trusting that the rehab work I was doing would do the necessary job. Unfortunately, things did not progress as I, or they, would have wanted. Now it wasn't just my rugby that was worrying me but my future quality of life. Eventually, we decided to go for the second surgery in September 2018. Then the whole process of rehab started again.

While all of this was going on, we also had to deal with a trauma involving our beloved dog Jay-Z.

I'd always wanted a dog. When I was young, we never had a dog in the house, probably because we were away a lot. But

I always played with and walked the neighbours' dogs. I loved the companionship you get with a dog, the unspoken bond.

I got Jay-Z early in 2010. I'd been living on my own for about 18 months. I had enjoyed having the space to myself initially, but in time I wanted company. I did my research, looking for a dog that didn't need a lot of exercise, that would be happy indoors, friendly, loyal and be a bit of a character. I decided to go with a Bulldog and found a breeder in Antrim who I was satisfied had a track record in breeding dogs in the right conditions. I went up during the snow of January 2010 and found this beautifully big-eyed but also very independent little character. It would prove to be one of the best decisions I ever made. I called him Jay-Z because I love all types of music, especially Hip Hop, and thought it would be cool to have a dog named after a rapper.

It was a steep learning curve at the start, with the toilet training, making sure he listened to commands and got enough exercise. The timing of my ankle injury in 2010 actually gave me the time to put in the training with him. That said, I was away from him a lot, travelling for matches and training camps, and it was around the time that Sheena came into my life. She's a dog lover too and she looked after him when I was away, and when we were both away we brought him to her mother's house in Skerries. Sharon already had one dog – and ended up with four – and Jay-Z loved his 'holidays' over there, battling with two German Shepherds to be the top dog.

The great thing about having Jay-Z was the escape he provided, the responsibility of giving him his food and walks, the companionship of scratching the inside of his ears. He got lots of late-night and early-morning walks after games, around Rathmines or Sandymount beach, or through Irishtown Park. I always felt better by the time I got home with him.

It was one of the worst days of my life when we learned in late 2016 that he had a form of canine bone cancer. I say 'we' because Jay-Z was as much Sheena and Sharon's pet as he was mine. We had noticed a little lump on his leg and brought him along to the vet. Straightaway I went into 'solution mode', but very quickly the vet let me know that there wasn't really a solution to the problem and that all we could do was slow the progress of the cancer and make things comfortable for him.

At first nothing really changed, but then Jay-Z started to slow down, then limp, then reluctantly get out of his bed. In his final weeks, we had him out in Skerries as we were then staying with Sharon for the summer of 2017. Those weeks were horrible and very upsetting to us all, watching as our little Jay-Z declined. It was horrible to see a dog who was once so vibrant, energetic and friendly struggle to even limp out of his bed. The right thing to do was put him out of his misery and all of us – me, Sheena and Sharon – cried about it. We haven't got another dog yet.

I started doing other things. In the summer of 2017 I did a short course at Harvard Business School, run by Anita Elberse, Professor of Business Administration. Professor Elberse is a leading expert on the entertainment, media and sports sectors and has published a great book called *Blockbuster* that is about creating and capturing value in those businesses, both for the corporate and the individual. I'd read it shortly before I was injured. The course was booked up, but Damien O'Donoghue had done it the year before and he worked his magic and got me a place.

It was a short, intensive course, from Wednesday to Saturday, very full days of lectures and evening reading. I checked in at the same time as the actress Katie Holmes, who arrived with a little golf cart full of all her stuff, which I presumed was her wardrobe and course materials. Gerard Piqué, the Barcelona and Spain footballer, World Cup winner and holder of multiple other titles, was there too, as well as former women's NBA players, former NFL players and a famous New York DJ. It was a collection of cool and interesting people from all over the world. I have a photo of me with Katie and Gerard, among others, as the header on my Twitter profile.

I downloaded all the case studies before I went over and read them. The classes were taught in a really interesting way. At first I thought it was meandering, but then I realised that it wasn't, that Professor Elberse was the orchestrator and we were all part of the band and she was directing us to where she wanted to go. I enjoyed it enormously, especially as it confirmed many of the decisions I had made over the years as well as opening my mind to new opportunities.

I hadn't written off my hopes of getting back to rugby, but I decided that I would keep details of all my efforts to return and my injury private. I did have some media responsibilities for sponsors, however, and inevitably questions came up. I admit that I did become a bit testy during one media briefing, especially when I was asked about having a second operation.

Question: 'We'll ask the obvious question first . . .'

Me: 'You'll get the obvious answer . . .'

Q: 'How are you feeling?'

Me: 'Good.'

Q: 'Any update on the prognosis? When you'll be back?'

Me: 'Nope. Nope.'

Q: 'No deadlines or timeline?'

Me: 'Nope. Nope.'

Q: 'I want to ask about the second operation . . .'

Me: 'Which operation? Who said I had a second operation? Who did?'

Q: 'Did you have one?'

Me: 'I am not going to give you an answer.'

Q: 'Are you definitely going to return?'

Me: 'I am not going to give you an answer . . . I have been very clear regarding my medical information. It's private. I'll get back on the field when I get back on the field. That's as best as I can give you. I don't mean to be hard on it, but medical information, I've been quite clear about [keeping it private], return to play . . . I'll be on the field when I'm fit and healthy.'

In retrospect, I don't regret keeping it private, at least while I still held out hope of returning to play. I realise that it led to all sorts of speculation and confusion, but as far as I was concerned I was in the most difficult period of my professional life, with my career on the line, and that wasn't up for public consumption. I'm sorry if the journalists didn't see it that way, but they had other stories to chase, matches to report on, and this was all I had.

It was in early February 2018 that I called a halt. I'd known from September, and from the time of the second operation, that, no matter how optimistic I always was, I was now seriously up against it if I was going to get back, but I couldn't say anything publicly without opening the door to more speculation. I'd had five months of dodging questions, trying to stay positive but wondering, fearing, trying to come to terms with the possibility that it could all be taken from me. I was training hard, some days I felt I was making a small bit of progress, other days I didn't. It really started to hit me from January, just how bad my situation was. I simply could not do the things I needed to do on the field to be a top-class number 8, I couldn't do my job.

I was reaching the point where I was able to make the decision when it was suddenly taken out of my hands. The surgeon, Ashley Poynton, called it: 'You're done, Jamie. You've tried everything and you can't go on. You are not able to continue your career as a professional rugby player as a direct result of the injury from the warm-up and, medically, I'm not signing off on you playing again. It's over.'

I knew he was right, so I didn't argue with him. I've always believed in getting the best to tell me about the things I'm not the best at. The surgeon was the expert, acknowledged to be the best in Ireland, one of the best in Europe. Did I want to play more? Yes. Did I want to go to the World Cup? Yes. Did he say I could do that? No.

My body wasn't able for professional sport any more. Worse, it wasn't quite right for day-to-day life any more. It took somebody from outside the rugby bubble to tell me. Bending, simple bending, had become a problem. Any heavy weight, what we call vertical loading, was an issue, which meant tackling, rucking, mauling were all difficult, as was lifting anyone in a line-out. It was tough, given the peak physical condition I'd been in and how hard I'd worked to reach and maintain it. But I was pragmatic. I'd enjoyed 14 years of this sport without any significant lay-offs. It wasn't as if I'd been cut off before I'd had the chance to do what I wanted. I can't say that I was too upset. Sheena was pregnant, we'd just bought a house that we were renovating and there was plenty of life left to live, things to do, places to see.

Sure, I would have loved to have been part of the 2018 Grand Slam team, to have played at the 2019 Rugby World Cup with possibly the best Irish squad ever, but it was the turn for other people now. I wasn't going to become a bitter ex-player. I was going to be happy with what I'd had and with what I would have to come. My optimism came through for me. I knew that very few people got the chance to go out on their own terms. It didn't happen for Paulie and it didn't happen for me either. Only Drico pulled that off, with a whole year to take a bow, two testimonial dinners and a farewell tour, but I don't begrudge him it because he was one of the game's iconic figures.

It was over. After meeting the surgeon, I rang my wife and then my parents and they weren't too surprised by the news. Then I rang Joe and that conversation was pretty matter-of-fact. There wasn't much he could say but sympathise and move on. I wasn't of any use to him now.

The next point of contact was David Nucifora, performance director at the IRFU, who I informed of my decision the week of the Wales game in the Six Nations. I was asked when I was going to announce it publicly. We agreed that I should do it on a down week during the championship, in case it was any distraction for the lads. What was really disappointing from my perspective was that they had a down week, then the Italy game week, then another down week and in those three weeks I had no contact from anyone in the IRFU. Then the HR department sent me my P45 and told me I had one more month's wages coming to me and that was it. I would have been covered by the IRFUs insurance for another 12 months after the injury, but after that I would be left to look after that my health insurance and other things.

The contrast between the IRFU and Leinster was remarkable. Leinster was unbelievably good, sympathetic and responsive. Mick Dawson was great. He tried to sell me a season ticket immediately, always the salesman, but I knew he was doing it in the right spirit. He invited me to the home quarter-final in the European Cup, so we could do an on-field sign-off. Later, there was a presentation at the end of year awards. It took the

IRFU two years to do anything to mark my departure, and
then only because the senior players kicked up a fuss. I was
a bit hurt and disappointed by it, and I'm not embarrassed
to say so, but it only emphasises how much the game is
a business. And I had prepared for it – what about those
who haven't?

I had invested a lot in rugby. It's a complete lifestyle and it
demands so much of you. There is much talk about the values
of the sport, but there is a contradiction in that it has become
all about business. Too many players don't realise that fact
until it is too late in their career. I was prepared for the end,
but I can see that for many players it will be a massive shock,
both how their career comes to an end and how there is not
a whole lot of process to make it easier for them to move on.
I don't know if the IRFU or Leinster as employers should be
legally bound to look after players in that transition period or
not. It felt like a very clear-cut transaction: we pay you to play
rugby, we don't pay you to look after you.

We organised a press release, making the announcement
on Monday 26 February 2018. Leo made a statement on behalf
of Leinster that I greatly appreciated, an acknowledgement of
what I'd done for the club. I went into the Leinster dressing-
room the weekend before the announcement and removed
my name from my hanger. I sent this message to the Leinster
WhatsApp group:

Brothers,

It's been a hell of a ride. First got to wear the blue of
Leinster in 2001 for Leinster schools and the sense of
pride I have in that jersey and this club ever since never
wavered. Some of you I've played with, some only

against and some I've only eaten with. What we've all shared is that drive to leave the jersey in a better place.

I hope I've played my part in that.

I'll miss a lot of things but grateful for the memories. You all know I love a brew, so always around to catch up.

Catch you in the afterlife.

Jamie.

I immediately removed myself from the group, before anyone could comment.

Announcing my retirement was a massive weight off my mind. There was almost a sense of relief when it was done. I think I had prepared myself for it, consciously and subconsciously, even as I was trying to make a return. As a result, I was ready to go, to move on to the next part of my life.

CHAPTER 16

MORE THAN A GAME

I stayed with Leinster and Ireland for my entire career, but I never allowed my heart to rule my head when it came to negotiating contracts. I was never shy about looking for my financial value, particularly as playing rugby can be a very short career. I always reckoned I'd do well if I got six years at the top level, to win titles but also to make the money I would need to set up me for life after rugby.

The sport is a commercial operation. Our problem, as players, is that the professional game is young and still rooted in its amateur past. It means that we don't always get what we should. The cards can be stacked against us. Young players are reluctant to ask for what they are worth, which is probably an Irish thing as well. I made a conscious decision not to do that. I approached it like any other business deal, aiming to get my maximum fair market value. I utilised my hard-won position in the team by negotiating from a position of strength at key points in my career. Plenty of players have had to take deals that weren't the best for them because of injuries or loss of form at negotiating time, or because they were getting older and could see the end line if they didn't make the deal. In my experience, the clubs don't do sentiment, so why should the players?

Academy players were probably better paid when I broke through than they are now because there were fewer of us then. There are so many kids now who will take what's offered just to get on the ladder. I was lucky that my brother Graham had played professional rugby and knew enough to help negotiate my first professional contract with Mick Dawson, the chief executive at Leinster. Graham had an idea what players were being paid and he secured what was at the time probably the best contract a new player like myself would have been able to sign. It was great money for a young fellow of my age, about 40 or 50 grand a year. There I was, effectively a college graduate, getting that money, with bonuses on top and match fees. Insane.

Even better, Leinster started talking about a new, improved, longer deal by Christmas of my first season in the senior team. Graham quickly realised that it was going to a level beyond which he could guide me. 'Look, we're going to ring around, we're going to find out who the best guy is,' he said. 'We're going to meet a couple of different agents.' I was happy to listen to him because I knew that, at the time, I was out of my depth at the negotiating table.

That's how I ended up with Fintan Drury, who owned the Platinum Agency. Fintan represented a wide variety of athletes and had experience of doing proper contracts in more established disciplines, like soccer. He also knew the business of sport outside of Ireland. He didn't have many rugby players on his books and that suited me. If an agent has lots of players, he might start cutting deals on some to get benefits for others. You could become a bargaining chip in a bigger game because the pool of money the employers can negotiate with the agents is finite. Fintan took over the negotiations in late 2005 and got me onto a better contract with Leinster. We agreed that once I had made a certain amount of international starts, I would automatically be offered negotiations on an upgrade to a national contract. This was before I had ever played for Ireland. Then that happened very quickly and I ended up negotiating a new contract in 2008, when I got onto the Six Nations side. We added a clause for extra payment if I was selected for the British & Irish Lions in 2009. I made the Lions tour and got some really great bonuses from the IRFU off that, as well as being paid by the Lions.

I always sought longer contracts, to ensure I wouldn't have to continually worry about the state of play. On a two-year contract, you basically have only one year where you aren't anxious about the next contract. The minute you start that second season, you're worrying about the next deal. With this in mind, we negotiated a three-year contract in 2008. There was another benefit to this because it would be revisited in June 2011, when I would be only months away from the World Cup. All going well, that would put me in a strong negotiating position if things were going well and I was starting regularly for Ireland going into the World Cup that autumn.

In 2011, I genuinely considered taking some time out after the World Cup, even though it would mean missing the 2012 Six Nations. My idea was to play in Japan for a time after the World Cup, then move to the Southern Hemisphere and play some Super 14 rugby and return to Ireland in the summer. The IRFU wouldn't hear of it. Instead, earlier in the year, to get it out of the way quickly, I was offered a three-year contract.

By that stage, Fintan had left the agency game and I needed a new representative. I contacted Damien O'Donoghue, who had worked with the music promoters MCD. He had set up his own agency, Ikon Talent, and was looking after Church. I decided to join him. Damien was cut from the same mould as Fintan, who'd had no interest in scratching the backs of the IRFU. Fintan's only interest was in what was best for me. If that had meant me going to France instead of staying in Ireland, then that's what he would have recommended. He explored my options. Damien would do the same. The two of them were very similar.

I left it largely to them. If the IRFU tried to drag me personally into contract talks, I refused. 'I have an agent for this, I'm not dealing with this,' I told them. Coaches and managers would try to pull you in, separate you from your agent, and I always thought that was unfair, particularly to the younger players who might not be confident in their positions. It was hilarious what Joe tried to pull with me once. It was January 2011 and the contract talks were under way when he called me into his office. 'Look, what's the story with your contract?' he asked. 'I don't want to particularly talk about it, Joe, because that's why I've got an agent,' I replied. However, I did tell him that I was looking at the market to see what my value was. And he said, 'Okay, yeah, that's fine, but can you hurry up and make your decision because I've got this guy lined up to come in as 8 from the Southern Hemisphere?' I didn't know what to believe. I just said, 'Oh, okay.' I have no idea if he did or didn't have a new candidate or if he was trying to pressure me to sign quickly, but I suppose he had to know and if I was going, he had his own decisions to make. I had no problem with him about that. I preferred people to be blunt and upfront with me, which Joe always was.

The 2011 contract I signed was for three years. In 2014 I signed for another three years, and in that one Bank of Ireland was involved in topping up the money I got from Leinster and Ireland with a separate commercial contract to do some sponsorship work for it. It was one of the first of these kinds of deals done in Ireland to allow the IRFU and clubs compete with what French clubs could offer, and it has happened many times since. It was reported in the media that it was the best deal ever signed by an Irish international at the time, but I have no interest in confirming to anyone if it was or what I was being paid. That's personal. When negotiating that 2014 contract, Drico was in his last season and it was clear that Paulie didn't have too much time left in his career either. Johnny was in France with Racing 92, a move that had caused consternation. I was able to leverage all of that with the IRFU. However, this was also the time that I came closest to leaving Leinster and Ireland.

I gave serious consideration to moving to France to play my rugby and I made no secret of that. Just because I had apparently become the country's highest-paid player in 2011 didn't mean that I should be grateful for that come 2014 and resign on terms that weren't good enough. The initial 2014 offer was actually less attractive than the 2011 one. The talks with the IRFU had started in late 2013, on the back of my time as captain, which was coming to an end. Damien spoke to Montpellier, but that didn't look too attractive and the discussions didn't go too far. Then Toulon, the richest club in France, got involved and given the money they were spending, I had to be interested. Bernard Laporte was in charge at the time, so I flew down to Toulon to meet him and we walked around the facility. Damien and I looked at a house overlooking the Mediterranean and it wasn't a bad place to live, to put it mildly. I examined the idea closely and I was serious about it. I wasn't bluffing.

There was an extra factor, however, in that I had to take Sheena into account. We were now living together and if she was going to move with me to another country, she'd have to make sacrifices too. There were a number of different aspects in play, not just the lifestyle in the south of France and the money. Damien told the IRFU what Toulon had offered and what it had to do to match that. There was a stand-off. The IRFU said it had reached a point from which it wouldn't budge; I was happy to leave if it didn't.

In early 2014, I drove out to Carton House to join the Irish camp for Six Nations training with a Toulon contract in my glove compartment. I knew this was a do-or-die moment in my career, that this season's internationals could potentially be my last for Ireland, that I might not get the same level of flexibility about playing for Ireland that Johnny had been granted. Damien had scheduled one last meeting with the IRFU. I knew what my market value was, but I also put a price on going abroad. If I went, I was in danger of not being picked for Ireland again and I had to put a value on that. It had to be worth my while to leave. Let's just say a contract abroad is paying €100,000 and a contract at home is paying €50,000; the gap is the value that you put on living abroad and not playing for Ireland. But there is more to it than that. I had to weigh up the fact that I'd get better looked after in Ireland when it came to physical demands, the number of matches played and the gaps between games, and that in turn might lengthen my career and earning potential. It was mad, though, that Damien was negotiating this the same week as I was playing a Six Nations international.

I tried to take emotion out of it. I wanted to stay, but I wouldn't have worried about it had I gone somewhere else. I wouldn't have felt like a traitor for playing with Toulon. Nobody called Johnny a traitor for going to Paris. Paulie would have played for Toulon after leaving Munster if his career hadn't been ended by injury. It wouldn't have been my preference, but if it was the better deal, I was prepared to go to Toulon.

I arrived at Carton House and was just pulling into the car park when Damien phoned me. It was good news about the IRFU and the contract. 'They've moved to that point at which we need to be,' he told me. The relief was enormous. It was like getting my Leaving Cert results. Decision made. I had a line and the IRFU had reached it. I had a good three-year contract in the bag and I could throw myself into my work once again.

I signed another contract, my last, in February 2017, only weeks before the England game that would prove to be my last time pulling on the green jersey. It was an even better deal financially than the one struck in 2014, taking me up until after the end of the 2019 World Cup.

It helped that I was shortlisted for the World Player of the Year in 2016, for the first time since 2009, but I made it clear I didn't see that as a finishing point. I was focused on doing much better at the next World Cup. I wanted to win another Heineken Cup, a Grand Slam, go on another Lions tour. I was greedy, but if I hadn't wanted to do those things, what would have been the point of signing another contract with Leinster and Ireland?

I earned my salary and I provided value to my employers for it. When I signed my 2017 contract, I had started 36 of Ireland's previous 41 matches. I had averaged 30 games per season for club and country over the previous 10 years. My reply to anyone who cribbed about it was, 'Cheapest player by minutes played.' Isa Nacewa was one of the best players ever to play for Leinster, but I used to ask him, tongue in cheek, 'Isa, can I get one of your contracts where you don't have to train on a Monday?' Or I'd say to Seanie, 'Can I get one of yours where you don't have to train on a Tuesday and a Friday?' I'm not complaining about what they got, because when they were on the pitch they were great for us, but I had a track record, an injury record that was one of the shortest of any Irish player and a reasonable expectation that I could continue to deliver for the money I earned.

David Nucifora, who manages all the players in the Irish system in tandem with Joe, publicly explained the decision on the basis that I was one of the top performers in international rugby and that I delivered a high level of performance every time I pulled on the green or blue jersey. Mick Dawson said that I continued to set standards for others at Leinster. I was happy with the money, but also with the level of ambition that had been restored at Leinster. Stuart Lancaster's work as our head coach, since taking on the role in September 2017, filled me with optimism.

My last three contracts may have broken down some sticking points the IRFU had about what and how they paid their players. I wasn't always paid according to games or minutes, but once I crossed a threshold of a certain number of games in a season, my retainer went up in addition to the match fee and other bonus stuff that was fairly standard. One contract increased my base layer, another focused on bonuses for games played. On my last deal I secured a set fee per international game that would increase every year.

Players on the same team don't get paid the same, there isn't a standard rate of pay. It's a team game but it's not socialism. It's only human that players sometimes think they deserve more than what they're getting and are jealous of what others are getting. But if one player pushes for more, it tends to set the bar higher and everyone can benefit from that. Although there is a finite pot of money, so if someone is getting more, somebody else may receive less. I've never found any animosity between players over it – at least, not to my face.

When I started playing, all some players were interested in was getting a discount at Eden Park when buying clothes and little bonuses on top of their salary. They were just happy to be on board, viewing their contracts as a means to allow them to do what they wanted to do. They didn't realise that they were worth more and that they needed to provide a buffer for the future, for when they weren't playing. They didn't see themselves as brands with individual power, but rather as part of a collective brand, the team of which they were a member for a period of time.

It can be hard for a player to think of himself as a brand in order to generate money away from his core contract. I looked at American sports, at what the top American athletes did. I always thought Michael Jordan was amazing in the way he used his brand. He had money from his playing contracts in basketball, but he was a billionaire off the back of the deals he struck to receive equity in other ventures, instead of just fees for lending his name to their advertising campaigns. He took less money for endorsements with Nike than he could have got from other sportswear firms, but he took equity in the company. LeBron James and Kobe Bryant did that, too. I know I'm not remotely near their level, but I took the lessons and applied them to the Irish market, looking at the deals on offer, trying to create longer-term value rather than short-term gain.

I didn't regard my contract with the IRFU as merely a platform to get money from deals outside the game, to allow me to capture the value elsewhere. The contract had to have its best value in itself. But it also shouldn't stop me from doing other things. The brand being sold by the IRFU is the team, not the player. You have to step away from that occasionally as a player and think of your own individual brand, to generate money away from your contract. The players are slow to think of themselves as brands, but you can be sure that when the IRFU ties up with a sponsor, it's thinking of the group of players as a brand it can leverage, and very often for little additional money to the players used in campaigns.

Look at the situation with image rights, for example. If you see an image on an advertisement, be it television or a billboard, and there are three or more players pictured, then none of those players is getting paid for that. All the money goes to the IRFU or the club branch. The best the player can hope for is that the advertiser pays him a fee to be available for the photoshoot on the day. My belief is that if the IRFU holds the image rights, then they should do a revenue share with the entire pool of players, not just those appearing: the rising tide should raise all boats.

Fintan Drury bought into my belief of being a brand, of getting value from it by not overexposing myself with too many deals outside rugby. When it comes to outside opportunities for extra income using the personal brand, too many players look for volume. They do a lot of things for what seems good money, but they almost kill the marketplace for everyone else if they're doing everything for a fiver and they make your €25 by doing five events when it should really be €25 for one. Really good players, like Dan Carter, have been really clever about this over the last couple of decades, and Brian O'Driscoll and Paul O'Connell were good at it too. I'm aware that some people perceived me as paying too much attention to my brand and commented upon it, but I wasn't the first player to do so and I surely won't be the last.

Unfortunately, the marketplace in Ireland isn't as competitive as somewhere like the UK or France. There are not as many big brands in the country that have that kind of money to spend, but that's not to say that players should do things cheaply. More quality in terms of value for yourself should be the watchword. Both Fintan and Damien saw it, Fintan from football, Damien from music. Damien is big into the blockbuster philosophy of creating value and then capturing it at its maximum point, and that's what I always did.

I know the economics of rugby are not the same as Premier League football, but it's possible to bring to it the same philosophy of getting more for the players. In rugby, the players' group does not get a slice of the revenue as a collective. I looked at the NFL, at the NBA and I saw how the players came together as a group and used their collective bargaining agreements to extract value from the game. I would love to create more value in the game of rugby so that players are better off when they finish, so that their personal value is rewarded and trickles down to them financially.

I realised quite a few things about my personal finances early on. One was that I would have to work after I had finished playing, but that I most likely wouldn't ever get a job that would pay as well as rugby unless I became the chief executive of something, and that would probably have to be of something that I was involved in creating. But I have also seen too many friends in careers or jobs that they had come to hate, even at a young age, but continued to do because they needed the money. I knew I didn't want to do post-rugby jobs just for the money. My big fear of life after rugby was doing something I didn't want to do out of financial necessity. I'd seen that happen to a lot of guys – they have outgoings, a family, and the real world comes in on top of them. I was lucky in my twenties and early thirties to be doing something that I absolutely loved, but I saw how miserable some of my friends were when they were in jobs they absolutely hated. I never wanted to be in that position.

I don't expect to ever make the money outside rugby that I did in rugby. I'd be amazed if I did. Some guys think they're going to walk into a job that pays them six figures straight out of the gate, which is ridiculous when you think how hard it is in general to get a job that pays you six figures. I was aware from an early stage that I would leave the rugby bubble and join the workforce, where my peers would have had a 10- to 15-year headstart on me in building careers. Some players want to stay in the bubble by getting jobs in coaching, but that never appealed to me. I can see why lots of players want to remain on in the sport, particularly if their whole life to date has been dominated by rugby. It's easier to stay than to go out into the real world.

There's an illusion, however, that there are lots of options available in rugby, lots of jobs. There aren't. If you want to do coaching, your family is going to have to be pretty mobile, moving to wherever jobs are available and usually not for long enough to put down roots. The time involved in going to so many games, being at your own games before and after the players, the preparation and reviews, I wouldn't like that lifestyle. It would be too demanding. If I were to be involved, I'd much prefer helping out on the performance side of getting players match-ready. I've toyed with the idea, but never seriously. While I'm enjoying some time now in rugby media (in 2019) and like the idea of developing a career in broadcasting, especially podcasting, radio and some television, my preference, if I were to stay in rugby, would be in the business end of running a club. There are few enough jobs in that, however, and now that I'm settled with family, the idea of dragging Sheena and the baby around from job to job doesn't really appeal. I like Dublin, so I don't particularly want to leave Dublin.

I also realised that once a rugby career finishes, a lot of doors that were held open because of celebrity are closed. I used to get slagged by the lads in the dressing-room a lot, 'Oh Jamie, who are you going off meeting today on your down day?', or 'Who are you meeting for a coffee today?' Big laugh. I kept saying to them, 'Like, lads, when you're playing, there are people who want to know you, so pick one and it can be a great door-opener for you.'

My goal was to retire with a financial cushion that would give me flexibility in making choices for life after rugby. I wanted to have the mortgage paid off, or near enough, so I wouldn't be worried about repaying debt, and to have enough in the kitty to do as I wanted. That, I suppose, is what most people look for at the age of 65 or so, when they retire. I was going to be retiring sometime around the age of 30 and even if I continued to work, it would be for a lot less money. I set up a pension as soon as I signed my first professional contract, a direct debit taking the money every month so it never went through my hands.

I was still able to enjoy myself being on a six-figure salary in my early twenties, something very few people of that age can do. I spent a lot on gadgets, clothes and nights out. Gadgets are to me what shoes and bags are to some people I know.

From the start I put a lot of my money beyond my reach and saved it. I set up standing orders and savings accounts and denied myself access. It wasn't just the pension that I put money into, I also decided to invest. Someone, can't remember who, told me to buy a property every two years and build a portfolio, then to use the special tax refund available to Irish-based professional players at the end of my career to pay off the balance of the mortgages. The idea, as proposed to me, was to live off the rent from them at that stage or to sell them and use the money for other things. It was pure Celtic Tiger advice. I bought two properties before I reached the age of 25. Everyone was doing it at the time, the height of the boom, before the 2008 crash. I bought my first apartment in 2006, when I was 22. It was on Cork Street, near Dublin city centre, and I loved living there. Two years later I bought my house in Irishtown. It seemed like I bought it on a Monday and the recession kicked in on Tuesday. The property crash left me in negative equity on two residential investments and I didn't buy any more. But at least I was young and had time to recover the loss. I was lucky, I was getting paid very well so I was able to ride the wave.

I enjoyed the opportunity to invest in companies. I decided that if I was going to create long-term value for myself, I would have to own things rather than just be an employee. I leveraged my worth. If somebody came to me looking for a commercial endorsement that I valued it at, say, €5,000 but they only had €2,500 to spend, I'd say, 'Okay, it's two-and-a-half K in a payment, but you're going to give me two-and-a-half K worth of equity in the company as well.' That worked.

I invested in CocoFuzion 100, a coconut-water sports drinks business. I used to give out bottles of it to the Leinster players. It was part of C7 Brands, which became part of Prime Active Capital (PAC), where I then owned a 2.6% share. I became involved in the website Lovin Dublin, founded by Niall Harbison, which is all about food and social life in Dublin. I also got into restaurants myself.

I didn't actually own or part-own the restaurant Bear, as everyone thought. I gave it a loan on commercial terms – at a premium rate – and the use of my name, for which I received a revenue share but no downside. We positioned it as if I was a part-owner and they got plenty out of that deal in terms of exposure and marketing. I'd eat at the restaurant, do photo shoots, a couple of events, standard enough ambassador-type stuff. I was trying to get more involved in the business, but as I did, I realised I didn't want to be in the restaurant business because it's so bloody tough. My accountant/advisor Ciarán Medlar was the one who came up with the idea of a loan instead of a straightforward investment. I did it for two or three years and then got out of it.

I have stayed in the pub business, though. I invested with Noel Anderson, the main owner of The Bridge 1859 in Ballsbridge and Lemon and The Duke off Grafton Street. The Kearney brothers, Rob and Dave, and Sean O'Brien are in on those, too. We own a leasehold at Lemon and at Duke and we own the freehold and building at Bridge 1859, which is located just around the corner from the RDS and the Leinster home ground. We bought the building in 2014 and we've traded well since.

I always chose to invest in things that I was interested in, partly to figure out if they were one of the industries or businesses I wanted to go into after my rugby career ended. The very first thing I ever invested in was Providence Medical Technology, which my brother was involved with at the time, an innovator in tissue-sparing surgical equipment and implants for cervical spine fusion surgery. It produced a neck implant for people who might have degenerating vertebrae or discs or who had suffered from an impact where the disc and the nerve were impinged. I understood the concept from my time studying medical engineering, so I was comfortable investing in it. I'm still involved, and the company is looking to the American market to try to expand to the point where it can be bought out, which hopefully will happen. Providence has raised a total of $53 million in equity financing since its 2008 inception, so obviously my stake has been diluted a lot.

Through these investments I was trying to learn more about the different industries, but it meant I became sort of known as 'the tech guy' among rugby people. That became part of my brand, I suppose, and people started coming to me with ideas in which I could become involved as an investor. It wasn't obvious that a rugby player would be involved in these kinds of company, but when I showed a real interest in the people and their teams, and in the technology, it snowballed from there.

Kitman was a no-brainer to me as an investment because I understood exactly what it was and could achieve. It's a sports analytical company that collects data and analyses it using artificial intelligence and machine learning to predict future performance. The aim is to get the player performing at the optimal level. The original idea was developed by Stephen Smith, who was Leinster's expert on rehab and prehab under Cheika. Stephen posed the question as to whether it would be possible to use the data gathered by the players' GPS trackers, which he had introduced, to assess the indicators for the occurrence of injuries. Kitman looks to protect what vulnerabilities players have to injury and reoccurrence, based on analysis of their personal data.

Stephen left Leinster to set up the company and then won a competition for some seed funding. They needed more, so he came to me. I understood what he was trying to do and signed up and gave the startup some money. I used my contacts at the Web Summit – which I had attended as a guest in the early years when Paddy Cosgrave put it on in Dublin, before moving it to Lisbon – to put Kitman in touch with Bluerun Ventures, run by an American called John Malloy, which was one of the first investors in PayPal. Bluerun ended up being our big angel investor in Kitman Labs. Malloy had played some rugby himself in the US and understood quickly what we wanted to do. Some of the investments I make I don't expect to exit for five to ten years. Kitman is about six years old now, so I keep in touch regularly because I want to know where it's going, whether it will pay a dividend to me or whether it will accelerate growth to be bought out.

UrbanVolt is another of my favourites. It installs LED energy-saving lights as a retrofit. The shareholders take little enough money upfront for the capital expenditure involved in providing and putting in the LED lighting, but a percentage of the savings that the client makes over the following five years accrues to us. After that, the product belongs to the customer. We're currently looking at expanding into solar and other forms of renewable energy, all with a view to improving efficiency. We've gone international and into retrofitting old buildings.

I also got involved in Flender, an online peer-to-peer lending company, where small and medium-sized businesses can arrange debt finance. It enables businesses and consumers to lend and borrow money through an app that links in with social network connections. There are no lenders' fees attached, unlike most platforms, but there is a success fee and what the company calls 'a small interest margin'. It has full authorisation from the UK financial regulator to operate in Britain and a number of successful entrepreneurs have invested in it as the business rolls out into Europe. It's going up in value, but until it is bought by someone else or starts paying dividends, I'm not placing a capital value on it.

That's a lesson my advisors have taught me. John Malloy has been very helpful in that regard, explaining how to understand value. I also apply basic common sense. It's great hearing, 'Oh that investment you made at x is now at x plus whatever', but I say, 'Okay, that's great, but can I sell that share now? If not now, is there going to be an initial public offering (IPO) because I want to know if there's a market into which I can sell my share. Am I able to sell it to someone else or does the group buy it off me? Are my shares liquid, easy to sell?' It's more prudent for me to plan for them not to come through than to plan for them to come through. Patience is the key. So somebody tells me I've made money, but as far as I'm concerned I haven't yet because no cash has gone into my company account or personal accounts. It's good to know that valuations have gone up, but that's all there is to it … as yet. Have I invested in any duds? I can't say that I have yet.

Enda McNulty, the sports psychologist I worked with for years, persuaded me to look at my business interests with the same level of attention I gave to rugby. He told me to add value wherever I went, even if I didn't necessarily always have confidence in that regard. In business, I've always been conscious of going from being an expert in what I did, rugby, to not being an expert at all. But I still think I can bring value. I made it a rule that if I was going to a board meeting, for example, I would know the numbers and understand the board pack given in advance of the meeting. It's not like I'm going to be telling the finance director what the numbers really mean, but I'm not going to be left there not understanding what's going on and not being able to say something if asked. I have to bring some value to the process.

As a successful rugby player, I'd got used to the pats on the back, being told what a good player I was, how good a game I'd played, but that didn't happen any more when I stopped playing. I was Ordinary Jamie now, determined not to go off the rails and to have a new structure ready to step into.

There has been one drawback. Since retiring I have been caught in a legal dispute with my insurers, who refused to pay my claim for compensation upon retirement. It is heading towards a High Court hearing. I have filed an action against two insurance companies, International Insurance Company of Hannover SE and Great Lakes Re-Insurance (UK) SE, looking for what is legally called specific performance, which means an order to compel them to fulfil the contract by paying out the sum insured.

The insurance issue has been a major frustration because I had done the right thing, the sensible thing, by taking out insurance. It wasn't to make money, it was a protection and I purchased it as that. I knew what my contract was worth and my insurers knew, and they provided cover, at a price, for circumstances in which I was unable to earn money from the IRFU and Leinster. If players actually looked at the insurance on their own playing contracts, they'd see it's pretty pathetic. You need your own insurance. The insurance contract, when I signed it, provided me with a degree of reassurance should anything happen to me.

Unfortunately, something did happen.

The insurers knew my medical history before selling me the policy, had signed off on it and took my premiums. But when it came to making the payment, they refused. It's as if they said to me, 'Tough, you were getting old'. So I'm suing to get payment. By the time it gets to court it could be more than two years after my date of retirement, three years after my last game. Although

I remain an optimistic person, the insurance has been a bit of a stress, particularly as it is out of my hands.

I've been lucky in that I've never suffered depression, even if the issue about the insurance has upset me. I've always been quite positive about things. They say three of the most stressful things in life are changing career, having a child and moving home. I did all three in the year I retired from rugby.

Initially when I retired, I did get antsy. It's not just the money that players miss when a career ends. It's the emotional highs and lows, the respect you earn for being among the best at what you do. In a new environment, you find you're bottom of the totem pole. The life you lead after a career as a professional rugby player is a lot tougher. It's very hard to keep believing in 'Next Ball' then.

Despite my preparation and awareness of the looming issues, I missed the structure of my daily life as it had been for nearly a decade and a half. I tried to create my own structure but the income issue, its inconsistency, dragged on me. Just because I had tried my best didn't mean that things were happening as I'd expected. I tried to address things head-on and not run away from them, but it was difficult without set goals to achieve. I no longer had an injury to overcome, with the potential of playing at another World Cup to follow. I became aware of the things that might never happen. I had to come up with new plans. Control the controllables, as Joe would say, but be comfortable in the new chaos, as Stuart would say. Trust in myself and go with it.

I thought of returning to full-time education. When I did engineering at college, we had one business module in the whole four years of study, yet I was curious about business. I followed my interest and did a master's in management at the

Smurfit Business School. I started it in 2008 and finished in 2014, doing one or two modules a semester, working around my training and playing schedule, which is why it took nearly six years to complete. It gave me a grounding in accounting, HR, marketing and other things. Since retiring, I've toyed with the idea of doing a master's in business administration, but decided against it because it would merely be an extension of what I've already done. I'd pay loads of money for it, take 18 months out to do it and still really be no better off career-wise.

I knew that what I really needed was relevant experience that I could put on my CV. I'd done several business internships over the years, during holidays from rugby, and one of the contacts I'd made during my time with the Irish squad helped me. John Herlihy, then head of Google Ireland, now at LinkedIn, came to camp once to speak to us. Mick Kearney had a great network of businesspeople and others that he used to bring in to talk to us, to break the boredom and to open our minds. I wrote John Herlihy a note of thanks after his talk and asked if I could see the Google offices in Dublin sometime. He invited me in, walked me around and set up a week-long placement for me, allowing me to visit various parts of the Dublin campus. John then left for LinkedIn, but I kept in touch with Ronan Harris at Google. In late 2018 I was told that there were jobs coming up and I applied. I had to work hard to get selected and I did a lot of preparation for four interviews back-to-back, two weeks after my daughter was born, so I was surviving on very little sleep and Sheena was an absolute hero, giving me the time I needed to prepare for them. I got the job in December 2018.

So now I'm with Google as a senior account manager in an Irish large client services team. I'm a consultant, a project manager, with a little bit of sales, advertising and marketing thrown in. I'm across four different verticals, or industries, with a couple of different clients in each. There's great variety in the job and in the organisation. It's like drinking from the fire hose right now. There's so much information coming at me that it's almost impossible to take it all in. People think of Google as a search engine, but it's way more than that, with cloud services, Gmail, YouTube and other businesses and billions upon billions of users. It's an organisation that really looks after its staff, but it's also big enough to allow me to switch areas, to learn more. Even if they move me on or I decide to leave, it's great to have on my CV. My country manager Cera Ward, my manager Ross Mooney and the rest of the UKI team led by Conor Jones have been a great help to me.

I'm in a work environment now where I have to reboot my responses and reactions to situations because they're so hardwired from my time in rugby, where they worked so effectively for me. I can't necessarily be as demanding of others as I was in the rugby environment because I may not understand all the factors at play. I can't demand immediate actions because they may not be the right ones. I have to learn something new.

There are other things of value from rugby that I can bring to my new career. Over the years I've learnt so much about working with people, leading and reading them, being led, the need for different skillsets and development of them, seeing people react under pressure, be it constant or unexpected, how they deal with it when times are good and when they are bad, how disciplined they are, the processes they go through to get ready for high-pressure scenarios. In my work I want to be in high-performance environments because that's what

I'm used to. I've used my profile to get meetings with chief executives over the years, to learn from them, because while I have developed certain skills, I don't have others and there are industries I don't know or understand. I have confidence in myself that I'll learn the hard skills part, but it may be harder to develop the emotional intelligence as quickly as I did in a sports environment. That realisation is important because it enables me to realise where my shortcomings are and what I need to improve. Feedback is something I crave and I get it at Google, direct, honest and constant. If I make mistakes, I learn and move on. I love the problem-solving environment we have here, both internal and external. I love the structure, the processes, the scale and the team I'm in.

I still like working in teams. I like the discipline and the routine in any effective team, how you prepare, recover, achieve a balance, review, give honest feedback. I suppose I use my experience in rugby as a metaphor, but I am aware that I'm going through a major transition. I remain interested in performance. I liked the book by Tim Ferris, The *4-Hour Work Week*, because it goes into optimal performance. I like the deep dives, the insights, such as that 20% of the things you do will give 80% of your return. When you dive deep, you find these little nuggets that give you the marginal gains.

In business I would eventually like to be involved in big, blockbuster events instead of high-volume, low-value transactions. I like helping clients get to a high-performance environment themselves. I like where I'm at with Google and I'm grateful. How far I'll progress within the company I don't know, but I like it and I'm learning every day. I say to myself, 'Amn't I lucky to be 35 years old and learning something brand new again?'

THE AFTERLIFE

I have ongoing issues with my back. It gets sore a lot and if I do too much, I get weakness down my legs. I can't sit or stand for long periods without moving or it starts going all tight on me, the same way as it did when I was doing my recovery training after the operations, the training that didn't work for me. I lose power. I have to be careful travelling, getting plenty of leg room and ensuring I can lie down or move around when flying long distance. I certainly won't be able to play golf. I've been told that I have to stay fit, to be healthy and strong, as anyone would, but it won't be to my old athletic standards. I lost a lot of weight after I retired, dropping to 101kg, but I thought I was getting too skinny and built back up a little bit, to about a healthy 104kg.

I will remain in touch with rugby for as long as I can. I like doing match commentary and punditry and other media work and ambassador work, but how long will I get out of it? The number of players coming out of the game looking to do just that, and the media and corporate desire to have the new person, new voice, new hero, means that might be a limited career.

I'm giving time to the International Rugby Players body, speaking up on the issues I believe are important. I was at a World Rugby anti-doping committee meeting recently and people were saying, 'Oh, everyone's getting bigger and faster, stronger,' as if that was a bad thing. I believe it's a logical consequence of professionalism. Lads are training in a more systematic way and because there's money behind it, people are investing in the science of strength and conditioning. That's what anyone in a business would do. I think rugby can learn from the mistakes made by other sports, given that the professional game is young and still evolving.

I worry about the level of physical impact and the issue of 'player loads' as much as about the actual game time. An enormous amount is demanded of players that is not necessarily normal in a work environment but remains a product of the old amateur days. It is not 9–5 at the best of times, but the demands are enormous. If you go to a World Cup or to the Six Nations, you are required to sleep away from your family, sometimes for weeks at a time. You may struggle to get sick leave or parental leave, to get time off when needed. You have to deal with the media – often about personal things – in a way few employees have to do. It can be tough mentally as well as physically and this is not always acknowledged, let alone addressed. Players aren't always treated as assets but sometimes as expenses.

I also have serious concerns about the bubble into which the modern generation of players steps – straight from Academy to professional game, without the advantage of enough education – and how they will cope with what happens when they finish playing. Do we want rugby to be like the NFL in the USA, where 80% of the players are either bankrupt or divorced or both within three years of finishing up? One of the things I've become more conscious of since retiring is the friendships I've made in the game. When I first came into the Leinster squad, I did feel a little distance, partly because of my age and partly because, having gone to school in Kildare, I didn't know guys from the rugby-playing schools in Dublin who dominated its make-up, but people like Malcolm O'Reilly, Keith Gleeson, Ronnie McCormack, Brian Blaney and Reggie Corrigan were good at getting me in. Then younger lads came in like Rob, Ferg and Sexto, and others like Chubbo and Paul O'Donohoe. Then later Seanie, Dominic Ryan and Mike McCarthy all became friends.

I keep in touch with current players, conscious they have the demands on their schedule that I used to have on mine. Church, obviously, is the one I see most. We've always got on, and have spent so much time together over the years, rooming when away with Leinster and Ireland, having so many similar interests outside the game. He was brilliant during my attempt to come back, encouraging me because he had a near career-ending injury himself at one time. But a constant to me over the years are the friends I made at Naas underage and at Newbridge: Sweets, Danny G., P. Diddy, Tea-Bag, 1800 Ryan Line, Figo and Archers. They've been with me through it all and clipped me if I got above my station.

I look forward to watching Leinster and Ireland because they are so well set up for future success, even after Joe's departure following the 2019 Rugby World Cup, when Andy Farrell takes over. Things move on so fast. I'm only out of the game a couple of years, but I never got the chance to play with imports like Scott Fardy or James Lowe, or with the new lads coming through like James Ryan and Jordan Larmour. They're the present and the future, I'm the past. Joe has laid a really good foundation. He has created a system that produces very smart players. They can play with ball in hand and offload, but where the real smartness lies is in playing in the right areas, no problem kicking and playing territory games, able to choose their moments well, don't force things, remain patient, build pressure and exploit it. And it's done at pace. We're getting like New Zealand, which is why we can now beat them.

Since I've retired a lot of people have asked me if I miss rugby. I tell them that I miss the big days but that I came to terms a long time ago with knowing that would happen. I know I'm not going to repeat those days, so there's no point in wishful thinking for something that can't happen. I don't miss the grind of rugby, I don't miss the sacrifice of rugby. You invest so much in the game, it demands a lot and it becomes a complete lifestyle. This was the advantage of not being 'anchored to' rugby – when I was cut adrift, I was able to cope.

The visualisation techniques I used as part of my match preparation I was also able to use for life beyond rugby. I was always aware that I couldn't just live in the rugby bubble, that I had other obligations, responsibilities and interests and that those were equally important. I always kept to the forefront of my mind the fact that rugby would come to an end and I didn't want to be left devastated by that. I developed the five Olympic rings as a visual aid, to keep it in perspective. I put the different important aspects of my life into the five intersecting rings: rugby; recovery; Jamie Inc; community and charity; friends and family. Each in its own ring, all intersecting, all needing balance and then, in their own way, providing balance for me. I always wanted to be more than a rugby player. I think I achieved that and now I'm grateful for my foresight.

The priority for me now is my family. I proposed to Sheena on Christmas Day 2015 and we got married in August 2016. Sheena is an amazing woman, as a partner and now a mother. The support, understanding and patience she has shown me over the years has blown me away. She is always ready to give me honest feedback, especially to pull me up on not striking a good enough balance between rugby and the other things in my life. I'm the kite and she's the rock, providing the most important anchor in my life. In simple terms, she has made me a better person since she came into my life.

Our wedding was in Dublin as I just didn't want to travel out of the country; I travelled enough with rugby. I also wanted to make access relatively easy for everyone coming. We had a ball. There were lots of rugby people there but more from outside the sport. It was a great day and night, a big party, a big blow out. Nothing in rugby came close to the excitement of that day.

Harper then came into our lives in July 2018 and her arrival surpassed everything before. She came at such a busy time, after my two surgeries, my retirement, our move to a new home, but before I took my new job. She provided a real 'taking stock' moment and helped put everything in context, a reframing of what was really important in life for us, and for me in particular by making me realise that there is such a life to be enjoyed beyond the end of my rugby career. Sheena had asked me when she was pregnant if I'd prefer a girl or a boy, and I said a boy, not because I wanted to bring up a rugby player, but because part of me was a little afraid of being a father figure to a girl, that having a boy would be easier. But I'm so happy and proud to be a father to a girl and I'm looking forward so much to our years ahead.

Being a father makes me realise even more how my actions and behaviours affect others. It has made me realise that I can't simply just look after myself and everyone else will follow. I have to show the way, lay down the road, show her how to drive and then hope that I've offered enough knowledge and values to take her wherever she wants. In writing this, I think I can see the influence of my own father.

I won't ever be able to replace the thrill of running out onto a pitch to play for Leinster or Ireland, or for the British & Irish Lions. I used to love the RDS, that terrace as you come out onto the pitch, all the Leinster fans there in that little Lions' pit, as I call it, right beside the tunnel as we come out, sending shivers down my neck, providing a surge of electricity as I came out to play. There are no other jobs that can tick those boxes, that can give me that adrenaline hit, but knowing that I can't replace it is important. It doesn't mean I won't put everything into other things I do. I will, but they'll just be different. And I'll get the wins in another way.

When I look back at my career, I'm really happy because I got nearly 14 years as a professional. I had a good run. I had a lot of success. I played 229 times for Leinster, the most capped forward of all time, scoring 38 tries. I completed the full 80 minutes for Ireland in 72 of my 95 caps and scored 13 tries. I got two Lions tours and played in five test matches. I won three European Cups, one Challenge Cup, three league titles, three Six Nations, two Triple Crowns, was part of a Lions series win and, of course, the Grand Slam in 2009. The statisticians tell me that I'm ranked in the top two players in the history of the Six Nations in each of the categories of ruck clean-outs, carries, metres made, tackles and turnovers.

I have been extremely lucky. No one needs to tell me the dice rolled kindly for me. I got paid to do something I love. I did it as well as I could have, made an honest effort and got the rewards for it. I feel I was the best pro I could have been and the people I respected most confirmed that. I made good friends, for life. But I always knew there was a life beyond, a next ball to go after. All in.